GOLDEN GIRL

BY

SHIRLEY EATON

B.T. Batsford Ltd • London

Printed by Polestar Wheatons Ltd, Exeter

For the Publishers
B.T. Batsford Ltd
583 Fulham Road
London SW6 5BY

A catalogue record for this book is available from the British Library

ISBN 0 7134 8458 6

Acknowledgements

Credit is given to the following for all photographs published in this book from the film GOLDFINGER.
© 1964 Danjaq, LLC and United Artists Corporation. All rights reserved.

I would also like to thank the following people for the many diverse ways in which they touched my life.

Richard Stone, John Pawsey, Jonathan Coe, Gary Reed, Guy Perry, H D, Jack and Connie Luffman, Olive and Bill Ladmore, Dolly Frankel, Maureen Timms, Barbara and Bobby Hester, Lady Mary Meany, Dennis Lotis, Jean Englander, Annie Hicks, Jill and John Pettigrove, Louisa Moore, Melanie Toso, Patricia Kleine-Brockhoff, Brenig Hester, Robert Mansfield, Richard Reynolds, Robert Ross.

Cornell Lucas, portrait photographs
Paul Hancock, portrait photographs

Contents

Foreword

by Mickey Spillane

There are some people who can pull beauty out of the morass of this world and make you know what it is like and that it's there for you too. Knowing Shirley Eaton is like a gentle explosion of pure pleasure and adding her own thoughts and words for us to peruse is a sheer delight, a fiery, emotional experience, as wonderful now as it was then.

Introduction

By Jonathan Coe

Over the years, I've noticed something strange about the name Shirley Eaton. Mention it to any male who was a regular film-goer around the start of the 1960s, and he'll go weak at the knees. Still, even to this day.

For my own part, I was born in 1961, so I was too young to experience the Shirley phenomenon when it first came around. My earliest memories of her date from school holidays in the 1970s, when the TV channels would fill up their afternoon schedules with old black and white British comedy films, and among all the familiar faces – Kenneth Connor, Charles Hawtrey, Terry-Thomas – I soon began to watch out for one in particular – a drop-dead gorgeous platinum blonde, full of sexy good nature and a first rate comedienne to boot. Granted, the nicest thing about her, to any young man in my hormonally-challenged state, was the regularity with which her bath-towel or bikini top seemed to slip off whenever the script required it. But I could also tell that here was something rare: a British actress who really looked as though she belonged in the movies, with a face that the camera loved.

That quality was quickly recognized, and Shirley was soon plucked from the ranks of the Carry On and Doctor films to die a gloriously kinky death in the third Bond movie, Goldfinger. The image of her naked body covered from head to toe in gold paint has become one of the key symbols of the 1960s and, quite rightly, she begins this fascinating book with an account of how it all came about. But there is much more to her story than those few minutes of immortal screen time. Her roots go right back to the variety tradition, and after accompanying her, in these pages, all the way from her early song-and-dance days right up to the painful and deeply-moving account of her husband's death, there can be no doubt that we're dealing with an incredibly versatile and sensitive woman. A true artist, in short.

She could have been the British Bardot, in a way – a homegrown Monroe or Lollobrigida – if our film industry hadn't proved itself so good (as she points out herself, with typical insight) at taming her sex appeal, keeping it penned within the cosy limits of comedy instead of giving her the dramatic roles she craved. It was largely her frustration at the kind of parts she was being offered, combined with her very strong maternal, home-making instinct, that led her to abandon the movies at the end of the 1960s. This was bad news for her fans, but the right decision for Shirley, and you can tell she's never regretted it. Today she's one of those lucky people, it seems, with a healthy attitude to her own fame. Not for her the Sunset Boulevard option, sitting at home surrounded by faded memories. Shirley in her sixties is a whirlwind, full of creative energies that continue to drive her with unstoppable momentum: get her on the phone, ask what she's been doing this week, and you might as well set aside the next couple of hours.

It remains a mystery to me, in fact, how she finds the time to sleep in the midst of all her writing, travelling, jetting off to film festivals, being with her family and, yes, answering her fan letters that still pour through her door. There are going to be even more of them after this book, as well. She may have been off our screens for thirty years, but for most of us that glittering comeuppance in Goldfinger seems like yesterday. Pretty young actresses come and go, you see, but the public never forgets a twenty-four carat star.

Jonathan Coe
London, 1999

Dedicated to Isla, Jake, Morgan and Jessica

To Colin for his eternal love; Grant, Jason, Jill and Dulcie for being there when it matttered; my parents who began it all and the little people, Isla, Jake, Morgan and Jessica who continue...

1
Striking Gold

I am the girl covered in gold paint in *Goldfinger* and, in a sense, I always will be. That's the movies for you, they grant some of us a kind of immortality. That image of me covered in gold paint is perhaps the most famous single image to emerge from the Bond series and am I happy to be recognized in that way by people all over the world! Every week I still receive fan letters from round the globe and although the writers mention the many other film roles I have played, the part they most often refer to is the Jill Masterson cameo in *Goldfinger*. There clearly is something about that image that has struck a chord with millions of people, women as well as men. Perhaps it is the association of the most precious metal in the world with the beauty of the female form. It is a sensual, luxurious and exclusive image and I was very fortunate indeed to have the chance to appear in *Goldfinger*, although in terms of screen time my appearance lasted less than five minutes in total.

By the time I made *Goldfinger*, I had already made twenty films, some of them in leading roles, so in 1964 I was no novice starlet, but when the chance came up to be in the third of the highly successful Bond series (the first two were *Dr No* and *From Russia With Love*), I was not going to say no. I am very glad I had the good sense to accept the part, because that gold-covered image of my almost-naked body has become a part of twentieth-century iconography.

As I say, I was already an experienced film and stage actress before I was cast in *Goldfinger*. Let me tell you how exactly I got that role, because I know you will be interested in the details. The late Harry Saltzman, the rather gruff and earthy Canadian co-producer of the Bond series, was at a party to which a very good friend of mine was also invited. Harry was bemoaning the fact that he couldn't find a British actress to play the part of the 'golden girl' Jill Masterson in the next Bond movie. I'll just have to use an American actress, he said, there just aren't any British actresses sexy enough for the part.

'Nonsense!' roared my loyal friend, to whom I will be eternally grateful, 'I know just the actress you are looking for. In fact, I know two.'

'Oh, yeh?' said Harry dubiously, 'and who exactly are they?'.

'One is Shirley Eaton and she's already been in about twenty movies. The other is Shirley Ann Field.'

'OK, but are they sexy?' Harry asked. 'I need someone who is attractive and sexy but not in a vulgar, obvious way.'

'I'll tell you how sexy this lady is,' my good friend replied, referring to me. 'Whenever I give a party and Shirley Eaton is there dancing, and, believe me, this girl can dance, all the men in the room get erections!'

'This lady I have to see,' said Harry.

So Mr Saltzman arranged to watch *Three Men in a Boat*, which I had made a few years previously with Laurence Harvey and Jimmy Edwards. That movie is, of course, a period picture so I was dressed in Edwardian clothes all buttoned up to the throat and dropping to the ankle. Not exactly the sexiest role in the history of the cinema, but it must have made some impression because, after I came back from filming *Rhino* in Africa, I was summoned to Harry's office. Luckily, I had acquired a lovely tanned look during the location shooting so when I walked into the office dressed in a very sixties outfit, a simple white mini dress, I was feeling very confident and attractive with my brown face and tanned legs.

After the initial discussion, Harry got straight to the point. 'How do you feel about being filmed nude except for a covering of gold paint?' I had never appeared naked in any of my film roles up to that stage in my career. I replied that if it were done tastefully, then I wouldn't mind at all. 'Actually', I added, 'if you're covered in gold paint, I would guess you might feel almost fully clothed.' And in the event, that was true.

At the end of the interview I was not sure about Harry's decision and I knew that the producers were seeing other girls for the part. I left the office and wandered down Park Lane into the beauty and peace of the park, thinking about the film and how marvellous it would be to be offered the role. I wanted it very badly indeed. The two previous Bond movies had been great successes and *Goldfinger* was to be their most lavish production to date. There was just so much excitement building up around the Bond series that I knew I had to be part of it.

The next day my agent rang me to say that I had got the part and that filming would start in a few weeks. I was overjoyed. It seemed like a very big break indeed and so it proved. *Goldfinger* was to end up costing four times as much as the first Bond movie, *Dr No*, and you can see every pound spent up there on the screen in the lavish sets, such as *Goldfinger*'s headquarters in Kentucky with its operations room which is transformed by a few flicks of a switch from a ranch-house lounge into a superbly-equipped centre for military planning with wall-sized maps, instrument panels and a model of Fort Knox. In addition, the Fort Knox set itself is a full-scale model, a fantasy version of what the designers thought Fort Knox might look like inside, which cost a fortune to build at Pinewood. The elaborate action sequences and gadgetry, such as is incorporated into Bond's Aston Martin DB5 (rotating licence plates, passenger ejector seat, tracking devices), also were expensive, but the high production costs were justified because the movie made a huge amount of money and is rated as probably the best of the series among Bond fans.

Naturally, I was delighted to be appearing in a Bond film and opposite Sean Connery, but I had no idea at all at that time that my brief role in the movie would

Taking a break on set during *Goldfinger*

cause such waves and create such a personal resonance for the rest of my life. In showbusiness, you never can be sure what impact something you are involved with is going to have. For example, how could anybody involved in the making of *The Full Monty* have foreseen that this small-budget British film would end up earning more at the box-office than any other British film in cinema history and that it would be such a hit across the world? No one could have guessed that. Similarly, at the time of getting the part in *Goldfinger*, I had no way of knowing that it was going to be such a milestone in my career and that it was about to transform me into one of the enduring icons of this century.

The Filming of **Goldfinger**

I was covered in gold paint twice: once for the shooting of the scene when James Bond discovers me dead in the hotel bedroom and again for publicity shots for the movie. Getting the gold paint on wasn't the problem, it was getting it off afterwards! The first time I had the help of the wardrobe mistress who helped me scrub and scrub until the last gold flake had disappeared, but, believe me, it was not that easy! Just to make sure, I had a Turkish bath a week later to sweat out every last gold particle.

The advice given by doctors employed by the studio was that it might be dangerous to have the gold paint covering my body for much more than an hour, so the shooting of the scene and the publicity shots had to be completed fairly speedily. Apparently, the paint might have blocked my pores had it been allowed to stay on for much longer. So, although the image of my gold-painted face and body still turns up all over the place over thirty years later, the span of time during which I was covered in the stuff was comparatively brief.

On the morning of the gold scene I arrived in the make-up room at the usual unearthly hour. The make-up artiste was French and I stood there in my G-string while he slowly and delicately painted my entire body with a large, soft paintbrush, except for a small area down my front, which was a precaution advised by the doctors. The make-up was a cream foundation with millions of tiny gold particles in it. The sensation of being softly brushed all over was tingly and sensual. It only became uncomfortable after I had had it on for a while.

Yes, the day when Shirley Eaton was going to be filmed in the 'gold scene' caused quite a buzz at Pinewood. It must appear surprising nowadays but the filming of the scene was done on a 'closed set', in other words, only the actors and technicians who were required for the shooting of the scene were allowed to be there. However, the buzz about the scene permeated to a nearby stage where a British film called *The*

'Mirror, mirror on the wall…'. Preparing for my golden moment

Guns at Batasi was being made. Graham Stark, that very talented stalwart of many a British movie, was involved in filming that day when Sean Connery, who was, of course, James Bond in *Goldfinger*, visited the set and whispered to Graham that Shirley was doing the gold scene!. Sean had, and presumably still has, his mischievously naughty side and he brought Graham over to my dressing-room where I was busily being covered with the gold paint and was almost in my birthday suit!

Suddenly, the door of my dressing-room opened and there were Sean and Graham standing grinning from ear to ear 'Get out of here, you two!' I cried, although I did it nicely because they were so much like a pair of naughty schoolboys that I couldn't really be angry with them. But I did want my privacy, as I was feeling nervous and excited about what exactly would happen on set during the planned sequence.

'OK, OK, Shirley', said Graham, 'but before I go, give me a kiss.' To get rid of him, I went up to Graham and put my arms round him and gave him a big hug. When he stood back from me, the inevitable had happened. He was wearing an immaculate white sailor's uniform for his role in the film he was shooting and now it was covered in gold paint all down the front. When he returned to the set and was required in front

13

of the cameras, you can imagine how his co-stars and the wardrobe people felt when they saw what had happened to the immaculate white. In fact, Richard Attenborough, now 'Sir Richard', was in the middle of a dramatic scene and caught a glimpse of Graham standing behind the camera and completely dried up! However, when he explained that he had been embraced by the *Goldfinger* girl, all was forgiven. Graham is definitely one of the best character actors ever to grace British films, a sweet man too.

I caused quite a sensation among the technicians and crew when I walked onto the set that day! But the fact is that for the 'golden girl' sequence I was not completely naked. I wore what is now called a 'thong' and it was also painted, of course, so it would not be apparent on screen. For my own modesty when I walked onto the set, I also wore a couple of gold-painted cones over my breasts. I'm sorry if that destroys any male fantasies out there, but that is the truth of it. This was 1964, after all. I've laughed many times over the years about that day at Pinewood Studios - what a weird and wonderful profession to be in!

If you are a Bond devotee, you will remember my part in *Goldfinger* is that of Auric Goldfinger's girl friend, who helps him cheat at cards for high stakes by a Miami hotel pool side. Jill (my character) does this by positioning herself in a hotel bedroom overlooking the pool and peering through binoculars at Goldfinger's opponent's hand. She then transmits the information to the villain's hearing-aid. Bond/Connery discovers me in the act, and soon afterwards we find ourselves in bed together. It must have been that glamorous bikini I was wearing in the scene!

Sean has an irresistible seductive screen appeal to him, so it does not appear that unlikely that Jill would jump into bed with this attractive Scotsman. In the bed scene that follows, I wear a pyjama top covering all my body except for my legs. The next scene has me covered in gold paint and acting very dead, because bad old *Goldfinger* (Gert Frobe) has taken his revenge for my betrayal. What a way to die!

I wish I had a pound for every time I have been asked what it was like to be covered in gold paint and to be kissed by Sean Connery. The gold paint was very special and fun and not exactly your run-of-the-mill day at the studio. Kissing Sean Connery was a job of work, although I have to say that he is the sexiest actor that I have ever acted opposite. He has that earthy, masculine, animal quality which is so attractive to women.

When we were on set together, he was extremely professional. Although he was friendly, he was quiet. In between takes, we would sit in our chairs next to each other and I would look at him and try to imagine what he was thinking. He seemed quite

Meeting Ian Fleming on one of his rare visits to the *Goldfinger* set

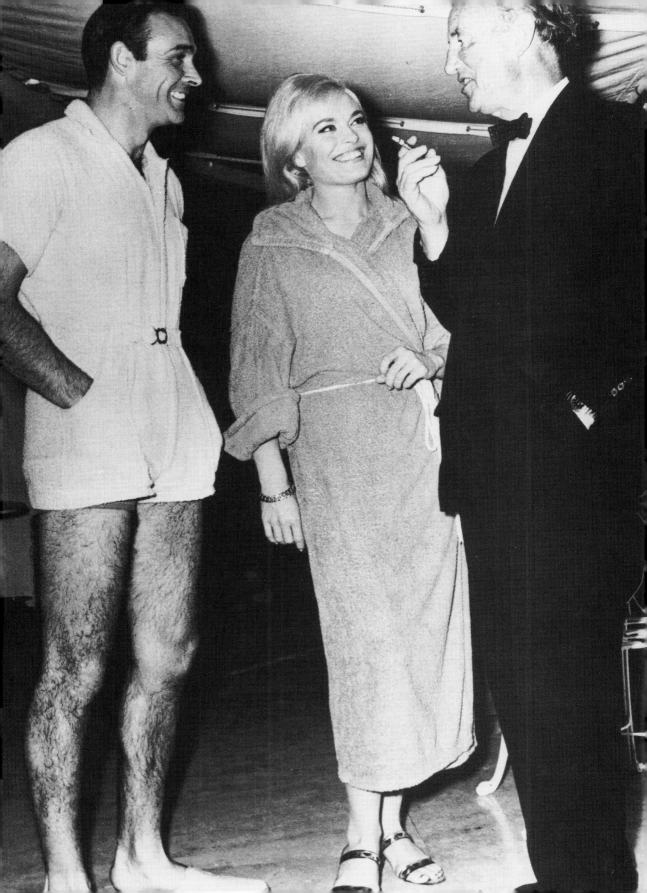

unaware of himself. He was self-contained and deep in his own thoughts, simmering with his natural Celtic appeal. But by the time we had finished our scenes, we had worked up a flirtatious relationship. We liked each other and I would guess that audiences can recognize the chemistry there between us when they see the film. But, to tell the truth, I never felt I got to know Sean very well. He has said himself that he hasn't always handled women very well. He strikes me as being very much a man's man, with interests that are usually classed as 'male'. Of course, he loves women and is attracted to them, but he is almost certainly more at ease in the company of men who share his particular manly pursuits: golf, riding, driving and all that.

I didn't really to get to know Honor Blackman very well during the filming, but I remember her arriving one morning at the make-up room at a very early hour (oh, the glamour of filmmaking!) and peeking in as I was in the middle of being made up. 'Good God, Shirley!' she said, 'no one has the right to look that good this early in the morning', which I took to be a very generous remark from a lady who was renowned in the glamour stakes herself.

I sue!

It is a very little known fact that I sued the makers of *Goldfinger* because of the billing I received when the film was first shown. In my contract, it had been stipulated that I would receive the same line billing as Honor Blackman (who, of course, played Pussy Galore) and Gert Frobe, but when I saw the credits for the first time, I was merely at the top of the list of the other cast members, and not on the same line as Honor and Gert, which was not at all what had been agreed in my contract. It was a similar state of affairs with my billing in the posters and related publicity.

Billing is very important to actors, and no small matter at all. By this point in my career, I had had my name above the title in numerous films and I was just as well-known as Honor or Gert. So, despite the fact that I had been delighted to appear in *Goldfinger*, my agent Richard Stone felt he had to act on this matter and take legal steps to make sure I received my contractual due as far the credits and publicity billing were concerned. Luckily, the producers settled out of court and the situation was remedied to my satisfaction. It caused no lasting damage to my relationship with the makers of the Bond series, it was just one of those things that happens in the world of showbusiness from time to time. People have said to me that it was courageous to take on such a powerful force in the world of movie-making, but I felt I was in the right and the peaceful settlement proved that.

Hot chemistry between our characters in the love scene

The premiere of **Goldfinger**

However, the credits were not the only surprise in wait for me when I first saw *Goldfinger* at the Royal Premiere at the Odeon, Leicester Square. Premieres are always exciting occasions and the *Goldfinger* premiere was particularly glamorous. But as I settled down into my seat to see the movie for the first time, I had no idea of the shocks it would contain.

First of all, there was the fact that the producers had used another actress, Margaret Nolan, who plays Ample Dink in the movie (the young woman who gives Sean a massage in one scene) as the gold-covered lady who slinks her way through the credits. There is a brief shot of Shirley Eaton in the credit sequence, but I am not covered in gold. Many people assume that because I play the 'golden girl' Jill Masterson in the film, it is my golden image in the credits and even on the movie poster, which, incidentally now sells for over a thousand pounds at auctions of movie memorabilia. However, if you look closely, you will see that the face and body are nothing like my features and figure!

To this day, I have never found out exactly why the producers decided to use another face and body for this purpose, but two explanations present themselves. Firstly, I know they had practised putting the gold paint on Margaret to see how it would take, before they shot the scenes with me. Having gone to this trouble, perhaps it made sense for them to film her covered in the gold paint and use what they had shot under the credits. Secondly, if they had shown me in gold paint at this stage in the movie, they would have been giving some of the story away and robbing the plot of some element of surprise. Those are the likely explanations.

The much greater shock came when I listened to the voice emanating from my character, Jill Masterson. It was not mine, they had dubbed me! Another actress's voice had been used. Immediately after finishing my part in the filming of *Goldfinger*, I had rushed off to Greece to film *The Naked Brigade*, an adventure movie in which I starred with Ken Scott, so I had no inkling at all that, while I had been out of the country, someone had taken the decision to dub my part. When I quizzed Guy Hamilton, the director of *Goldfinger*, about why that decision had been made, he declared that he too had known nothing about it.

You can imagine that I felt rather disappointed as I sat there that night in the stalls watching the first showing of *Goldfinger*. First of all, there had been the business with the billing, then the gold-painted other lady during the credits, and now this strange voice was coming from my mouth up there on the screen. But that's showbiz, as they say. You have to grin and 'bare' it! I still enjoyed the crazy excitement of the glittering evening.

To this day I have to field questions from fans about whether or not it is me in the credits sequence and occasionally people also ask whether it is my voice speaking Jill Masterson's lines. So I am happy at last to set the record straight. Obviously, I wish they had not dubbed my voice. However, the enduring aspect of my participation in *Goldfinger* is the image of myself covered in gold.

Promoting **Goldfinger**

The dispute over my billing had clearly caused no lasting damage to my relationship with the producers of *Goldfinger* because they asked me to undertake a three-week promotional tour of America to advertise the release of the movie in the States. I undertook a schedule that took in major cities such as Los Angeles, New York, Washington, Las Vegas, Chicago and New Orleans. One fun aspect of the gruelling schedule was that the tour promoters had arranged for me to wear a new gold outfit at every stop I made. So as I walked down the steps from the aircraft at each of the major airports I flew into, the photographers were able to capture me in these attractive gold outfits, a fresh one for every major city.

Then it was a matter of tuning into what I call the 'ordinary American madness' of morning, noon and night interviews for television, radio and the printed media. When I hear present-day stars talking about the burden of promotion work they have to undertake to publicize their films and how this is all a new phenomenon, I feel like pointing out that I was doing that kind of thing thirty years ago and the Bond series producers were very aware that even a prestigious series like theirs needed skilful promoting.

A promotional schedule like the one I undertook to promote *Goldfinger* may sound very exciting and glamorous and it indeed did have its exciting features. I was visiting these major American cities and was the focus of attention of a considerable media frenzy, which has its own particular buzz. However, it was tiring and, more importantly, I was away from home and my family, my husband Colin and my son Grant, who was five at that time. Naturally, I missed them very much, because Colin and I were always very close and supportive of one another. He always encouraged me in my career and never stood in my way, understanding that in the business I was in, I would have to, from time to time, be away from home. Colin was not involved in the world of showbusiness and did not want to be. He had his own successful building contractor's business, which took up most of his time. My marriage and the family life I enjoyed, including the support of my loving parents, provided a secure bedrock for me when I had to be away, so that the inevitable loneliness I felt was bearable because I had that emotional security and the knowledge that I was loved and needed.

I would, however, be less than honest if I did not admit that there were temptations associated with the kind of world I moved in. After all, I was working opposite some very glamorous stars in an industry that has an exciting aura about it. However, film-making is about hard work first and foremost and I like to think I always took a very professional attitude to my profession. That, and the fact that my marriage was so stable and rewarding to us both, and the joy I got from being a mother, provided me with a stability that I think some other members of the profession did not have. I do not want to sound like Goody-Two-Shoes and I quite understand how mutual attractions on set can lead to affairs, which in turn can result in marital break-ups, but my husband Colin and I had an understanding and a trust that was lasting and deep. For that I am profoundly grateful and it was the principal reason I remained sane and on the rails and did not succumb to the temptations of alcohol, drugs or serial affairs.

Thus, during the *Goldfinger* promotional tour, more often than not I would retire to my room after dinner and watch television and get on that transatlantic phone to speak to Colin and my small son. If that does sound like Goody-Two-Shoes, the truth is that_s the way it was with me. They were my roots. They were my emotional security. I was a beautiful blonde lady and there were always wolves around looking for that kind of prey, but I was well-chaperoned during that trip and at other times. Above all, I held my own reins very tightly. Sometimes, the loneliness I felt was almost unbearable and I knew with certainty that I needn't be lonely if that was what I wanted. However, I felt the complications that would arise if I took steps to stop being lonely were too many and too dangerous. Additionally, I believe that we are all children of our time and I grew up in a era of comparatively stable marriages and when the divorce rate had not yet gone through the roof. People expected to stay married. I certainly did and I found that, as our marriage lasted, the mutual trust grew and grew. The very thought of us divorcing would have been my idea of hell.

Naturally, there were flirtations and I am a naturally flirtatious and sensual woman, but I always made it clear where the line would be drawn. I have worked with male stars who were notorious womanizers (no names!), but I have never found that kind of man attractive. Womanizers are often more interested in themselves than in you and feed off their own egos and the score they keep. I was far more likely to find someone on the other side of the camera attractive - a member of the crew, a technician - than a vain leading man who was always thinking about his profile and potential conquests.

One evening, however, the organizers of the tour asked me whether I would like a night out on the town in New York, New York. I thought yes, why not, a New York night club should be fun. We were sitting at a table in this top New York club when I spotted Sammy Davis Jnr, surrounded by an entourage, at a nearby table. I had always been a great fan of Sammy's and had in fact gone to see him at his recent season at the Talk of the Town in London, when he had performed his cabaret act. I hadn't gone backstage afterwards because I did not really know Sammy, though I had stood beside him in the line-up at a Royal Variety Performance nervously waiting to be introduced to the Queen (more of that later!).

At any rate, one of the publicity guys at my table, realizing that I was a fan of Sammy's and sensing a great photo opportunity, suggested that he go over to Sammy's table and ask him to come over, which he duly did. Sammy was charming and we seemed immediately to be on the same wavelength. Then he asked me have a dance with him and I wasn't going to turn that down. We went on the dance floor and I can safely say we attracted more than a little attention because, if I say so myself, I can dance and Sammy, well, Sammy was a renowned hoofer and so we showed off a bit and enjoyed ourselves hugely. Sammy was a strange-looking man, some might even call him ugly, but I've never danced with a better dancer than him.

At that time, Sammy was married to May Britt, a blonde Swedish beauty. Later the marriage was to end in divorce, but in 1964 it was happy enough for Sammy to invite me to meet May and the family the next day at their home. Unfortunately, I was scheduled to leave New York for the next leg of the tour so I wasn't able to take up that particular invitation. I never met Sammy Davis again and I was very sad to hear of his death through cancer at a comparatively young age. I think Sammy lived his life burning the candles at both ends and in the middle, but as he said of himself, he had 'come a long way for a one-eyed Negro Jew', meaning he had had to fight against several sets of prejudices to battle his way to the top.

Another interesting feature of the American tour was the excitement generated among the publicity people when *Life* magazine decided to feature me covered in gold on their cover. The American publicity man who had arranged this was literally jumping up and down with excitement: 'I got Shirley on the cover of *Life* magazine! I got her on the cover of *Life*!' he kept saying. Then he and the rest of the team

Not really dead! After filming the golden scene – relieved that it's all over – I pose for a publicity still

wondered why I wasn't more excited. Of course, I knew that being on a *Life* cover was very significant in publicity terms and for me personally, it was stupendous exposure. Not many people in the world can say they have been on the cover of *Life*. I joined a comparatively short list of people that included Presidents, heroes and heroines, very famous movie stars like Garbo, Dietrich and Monroe, and many other world figures. Naturally, I was pleased and loved the cover when it came out, but I have always remained a very down-to-earth person and have never been overly impressed by the trappings of this business I have made my living in. OK, so I was on the cover of *Life*, I was glad for myself and the movie, but as someone said in another context, it wasn't a cure for cancer. Now that would be worth putting on a *Life* cover.

Cubby Broccoli

Albert Broccoli, known as 'Cubby' to almost everybody he came into contact with, was the co-producer of the Bond series with Harry Saltzman. Cubby was almost universally loved by the people he worked with and the announcement of his death on 27 June 1996 was greeted with great sadness among the many people he had helped in their careers, including myself. Cubby was like a warm Italian-American 'Papa' to all those who worked on a Bond film whether they be a star, a supporting actor, a member of the crew or the tea lady. During location shooting, he would cook huge bowls of spaghetti bolognese for cast and crew. If there were ever some altercation or dispute, as there inevitably was when creative people got together to do something as important as a Bond movie, then he would be the pacifier, the guy who could inject some calmness and sense of proportion into things, bringing the quarrelling parties together and seeking a compromise between them. As Donald Zec wrote in his introduction to the programme that was printed for the tribute held for Cubby on 17 November 1996, 'Despite all his successes, international awards, and distinguished friends in many countries, Cubby remained the gentle and unaffected character everybody liked and most of us loved. He may have been designated Albert Romolo Broccoli for his Order of the British Empire and similar distinctions elsewhere. But he was always 'Cubby' to intimates and subordinates alike.'

I was very privileged to be asked to take part in the tribute to Cubby that Sunday morning at the Odeon Leicester Square, where all the Bond films had had their premieres. Most of the leading personalities involved in the Bond series took part and were asked to add their tribute to the man we all loved. These included Roger Moore, George Lazenby, Timothy Dalton and Pierce Brosnan, as well as directors Guy

Hamilton, Lewis Gilbert and John Glen. Among the female stars asked to make their contribution to the tribute were Jill St John, Lois Maxwell, Jane Seymour and myself.

I was naturally very anxious to do full justice to Cubby and add to the occasion in a meaningful way. I was also very nervous about speaking in front of such an audience and after contributions by Prince Charles and other distinguished people. But I decided to take my courage in my hands and read a poem that I had written after the death of Colin, my husband. I thought it would be appropriate to the occasion and express some of my feelings about the death of this fine producer and human being.

My heart was pounding when it came to my turn to pay my tribute. I left my seat in the front row of the stalls and went through a side door, climbed a few steps and waited in the wings. Iain Johnstone, the critic and well-known writer on the cinema, who acted as presenter on that auspicious occasion, was introducing me and Shirley Bassey's wonderful voice singing the title song from *Goldfinger* was filling the theatre. Then on the screen came my scene in the hotel room with Sean Connery and then the scene where I am covered in gold paint and very, very dead. The clip ended and Iain beckoned me to walk onto the stage. I confess my knees were shaking as I walked those few steps to the microphone. The spotlight was shining on me. The audience, which I had been a part of a few moments ago, were applauding. I just stood there letting it all sink in. I hadn't been in front of a live audience for over twenty years. What a memorable moment to be part of that wonderful tribute to a fine man!

I smiled and thanked the audience. I preceded the reading of the poem with these words: 'I am very glad to be here today. Over thirty years ago while we were working on *Goldfinger*, nobody really knew what the James Bond films would become. I am very proud to be a small part of the Bond legend and will always thank Cubby for giving me the chance to be painted in gold. That scene changed my life and has lived with me ever since. After living for the past eight years in the south of France, I have now come back to England to be near our two sons and their families. Two years ago my husband Colin died of cancer. We had been married for 37 years. Before he became ill, I wrote many poems about the beauty of where we lived and of my love for him.'

I then dedicated this poem to Dana (Cubby's widow) and her family:

> *We're earthbound for a fragment of time*
> *To live fully and toil as we climb*
> *Onwards and upwards in our individual ways*
> *This path and that, trying them all*

Longing with grace not to stumble and fall,
Knowing our spirit will carry us far
To live once more like the infinite star.
The moment comes to leave this earth,
Peaceful and light to greet our rebirth.

The poem was heartfelt when I wrote it after the death of my beloved husband and it was heartfelt when I read it as my contribution to the celebration of Cubby's life, because that was what Dana Broccoli and her family wanted the occasion to be, a celebration, not a memorial. When I had finished reading the poem, I stood for a moment looking out into the sea of faces, then bowed my head and walked off the stage. Pierce Brosnan then walked on and gave his own moving tribute. Finally, Michael Wilson, Cubby's stepson, finished the tribute with a beautiful speech about his father and his work. The presentation had lasted an hour and a half. We had all, in our different ways, paid our dues to the man whom we respected and loved, the real creator of the James Bond movies.

I walked up the aisle of the Odeon to find Dana Broccoli. She was sitting with her family wiping away her tears and trying courageously to regain her composure. She is a brave, lovely, warm woman. Dana told me how much my reading of the poem meant to her and I was more than pleased to think that I had made a worthwhile contribution to the tribute, one that was appreciated by the people for whom the whole occasion had been organized.

Outside the Odeon, crowds of fans were waiting to see the stars leave. Those of us who had been part of the presentation were invited by the Broccoli family to Cubby's favourite restaurant, La Famiglia, where we had a great meal, relaxed and talked over old times. Cubby's spirit was with us that day in the cinema and in the restaurant afterwards. And the spirit of Colin, my husband, was there too. It was a very emotional experience for all who were there.

It was at Cubby's tribute that I first met the present James Bond, Pierce Brosnan and what a lovely man he is. I think we were drawn to each other right away because we had both suffered the recent loss of a dear partner, myself with the death of Colin and Pierce with the death of his wife. At the time of the Cubby tribute, he was still very much in mourning for his wife, as I was for Colin, and that kind of loss creates a bond between two people because they understand instinctively what the other has gone through and is still wrestling with. Our mutual loss undoubtedly leant additional emotional force to our respective tributes to Cubby Broccoli.

I had meant what I said in my introductory words to the reading of the poem:

Goldfinger had changed my life and it would be with me forever. It had given me a fame that I had never had before and which has never left me. I had become instantly identified as one of the icons of the century and that doesn't happen to many actresses. I mentioned at the beginning of this chapter how fans still write to me about my part in *Goldfinger* and I would like to quote a few brief extracts from some of these letters to illustrate the impact those few minutes of screen time have had. 'It might be a cliché,' one fan wrote in a recent letter, 'but it's true that no other Bond girl has made the impression that you did in *Goldfinger*. The relationship between Bond and Jill was just beginning to fizz when you character was killed. It wasn't just the fact that you had been murdered and sprayed in gold paint that made it shocking, so much as the unexpectedness of it all.' Another fan wrote 'Who could forget your sexy look in black bra and panties lying on a chaise longue in *Goldfinger*'s Miami Beach hotel?' That was no bra and panties, my friend, that was a bikini! 'I can honestly say that my favourite movie of all time is *Goldfinger*', another fan wrote. 'I remember very well the first time I saw *Goldfinger* thinking how beautiful you were and then for you to be killed off so quickly. I do hope that this letter finds you in good spirits and health.' A very touching concern for my well-being!

Of course, I will be eternally grateful to Cubby, Harry and that dear friend who told the latter about her mate who danced so sexily at her parties! But the path that had led to the glamour of *Goldfinger* had begun years ago in a suburb of North London where I had been born in 1937 and that is where we ought to return to now, so that you can know a little more about this particular 'golden girl'.

2

Beginnings

I have always been a very romantic person, believing passionately in the ennobling potential of romantic love between a man and a woman. Romance is perhaps not so fashionable these days, when the emphasis seems to have shifted to pure sex (not that I have anything against sex, on the contrary!). But perhaps how sex is represented in the movies and in the media in general has become too exploitatively crude and prosaic, robbing it of that essential element of good, old-fashioned romance.

I mention romance as a lead into a section on my early life, because I believe I got my sense of romance from my parents. My mother was seventeen and my father twenty when they met and fell deeply in love. This was over sixty years ago, a different era in many senses, especially in terms of what was considered right and proper. When the young couple asked my mother's father permission to marry, he refused outright. Frustrated by these strict Victorian attitudes, they knew there was only one way in which their dreams of being together for the rest of their lives could come true. Thus, I was conceived in the spring of 1936. I could accurately be described as a love baby. When they told my grandfather, my mother's father, that his daughter was pregnant, he relented and he gave his consent, which he had to do in those days because of my mother's age, for them to get married.

I was duly born on the twelfth of January, 1937, a year after the abdication of Edward the Sixth and over two years before the outbreak of the Second World War. The birth was not easy, but I arrived safely after a traumatic delivery by caesarean section, which was a much more difficult procedure than it is today. I have learned from my mother since that she was deeply affected by the birth and apprehensive about her new-found responsibilities. However, my father was calm and happy about being a new dad and helped her to cope with me during the first months of my life. Actually, he had wanted a son, but like most new fathers, once he saw his baby daughter, his heart melted.

My father was a rugged, working-class, red-haired young man, full of life and fun. His great love besides my mother and me was his motorbike. After I was born, he bought a sidecar and all three of us used to go camping at the weekends. Whenever I think of my parents, I am full of admiration. They really knew how to enjoy life. As I write about them now, they are still full of

The only time I was ever photographed nude! Two years old, on our last camping holiday before war broke out

life and laughter even though they are both in their eighties – it's just amazing!

The war and I

We lived in a small flat in Kingsbury in the Edgware district of North London. In other words, I was, or became, a suburban girl. Our home was not far from the huge mattress-manufacturing factory where my father worked.

When I was about two-and-a-half years old, everything changed. War was declared and my father was drafted into the army. At first he was stationed quite near to our home and my mother and I were able to see him from time to time. After a while he was sent overseas and he was away for three-and-a-half years. Many families experienced this disorientation during the war - the prolonged absence of the father I am certain leaves a lasting effect on children who have had this gap in their early years. It affects different people in different ways, but I am sure that, for the rest of my life, it gave me a great desire for stability in my life and for a close, lasting relationship with a loving man, who would not leave me.

While my father was away, my mother tried to make my life as normal as possible. She could not call on any help from an extended family because both my grandmothers were dead and she had no sisters. As it was for many wives and mother in her position during the war, it was a struggle. To help the war effort and to earn some money, she worked making soldiers' uniforms. Some of her friends looked after me until she came home from work. My happiest times were when I was with her in the evenings, because we were very close, my mother and I. The radio was the great home entertainment of the day and we would listen to favourite programmes each night and I would sometimes watch her sew. She made almost all our clothes, she was so good with her hands. These were the best moments when there were just the two of us together.

Meanwhile, we had moved to another little flat in Harrow Weald, which was the ground floor of a terraced house with a garden. To help supplement the food rations (and remember that during wartime, there was very strict rationing of food with everyone having to produce ration books when they bought at the local shops), we kept hens and I would look after them with my mother. The government of the day, under the leadership of Sir Winston Churchill, constantly told us to 'dig for Britain!', meaning we should all try to grow vegetables in our gardens. The Germans were trying to create a blockade round Britain hoping to starve us into submission and attacking the convoys of ships crossing the Atlantic with food supplies. It is strange now to think that in those dark days of the war a freshly-boiled egg was a luxury. I used to eat six slices of bread with one egg, just to make it last.

However, for each of my birthdays, my mother would make an enormous effort to make the day exciting. We would have a lot of my friends to tea and there would be a home-made birthday cake. I would sit at the head of the table on a chair decorated like a throne, a queen for the day. It made me feel quite special. That was one of the things my mother did for me: she always made me feel special. However, things were incomplete because I missed my father's love during those years.

A few years ago, my mother sent me a large, brown envelope containing sentimental mementoes from the past, including some photos of me when I was a child and my dancing certificates from the Royal Academy of Dancing, whose patron was Her Majesty Queen Mary. These dated from 1945 when I was eight years old. She also enclosed some of the letters she wrote to my father during the war. The letters were very moving in their simplicity. She told him about the ordinary everyday happenings, like bombs falling close to our house, did he need any cigarettes, was he eating properly, the fact she couldn't buy any coal to heat the house, the fact that she'd just finished knitting me a warm jumper and the way I always seemed to need her attention every time she sat down to write to him. They are beautiful letters, catching the atmosphere of everything that was happening during that God-forsaken period of history. No self-pity came across from those pages, only her longing for him to come home safely. I remember vividly missing my father and reading her letters from that time verified those feelings. When I saw the kisses at the bottom of the letters that my father wrote my mother, I would ask her, 'Are they for me?'. Here is a small excerpt from one of the letters my mother wrote to which I had added a postscript to my father written in my own child's hand:

I also remember vividly when the bombing of London became very heavy. The night raids were absolutely horrendous. We were undergoing the terror of the Blitz. We would hear the bombs coming down and they seemed to hover, to my child's imagination, just over our house. My mother would clutch me in her arms and we would hide under the bed or under the staircase, praying that the bombs would not hit our house. I can still hear the haunting, bellowing sound of the air-raid sirens. We were the lucky ones because we survived, but for many others, that was not the case.

Later, when I had children of my own, I asked my mother how she had coped on her own through this dire period of hardship and the horrors of war. 'Everyone was in the same boat', she shrugged, 'we just got on with life as best we could.'

The government decided that, because the Blitz was so intensive, as many children as possible should be evacuated from London (and other major British cities). This came to be known as the Evacuation and many people of my age will have memories of this uncertain period of their lives. My mother arranged for me to be sent to stay with the wife of one of my father's army friends, Annie Hicks. The Hicks lived in an area of Manchester called Middleton and soon I was calling Annie 'Auntie Annie'. Naturally, I didn't want to leave my mother, but, as it transpired, it was the happiest year of the whole war for me. Aunt Annie was wonderful. She didn't have any children of her own, so she lavished love on me and I will never forget her for that. Her house was in a typical northern cobbled street; it had a large kitchen with a huge fireplace. Every so often a big tin bath would be carried into the kitchen and placed in front of a roaring, coal fire and I would have a bath. At the rear of the house, the garden backed onto gorgeous fields and farmland. I had a friend called Jean and she and I would roam those hills and meadows as free as birds.

When the Blitz eased somewhat and my mother thought it was safe for me to return to London, I did so, but shortly after my return, my mother was taken seriously ill with a kidney complaint. You can imagine how frightened I felt. A young child can hardly cope with the idea of her mother dying, but happily after weeks of ill-health when she was very pale, languid and bedridden for weeks on end, she recovered. The care of our upstairs neighbour, a kind-hearted Dutch woman who happened to be the District Nurse, contributed to her recovery.

The Odeon, Kingsbury and Glamour

During the war years and the immediate post-war period, my mother, who was an avid cinema-goer, would take me to the local Odeon at Kingsbury. In fact, an Eaton family story tells of me as a two-year-old getting separated from my mother during a shopping expedition. My mother was panicking, of course, and ran home to tell my father (this happened just before he was called up) that I had disappeared. You can imagine the nightmare visions that came to them, but at last they found me. Guess where? In the usherettes' room at the local Odeon. I don't know how I got there, but perhaps, even at that early age, I had the intuitive sense that the movies were going to be important to me. The cinema at that time was a refuge and a form of escapism. I think many people still crave that from films, that it should be an escape from the nitty-gritty real world into a glamorous, fantastic dreamscape where they can leave their everyday lives behind them for a couple of hours. People need dreams and the cinema used to be able to supply them.

Who were the glamorous screen goddesses who impressed me when I was a girl? Rita Hayworth was definitely one. One big regret that I have about my movie career is that I never appeared in an American screen musical. You know, one of those great MGM musicals with Gene Kelly, Cyd Charisse, Howard Keel or Judy Garland, or the

RKO musicals with Astaire and Rogers. Rita Hayworth had the luck, and the talent, to star with both Astaire and Kelly in different musicals. And she had real glamour. The genuine article, authentic twenty-four carat, old-fashioned (if you like) glamour.

I'm not pretending that the Hayworth glamour didn't come with a price tag attached. We now know enough about her life to realise just how hard she had to work at being this glamorous star that Columbia Pictures and Harry Cohn, the executive in charge of production, wanted (Harry Cohn will crop up later in this narrative). They changed the colour of Rita's hair so she became a redhead, they raised her hairline through electrolysis (painful!) and they put her on a strict diet. In addition, of course, they got their skilled designers to dress her glamorously, make-up artists and hairdressers to work their professional magic, they served her up in roles that stressed her beauty and allure, and had her play opposite handsome top male stars, like Tyrone Power in *Blood and Sand* and Glenn Ford in *Gilda* (probably her most famous role), swooning at her feet on screen. A star is born! But the problem was, as she said herself, her husbands married Gilda, but woke up next to Rita Hayworth, the real, living human being with more than her share of emotional problems.

Her beauty and fame led her into marriage with Hollywood's then presiding genius, Orson Welles When that marriage ended, the screen princess married a real-life prince, Prince Aly Khan. But that too did not work out and eventually Rita lurched into alcoholism and was afflicted with premature Alzheimer's Disease before dying at the age of 69. A cautionary tale. Yes, perhaps, but Rita Hayworth never found the emotional stability she clearly needed in her various marriages and without that bedrock of security, she probably did not have the strength to withstand the immense pressures and demands made on her to be this eternal glamour goddess of the screen.

The Queens of Melodrama

Another feature of my movie career I slightly regret was the fact that I did not play more strongly dramatic roles. But the reality was that by the time my career in films started in the fifties, strong dramatic roles for women were on the decrease and that remained the situation until comparatively recently.

That was not the case, however, in the forties when I was going to the movies as a girl. Two Hollywood stars ruled the roost as far as strong dramatic roles were concerned: Bette Davis and Joan Crawford. Neither of them were 'glamour girls' of the same ilk as Hayworth and Gardner, but they had a glamour of their own and they certainly deserved the description 'screen goddess', because their name on the marquee during the heyday of their careers guaranteed good box-office returns. Both

Davis and Crawford acted the part of the great star both on and off screen. Nowadays with the intrusions of tabloid journalism, and with the stars seemingly falling over one another to bare all (literally and metaphorically speaking) to chat-shows and the media in general, it is difficult to view actresses with the same awe that we invested the likes of Davis and Crawford with.

Davis and Crawford invariably played strong women, who, realizing that it was a man's world, used their female wiles and cunning to get what they wanted: the man they loved, riches, fame, security, whatever. To achieve these goals, they would sometimes cheat, lie, blackmail or kill. These ladies knew what they wanted and they went for it, and if it didn't always end happily, then they at least had had a good time trying. Bette Davis schemed and fought in movies such as *The Letter*, *The Great Lie*, *The Little Foxes* and *Now Voyager*. Joan Crawford emoted in films like *A Woman's Face*, *Mildred Pierce* and *Humoresque*. And they became great stars because lots of women identified with them and thought they were glamorous icons in some ways. Both were sexy in their individual styles, but again that sexiness had nothing to do with overexposure or explicitness.

Judy Garland

Judy Garland was another favourite of mine. She wasn't glamorous like Hayworth or Gardner. In fact, she suffered all her life from an inferiority complex about her looks and waged a constant battle with her yo-yoing weight, which almost certainly contributed to her early death at the age of 45. Yet Garland had her own kind of glamour, the glamour that comes from inside herself, her great talent and sheer guts. She was also very vulnerable and she showed that when she acted up there on the screen and sang her heart out. When she sang, she was singing about her dreams, her sadness, her regrets and her courage. She was singing for all women and yet she appealed to men as well. Shining through all her performances was her sincerity. My goodness, she really could put her whole self into a song like 'The Man Who Got Away' or even her trademark number, 'Over the Rainbow'.

But it was a long, long journey from *The Wizard of Oz* to her last film *I Could Go On Singing* along a very bumpy path that was not like the yellow brick road in Oz. Her failed marriages, the tussles over child custody, her arguments with studio heads, her worries over her weight and her health, the pressure of performing and just being Judy Garland, that icon of showbusiness - all that took its toll and finally it defeated her. If only she had had a stable marriage and family life behind her, things might have been very different. But her highly-talented daughter, Liza Minnelli, who has had a few problems of her own, has warned us off being too tragic when we discuss her mother. Life with mother Judy Garland was a lot of fun at times, and I think that comes across in Judy's performances. 'Life is a cabaret, old chum', sings Sally Bowles/Liza Minnelli in *Cabaret*, and this could have been written about Judy Garland, one of the greatest performers of this century.

During my career, there were inevitable pressures on me, although I would not claim they were as intense as those faced by Rita Hayworth or Judy Garland. But I had the great good fortune to be married to my beloved husband, Colin, for thirty seven years before his tragic death a few years ago, and to have had two wonderful sons. My husband and family always came first before my career and I'm not ashamed to say so in this feminist age. The fact that my marriage was so enduring and that we loved each other so much, and adored our two sons, gave me a security and a safe harbour that helped me withstand the demands that came my way when I was seen as the 'glamour girl' of British movies. I am not saying there were not ups-and-downs in our life together (what long-lasting marriage does not encounter those?), but the knowledge that I was adored by my husband, and my feelings of love for him, sustained me throughout my life and my career.

Ava Gardner

Curiously enough, Hollywood made a 1954 movie *The Barefoot Contessa* that was loosely based on the real-life story of Rita Hayworth, and that provides a link for me to discuss the other Hollywood screen goddess of the time who really impressed me with her glamour, Ava Gardner. Gardner starred in *The Barefoot Contessa*, along with Humphrey Bogart, as the doomed and wilful star. In films such as *The Killers*, *One Touch of Venus*, *Pandora and the Flying Dutchman*, *The Snows of Kilimanjaro*, *Mogambo* and *The Sun Also Rises*, Ava projected a brand of glamour that was very womanly, but hard-edged, romantic, but raunchy as well. She often played the sadder-but-wiser gal, the slightly bitter woman who has been around but who still has a heart of gold under that tough, defensive exterior. A glamorous sexiness leapt out from Gardner, an alluring appeal that had nothing to do with taking her clothes off or appearing in steamy sex scenes. The sexual appeal was intrinsic in how glamorous stars like Gardner and Hayworth were shown on screen. There was nothing of today's in-your-face screen sex and that restraint, forced upon filmmakers by censorship and public attitudes of the time, only made their glamour more potent. You know that old line, 'A glimpse of stocking was something shocking...', well, there's a lot to be said for less meaning more. If you show everything, where's the mystery of femaleness?

The War Is Over!

Meanwhile, back in 1945...one day there was wonderful news. The war had ended and my father would be coming home. But a few months had to pass before he was finally demobilized. During that time I was full of anticipation for the return of the father whom I had missed so badly. Everyone was having street parties, that fine old London tradition. A state of euphoria seemed to have gripped the whole population.

Finally, the day arrived when he was expected home. My mother had made two dresses for herself and me especially for this red letter day. I washed extra carefully and shone just like a new-minted penny. All day I waited and waited for him to arrive and I kept looking up the long street near our house. It seemed like eternity before I saw a soldier in the distance at the top of the street. My legs turned to jelly as my mother and I walked towards him. We stopped a short distance away from him. My Dad stopped too. I saw this sturdy, young man with his kit bag slung over his shoulder. I ran towards him and just as I reached him, he dropped everything. He hugged me in his arms. I felt overwhelming emotion. Home, my father was home again.

Like millions of other families in Britain, we all tried to pick up the threads of family life and start to live normally again. My father managed to buy a small shop with his hundred pounds demobilization money to make and sell his own mattresses. My mother made the mattress covers, so now they had their first joint business venture. To this day, I admire their initiative. It could not have been easy in those days after the war. The dislocation and disorientation that came with the war affected people in different ways, but my parents got back on their feet and characteristically made the best of things and prospered.

Schools

I was going to a local council primary school, but my parents thought perhaps I would get a better education at a convent school. I tried my best to adjust to these new surroundings and ways of doing things, but without success. I wasn't a Catholic, so I felt a bit of an outsider. In addition, I found the atmosphere suffocating. My parents were only trying to do their best for me, but eventually they could see I wasn't happy there and so back to the local school I went.

Any musical talent I have probably stems from my father. He is very musical and plays the piano accordion. Every Christmas and New Year my parents would organize big parties and invite all their friends. They would eat, drink, sing and dance all through the night. Inevitably, my father would dress up and do silly, and sometimes outrageously funny, things. He loves playing the clown and making people laugh. I would sing and dance as well, but when I'd had enough excitement for one night, I would crawl under the mountain of coats and hats into my bed.

I had started dancing classes earlier, where I was learning ballet and tap. If I do say so myself, I seemed to be a natural performer, enough anyway for my parents to think that it might be worth developing my natural talent in a specialist school. I think there is a good deal of the frustrated performer in both my father and mother, although they never became what people refer to as 'stage

Eight years old! Rehearsing for a ballet examination – which I passed!.

parents'. My mother, who is half-Irish with fair hair and clear blue eyes, was intelligent and ambitious for me, but she was never a stage mum. Both sides of the family had no showbusiness background, so I cannot claim, like Judy Garland in *A Star Is Born*, that I was born in a trunk. But something was working its way out and my parents' love of entertaining and my father's musical bent were clearly an influence on me. From an early age, I was used to singing and dancing in front of friends, so when I had to do it in front of an audience, it wasn't too much of a shock, although I was usually nervous.

Proudly wearing an outfit my mother made

It was quite a step, then, for my parents to decide to send me to a stage school called Aida Foster's in North London. It was also a financial sacrifice on their part, because they had to pay the fees for my tuition, which was no light matter for people like them who were struggling to make a living. But it is a testimony to their love for me and their desire to see that I got every opportunity in life that they made the sacrifices and paid their hard-earned money to send me to stage school. My father, it has to be said, had some initial reservations, because he did not want his daughter to go on the stage, but my mother persuaded him and so, at the tender age of ten, I enrolled as a

With my parents. Together at last, with the war behind us

pupil at Aida Foster. This was the first rung on the ladder that would eventually lead to my career in the movies.

I was ten, thrilled but very nervous about being at Aida Foster's. Somehow I had to learn to present a confident facade to the world. Mrs Aida Foster, the head of the school, was also a theatrical agent for child performers. Soon after arriving at the school, I began to audition for stage shows, but modelling children's clothes at fashion houses was my first taste of being in front of cameras and lights. It was all new and fresh to me and I enjoyed it with a child's wonder.

My days at school were split in half. In the morning we had formal education, in the afternoons we learnt how to act, sing and dance. I especially loved singing and dancing because it gave me such freedom of expression. I quickly began to show promise for future things and, to her credit, Mrs Foster was pushing me all the time to improve, especially in how I spoke. Being a north Londoner from my social background, I had a cockney accent. In those days, the late forties, accents were a hindrance in the theatre because this was years before the breakthrough of social realism in the arts and so-called 'kitchen sink' drama when having a working-class accent was a positive advantage in certain quarters. So I had to have elocution classes to get rid of my accent.

Life at Aida Foster's was very competitive. I guess this was practical training for the world of showbusiness we were intended to enter, because actors are always in competition with one another and some can be quite ruthless in their desire for success in the business. I found the competition quite hard at that young age, but I suppose it did help to toughen me up and prepare me for the sometimes harsh world of the entertainment industry.

Jean Simmons had been at Aida Foster just before I joined and she was obviously one of their success stories, starring in British movies of the time such as *Great Expectations* (with John Mills) and *Hamlet*, playing Ophelia to Laurence Olivier's Prince. I think Mrs Foster was hoping to find another Jean Simmons. Barbara Windsor also attended Aida's and our paths must have crossed at some time, but curiously I haven't any memory of it. It doesn't seem possible that I could forget someone like Barbara, but this was a long time ago. When I met Barbara recently at Pinewood Studio on the occasion of their fortieth anniversary of the making of the first *Carry On* film (more of that occasion later), she told me she remembered me sitting in class one day in front of her (I was a bit older than Barbara). 'I was in such awe of you,' she told me, 'you were so sophisticated and beautiful.' Another charming story concerning Barbara was when she was a guest on the Terry Wogan television show years later and she asked the chat show host 'Whatever happened to that lovely Shirley Eaton?' What a generous remark to make!

My First Acting Roles

When I was eleven, I made my acting debut. It wasn't on the stage but in the comparatively new medium of television. Television in those days was mostly all live. Shows were seldom pre-recorded, so actors had to act live in the studio, which was, of course, nerve-racking. The show was part of a '*For the Children*' magazine programme. It was called *Parent-Craft*, a short series about a middle-class family and their various ups-and-downs. William Mervyn played the father. There were two children: I played the young daughter and William Fox played the son. Wilfred Hyde White, whom later I would appear in several films with, was in one episode.

My mother acted as my chaperone, but I was absolutely petrified before each live show was transmitted. I knew there was only one chance to get it right, it wasn't like films where if you fluff a line, you can do a retake. If something went wrong in the studio, then that was it. So, before each show, I could be found in the ladies suffering from nervous diahorrea. As far as I remember, the series consisted of six shows and I wonder how many of you reading this now can recall anything about it.

One thing I do remember was that on one occasion Robert Morley, the genial British comedy actor, who wrote the series and played a character called

Crossington-Tallboy, took all the cast out to a very grand restaurant. He turned to me and asked if I would like a prawn cocktail. I innocently replied, 'No, thank you, I don't like alcohol!' They all laughed at me and I laughed too when it was explained to me. I realised I quickly had to learn some social graces.

Naturally, despite my nervousness, this new world of professional entertainment that I had entered was endlessly fascinating and exciting. New experiences were piling up and my stage debut was not long delayed. In fact, I stepped on the professional stage for the first time exactly on my twelfth birthday. In those days, children were not allowed to perform on stage until they were twelve. The play, *Set To Partners*, opened two days before my birthday, so the actress who played me as an adult later in the play had to dress up as a twelve-year-old for those first two performances. It seems absurd nowadays that this had to be done, but there were very strict rules about using child performers in those days. Then on the third performance a nervous but proud twelve-year-old set foot on stage. We toured the provinces for three weeks with the play, my mother and I sharing theatrical digs together. But the play was not a great success and it did not make a transfer to London's West End. Still, *Set To Partners* marked my professional stage debut.

I Sing Opera

The following year I had the great privilege to audition for, and be cast in, an opera specially written for children by the great composer, Benjamin Britten. It was called *Let's Make An Opera*. To my utter amazement, I passed the audition and got a speaking and singing role, playing the girl of a pair of twins, among a cast of eight children in total. Singing Britten's wonderful music was a challenge I really enjoyed. It was during these two runs of Britten's opera at the Lyric Theatre, Hammersmith in London that I began to learn what being on stage really meant in terms of hard work and discipline. It was a successful show, having an initial longish run and then reopening at the same theatre in the following year (1951). In between runs, I went back to Aida Foster's.

I quickly learned how to project my singing voice into an auditorium and I was also learning about various aspects of stagecraft, so the experience of being in *Let's Make An Opera* was invaluable in so many ways. I suffered from stage nerves, but I found out to my relief that most actors had them.

I also learned theatrical discipline from the wardrobe mistress on that show. We all wore period costumes of pale colours and frilly styles. The wardrobe mistress was a good-hearted woman, but, my goodness, she ruled the children in the cast with a rod of iron. If we got one speck of dirt on our costumes, we were in serious trouble, or so it seemed to us at the time. I still take great care of my clothes to this very day and I think that partly stemmed from that lady. My mother had always been a skilled dressmaker and I learned the art from her. Both of us still get great satisfaction from turning a length of material into an original design.

I also had another experience of live television because there was a special transmission of a performance of *Let's Make An Opera* from the Theatre Royal in Stratford, East London on February 3, 1950. There was my name in the Radio Times: Shirley Eaton as Tina Crome in the English Opera Company production. The show was especially interesting because part one showed the various stages of the creation and rehearsal of a new children's opera and part 2, *The Little Sweep*, was the opera itself about a wretched sweepboy who is rescued by a group of children, one of whom was played by me. There was the innovative idea (for opera) of the audience joining in the singing of four songs.

I was also earning real money now. In fact, I was earning more money from appearing in the Benjamin Britten opera than my father was making from his mattress business. That was something I did not like very much. It made me feel uncomfortable that I should be paid more for acting and singing than he did for all those hours of hard toil. However, his first mattress shop had done well so he bought another bigger shop, selling furniture this time. He had had enough of breathing the dust that was inevitable when making mattresses. He and my mother ran this new business successfully. He bought a caravan to replace the tent we used to go on camping holidays with. When I wasn't appearing on stage, we had wonderful weekends in St Osyths by the seaside. One glorious day at St Osyths, my father and a friend went out to sea in a small engine-powered boat. They had intended to spend an hour or two out at sea. Not long after they left the shore, the boat capsized. When my mother and her friends realized they were missing, they weren't too concerned at first. I remember standing next to her on the shore searching for some sign of the boat. After a while, we saw two heads bobbing up and down. Much later, my father and his friend dragged themselves out of the water, having had literally to swim for their lives. This brush with disaster did not deter my parents from their love of the sea. Boats and the sea have always been a part of my life in one way or another.

My parents had both wanted another child very much since the time of my father's return from the war, but it was not to be. My father wanted a son and when I was a baby, he used to make toy cars and great balsa wood aeroplanes which I played with along with my dolls. Once it was clear they could not have any more children of their own, they finally took the step they had been thinking about for a long time and adopted a six-week-old baby boy, whom they called Johnny after my father. I was fourteen at the time and was as happy about this as they were. I had always wanted a brother or a sister because being an only child can be a lonely affair. I would take Johnny out in his pram and show him off proudly to all the neighbours, perhaps rehearsing for the day when I would become a mother. To have a husband and children was my ultimate aim in life. It seemed perfectly natural to me to want that. Working in showbusiness was thrilling, but it was, as far as I was concerned, a period of good fortune until the right man came along. Meanwhile, I helped to look after my new baby brother and learned much from my mother's example. Johnny was a good and happy baby and we were all devoted to him. Now there were four of us, a real family. An only child can be like an appendage to a married couple, but when you have two or more children, the whole family atmosphere changes. However, it took nearly eight months after Johnny came to us for his adoption to be finalized. During those months, my mother's anguish would often show. How could she ever part with this newfound baby they had wanted so much and were growing to love? Fortunately, she did not have to.

My first portfolio pin-up session, aged sixteen.
I thought then you had to *try* to look sexy.

Modelling, My First Agent and Sophisticated Revue

Meanwhile, back at Aida Foster's, my education, both academic and dramatic, continued with my going for very competitive auditions from time to time. One day at school, I asked to be excused. It was a dull, wintry February morning. I slipped downstairs to the cloakroom and heard a group of girls talking in hushed whispers. I heard the words, 'Dead? He's dead?' I popped my head round the door. 'Who's dead?' I asked. 'The King', they choroused. I rushed upstairs to all the classrooms shouting, ' The King's dead! The King's dead!' in a hysterical voice, almost laughing with the tension I felt. I couldn't believe it. I was having a very strange reaction to the news. I have often looked back and thought, 'Why did I have such a strange reaction to the death of George VI?' To this day, I cannot fully explain it, except to say that in that distant era, the Royal Family were much more remote from the ordinary people and were perceived as being almost of a different species from the rest of us, so for the King to die must have seemed earthshaking to my young mind.

The cloakroom and changing rooms at school were havens for us pupils when we felt we had to share thoughts and feelings. I can still picture it in my mind's eye as I write now and sense the atmosphere. Sometimes I would sit and watch the older girls putting on their make-up to go out and they seemed so beautiful and grown-up that I was in awe of them. They seemed to have such confidence. I couldn't wait to be grown up like them and acquire a similar glamour.

The highlight of my schooldays at Aida Foster's was the year I was voted the most popular girl in the school. We were all assembled in the large ballet room. It had been a neck-and-neck race between another girl and myself. When they announced the result, they called out my name. What a thrill! At the time, it seemed like I had won an Oscar and I was just as excited as any actor accepting that gold-plated statuette.

I was thought to be photogenic and so I was photographed modeling a sweater for the cover of a knitting magazine. It wasn't quite yet the cover of *Life* or *Picture Post* but it was certainly a start. I did other advertisements in magazines as well. In addition, when I was sixteen, I did some clothes modeling at a London fashion house.

It must have been around this time that I acquired my first agent, Richard Stone, whom I stayed with until I made *Goldfinger*. Having an experienced and active agent with contacts in the business is an essential requisite for any actor wanting to make it in the profession and I was lucky to have Richard who worked hard for me and was someone I also trusted and liked. It was Harry Secombe, one of the original Goons, who put me into contact with Richard, when I met him during the recording of a radio show. Harry, a genuinely kind man, suggested my mother contact Richard, a well-known variety artist agent. My mother did this and I met Richard, who decided to represent me. He is an extremely nice human being and we still keep in contact every Christmas.

When I was fifteen, I was extremely fortunate to be cast in a revue that ran at the Lyric, Hammersmith and which was called appropriately *At the Lyric*. Revue is a theatrical genre that has largely disappeared now, but then revue meant a mixture of comedy sketches of a slightly superior and topical kind, as well as sophisticated song and dance. The cast included such skilled practitioners in the art as Ian Carmichael, Dora Bryan and Hermione Baddely. Rachel Roberts, then almost at the beginning of her career, was also in the cast, and I shared a dressing room with her and another actress. At fifteen, I was by far the youngest in the show, but I learnt a lot about life during the run especially from Rachel, who was a talented, vibrant, sexy and emotional Welsh woman. In such company, too, I inevitably honed my performing skills, taking part in comic sketches and in light musical numbers. The stars of the revue were very helpful to me. Backstage was small and uncomfortable as many theatres were at that time. One thing I have always disliked about the theatre was the comparative squalor behind the scenes. Everything of value happens on the few feet of board we call a stage.

It was during the run of the revue that I had an infatuation with the Assistant Stage Manager. But the relationship was fraught with difficulties and it floundered because of them. I was an adolescent girl trying to absorb everything about me, never quite understanding what was happening, only that so much change was going on in my life. I felt that a part of me was still a child and the other part was longing to be fully adult. I would travel home after the show back to reality and think what was this strange life of the theatre. I didn't know exactly where it would lead; all I did know was that I was on the road to somewhere.

It was fun sharing a dressing-room with Rachel Roberts, who lived life to the full. Later she married Alan Dobie, but the marriage didn't last. Then, of course, years later, she was one of Rex Harrison's wives. I met up with Rachel in Hollywood in the sixties when both our lives had been transformed, but more of that later.

I left Aida Foster's when I was sixteen. My parents bought a pleasant house with a lovely garden. I was still living at home and I enjoyed with them the comparative luxury of this new home. I had done television and stage work and now I was to get a break into radio. One well-known show of the time was *Educating Archie* which featured a ventriloquist, Peter Brough, and his dummy, Archie Andrews. 'We'll be educating Archie, What a job for anyone' became a familiar theme tune to millions of radio listeners each week on what was then called the Light Programme. I used to join in comedy sketches and sing in the interludes between the comedy. Max Bygraves, who was by then very well-known, was also in the show.

I seemed to be flavour-of-the-month and work was not hard to come by, but I still had not done any films. However, that branch of entertainment was not to be denied me for very much longer. Soon, I was to make my first films in a movie career that would span almost twenty years. I had grown up with movies, watching them with my mother in my local Odeon. They had a special glamour all of their own for me and the glamorous stars who appeared in them seemed very special. I wanted to be part of that glamour and add to it myself.

42

3
MOVIES GALORE

You have to start somewhere in the crazy world of movie-making and my first brush with films was 'doubling' work. Doubling is when another actor stands in for a star in long shots or in scenes where the star's actual presence is not absolutely necessary. Doubling reduces the amount of contractual days that the filmmakers have to employ a star for and it also saves actors from having to be on set or on location all the time.

If I had to start my movie career with doubling, then at least I started by standing in for someone who was a big star at the time, the beautiful Hollywood actress, Janet Leigh. The picture was *Prince Valiant*, which also starred Robert Wagner, and it was one those historical romps that Hollywood was fond of making in Britain in the fifties. They needed a girl who looked reasonably like Janet Leigh, at least in long shots, and who could ride a horse well. My mother had had the foresight to send me to riding school in my early teens, so I could just about handle a horse, although it was not something I liked doing much. But when the chance of the audition came up, I gritted my teeth and said 'Yes!' to the question as to whether I could ride a horse.

The audition took place somewhere in the middle of our beautiful English countryside. The director of the movie was the legendary Henry Hathaway, whose reputation had been made with action movies such as *Kiss of Death*, *Rawhide*, *Rommel*, *Desert Fox* and *Niagara* with Marilyn Monroe. He was an intimidating man and I was nervous as he 'inspected' me to see whether I met his requirements as a reasonable Janet Leigh lookalike. 'Yeah, you look good, kid,' he barked, 'but you're just a bit on the young side. Let's see how you sit on a horse.'

This was the challenge. How was I going to convince this leathered Hollywood veteran that I could ride a horse? Hathaway had made lots of westerns and worked with famous western stars such as John Wayne. In addition, although I did not know it at the time, one of the things he had been quoted as saying about being a film director was, 'You've got to be a bastard. I'm a bastard and I know it.' Well, he said it, not me!

They gave me a sprightly nag and dressed me up in a period costume and asked me to ride it side-saddle. When I was asked to ride the animal, I dug it in the flanks and frankly, it just bolted! I was clinging desperately to it and trying to look dignified at the same time. After all, Janet Leigh was playing a queen in the movie and as her double I would be expected to look regal even on a bolting horse. In fact, my heart was thudding with fear and I expected to be thrown at any moment. This 'audition' was scaring the wits out of me and I longed for it to end. But somehow, I don't know how, after what seemed an endless gallop, I regained control of the horse and rode it back to the starting-point. 'Yeah', drawled Mr Hathaway, 'you got the job.' Somehow I had convinced this grizzled Hollywood director that I was a horsewoman of sorts. I was pleased, of course, to get the work, but it was an ambivalent pleasure, because I knew that a good proportion of the next few weeks would be spent on horseback, which was definitely not my favourite way of spending time.

The location shooting took place all over England. As the Queen in long shot, I had to ride through forests and across rivers. I was always petrified that I was going to fall off, spoil the shot and become the target of Henry Hathaway's blistering tongue. I was perhaps more apprehensive of incurring the director's wrath than concerned about my own safety because I was so anxious to do this well. Yet I managed to hide my fears and somehow or other, I stayed glued to the saddle.

Prince Valiant was my first experience of the American, fast-moving, aggressive style of making a movie. I was a very young seventeen-year-old and was making my debut on a film being shot on location. I wasn't involved in the scenes shot in the studio. I was like most seventeen year-olds, starry-eyed and terribly inexperienced in this bizarre new world. I just gazed at all the crew, stunt men and other doubles with bewilderment.

Yes, Henry Hathaway was tough and demanding. Whether he deserved his own description of himself, I will leave you to judge. I remember vividly one scene that had nothing to do with horses. It was a night shot, which was filmed round one of our ancient castles. The script called for me/Janet Leigh to walk down a long flight of stairs to the edge of the sea and climb aboard a Viking ship. It was very dark and slippery and the boat was already half full of water. I had a long, flowing costume on, which became soaking wet almost up to my waist. I was looking, and feeling, bedraggled. Try looking regal and beautiful in those circumstances!

Suddenly, from way up on the battlements of the castle where the camera was, the bellowing voice of Hathaway, magnified through a loudspeaker, pierced the darkness of the night. 'Act like a queen, dammit, can't you act like a queen? Otherwise, we're all wasting our time!'

At first, I just froze with fear. I had just been shouted at in front of everyone by the guy who was running the show. But I gathered myself together, decided not to have a breakdown on the spot and did the scene again. I was dripping wet and freezing to death, but, if regal was what they wanted, regal was what they were going to get. Eventually Hathaway seemed to be pleased. I don't agree with the late Mr Hathaway: movie directors don't need to be bastards to get results. However, he obviously felt it helped!

When the location shooting ended, I thought, 'I hope I shall never have to ride again in a movie!' Years later, when I was making *The Scorpio Letters* in Hollywood, I met Janet Leigh because she was working at the same studio. I told her that I had doubled for her in *Prince Valiant*. She was surprised and very charming about it. It's curious that I could spend all that time doubling for a famous star and never actually meet her during the shoot, but have to wait for years before our paths crossed in Hollywood. But that, as I was finding out, was just one crazy aspect of this odd world of making movies.

My First Film Roles

It wasn't long after my doubling work on *Prince Valiant* that I was cast as a harem girl in the British comedy, *You Know What Sailors Are*, which starred Donald Sinden, Akim Tamiroff and Sarah Lawson. I hasten to add that I was only one of a group of harem girls, but somehow I made an impression on Betty Box, the producer of the film. Betty Box was to be an important person in my early years in films. She decided to give me a small part in the next film she was producing, which turned out to be the phenomenally successful, *Doctor in the House*. The two really big hit British comedies of the fifties, apart from the first *Carry Ons*, were *Genevieve* and *Doctor in the House*, so I was very fortunate to have a speaking role in the latter. Needless to say, when my agent broke the news, I was absolutely thrilled to get the part.

Doctor in the House starred the current heartthrob of the British cinema at that time, Dirk Bogarde, as well as Donald Sinden, Kenneth More, Muriel Pavlow and a host of well-known British character actors, including James Robertson Justice as the irascible consultant, Sir Lancelot. This was my first speaking part in films so I was very nervous about acting in this kind of company. I was especially apprehensive about my two scenes on my own with Dirk Bogarde. He was such a big star and so

Publicity shot for *You Know What Sailors Are*. I pose with Shirley Burniston, a fellow graduate of Aida Fosters

handsome. For those too young to know much about this era in the movies and who only know him from his more recent films, I better explain that Dirk Bogarde was worshipped by millions of teenage girls (and older fans as well) and sometimes had to be protected from their over-zealousness when he appeared in public. Later in his career, of course, he graduated to more serious roles working with directors such as Luchino Visconti and Joseph Losey.

I need not have worried about acting with Dirk. To my enormous relief, he was thoughtful and kind. We worked well together in the scenes and looking at them now, I seem very confident in the role of Millicent Groaker, the landlady's daughter who goes after Simon Sparrow, the young medical student who takes up lodgings with Mrs

46

Groaker, my mother in the movie. She was played by that excellent actress, the late Joan Hickson, who years afterwards played Agatha Christie's Mrs Marple in a television series. When you are working with people of the quality of Dirk Bogarde and Joan Hickson, you are bound to learn about film acting and especially about playing in film comedy.

I am in three scenes in *Doctor in the House*. The first scene has me coming into the dining room of the house with a soup tureen. My mother introduces the new young doctor lodger and I gush, 'How nice! I always think it's nice to have a *doctor in the house*.' So I got to say the title line of the film! I make my intentions towards Dirk/Simon very plain when I follow this up by saying flirtatiously, 'Saw a lovely film about a doctor and a beautiful girl. He operated on her and then married her.' I am playing a cockney girl so, in that sense, the part felt close to my experience. I didn't mind playing the ambitious sexpot, but she was hardly subtle in her approaches. But then the *Doctor* films were fairly broad in their comic style, although certainly not as broad as the *Carry Ons*.

Still, Millicent Groaker was a good cameo part to play. In the second scene, I have Dirk all to myself. I go to his room and pretend that I have something wrong with my foot. I sit down on the bed and raise my skirt above the knee, but Dirk tells me to pull it down and tells me it isn't necessary to take my stocking off. 'You have such lovely soft hands,' I breathe as he examines my leg. When he suggests I might need a poultice, I ask him whether he would put it on for me. Seen from the perspective of the late 1990s, it all seems so innocent and tame, but I think it retains a certain charm. My last scene is when I knock on his door again late at night. This time I am in a dressing-gown

Donald Sinden enjoying the attentions of the harem in *You Know What Sailors Are*

At the Lyric Hammersmith with Hermione Baddeley. My first important stage appearance in a review called *At The Lyric*.

and my intentions are plain. 'It's gone and moved up to my hip now,' I complain. Dirk closes the door on me and soon after moves lodgings. As Kenneth More says in the next scene, 'The landlady's daughter, the oldest joke in the world,' but it turned out to be no joke for me because it was a part I was noticed for, and the film itself was stupendously popular. Although cinema audiences had dropped off in Britain since the peak of the immediate post-war years due to the impact of television, almost everybody in the country, it seemed, saw *Doctor in the House*. To have even a small part in such a raging success was important for my career and justified Betty Box's faith in my potential. There was my name up there on the screen in the cast list, not very high up perhaps in the billing, but I was listed with some excellent, famous actors.

It was three years later that I made my other *Doctor* film, *Doctor at Large*. It had largely the same cast with the addition of Michael Medwin as my boy friend, and the usual roster of British comedy actors including Joan Sims, later a stalwart of the *Carry On* series, Mervyn Johns, Lionel Jeffries, Athene Seyler, Wilfred Thomas, Barbara Murray and Kay Kendall, who was married to Rex Harrison and died of leukaemia at such a young age.

This time my part was appreciably bigger. I played Nan McPherson, a nurse at St Swithin's Hospital where Dirk and the rest are supposed to be house doctors. And this time I was billed at the top of the 'Also Starring' credits along with Derek Farr and Michael Medwin. So by that standard, a lot had moved on for me between *Doctor* films. I am in the very first scene of the movie flirting with Dirk/Simon, although I

My excitement at working opposite Dirk Bogarde in my first speaking role was immense

am meant to be involved with the awful Bingham (Michael Medwin), Simon Sparrow's deadly rival for a resident's job at the hospital and also his rival for my affections. But my character is somewhat calculating and although I encourage Dirk's attentions, especially when I find out he runs a natty sports car, I have the eye to the main chance and plump for Michael Medwin. Before that, I go away for an illicit weekend to a country inn with Dirk, but the stern hotelier keeps us apart when Dirk mucks up the signing in with phoney names. This was the mid-fifties and the idea that two unmarried people would share a hotel room was still thought to be a bit daring, so our plans are forestalled. Oh, goodness, what an innocent age that now appears! I have some good lines including one where I reply to a boring intruder at the hotel (played by Guy Middleton), 'I'm a lady, but no wife!' I had graduated from sexy cockney girl in *Doctor in the House* to sexy middle-class girl in *Doctor At Large*. And by this time, I was much more experienced in films and I felt much more at ease about acting with these big stars.

A few years ago, I met up with Dirk Bogarde - his last public appearance at Pinewood Studios - for a tribute to Betty Box, who had produced the *Doctor* films and many other successful British movies, as well as giving me my first break in the cinema. Much water had passed under the bridge in the intervening decades for both Dirk and myself. Dirk, of course, went on to become a major international star and well-respected novelist. He was a very cultivated, intelligent man and for many years he lived in rural France, which gave us something else in common, because I too love French culture and lived in the south of France. *The Times* printed a photograph of us together at the gathering and I couldn't help feeling that something of British film history was caught in that image of us two together. It seemed a long time since we had made *Doctor in the House* together, but, in another way, it seemed like it was only yesterday. We are all caught up in the web of time.

More Television and Stage Work

The famous long-running television show *Juke Box Jury* had been running for some time on the box. For those not familiar with the show, I better explain that the idea was that new singles were played to a panel of guests who then pronounced their verdict as to whether they would be commercially successful or not. I seemed to be making a name for myself so I was invited to be a regular guest on the panel. It was quite a showcase because it was a hugely popular programme at the time and watched by millions of people every early Saturday evening. It was also additional proof, if proof were needed, that I had indeed 'arrived'. David Jacobs was the urbane host of the show and other guests included singers, other luminaries from the world of music and usually someone who was not directly involved in the music industry. How I hated sounding the hooter that meant that I had to give the thumbs-down to a record's commercial potential. I knew only too well what hard work had to go into trying to forge a successful career in showbusiness, so I did not like to be discouraging in any way, but that was the name of the panel game and I had to be honest.

Around this time, Terry Scott and Bill Maynard, who were big in this era, had a television series called, *Great Scott, It's Maynard!* I did a singing spot on the show and acted in comedy sketches. I suppose I could deliver on at least two fronts: I could sing and dance and I could also act. Perhaps they also thought I added a little glamour to the shows as well! I was learning another technique by appearing in these shows: acting in comedy in front of a live studio audience. The shows were live transmissions from the BBC studios, which was nerve-wracking enough, and millions of homes up and down the country would be tuned in, because there was no competition at that time from ITV or cable stations. But the live studio audience added another dimension of pressure. However, this was all invaluable experience and added immeasurably to my skills as a performer in different media. I was the youngest performer in these Terry Scott and Bill Maynard shows, but I was well looked after and the leads showed interest in me and my career. We did several different series, with a few gaps in between. An interesting postscript to this series is that years later I appeared as a guest on the *This Is Your Life* that told the story of Terry Scott's life and career. I also came on when *This Is Your Life* did Hattie Jacques, with whom I worked on three *Carry On* movies. I was delighted to add my tributes to both these talented and likeable people, both of whom in their different ways had helped in my own career. I was also due to appear on the Bob Hope *This Is Your Life*, but I had to call off at the last moment because I had been stricken with flu. I had worked with Bob on a Hollywood movie and I was very sorry to miss the opportunity to pay homage to the great comedian.

I also appeared in the very early *Benny Hill* television shows. Benny and I shared the same agent at the time. Benny's shows have become something of a cult since and I know they are especially popular in the States, where they are constantly repeated on cable stations. It is a strange fact that Benny made his name by playing this lecherous guy in a raincoat always chasing scantily-clad females over fields and doing jokes that concentrated on sex and toilets, yet the real Benny Hill was a very shy man. He must have been working out something in himself by adopting such a comic persona. I never found him in the least lecherous or smutty and, if anything, I thought he was rather repressed, which may explain the content of his comedy. As the

With Leslie Bricusse and Lionel Bart at a showbiz party

Carry On movies prove, the British like their double-entendres and seaside postcard jokes. Perhaps the surprising thing is that the humour seems to travel so well because Benny Hill and the *Carry On* movies have fans to this day all over the globe.

Big stars of the day such as Tommy Steele, Cliff Richard, Ronnie Carroll and Michael Holliday had their own variety shows and I appeared in them singing solo. It was during one of these shows that I met Lionel Bart, who would later write the massive hit musical, *Oliver!*. I went out socially with friends of Lionel's. They were a young group of musicians and writers who were all struggling to make their name in the entertainment or literary worlds. One of them had a small flat in Chelsea where we used to gather sometimes at the weekends. It was fun. I was just seventeen and everything was happening to me so rapidly. I was meeting all sorts of people from all different spheres of showbusiness and the arts. The press called for

Posing to publicize *Picture Post* magazine at a news kiosk, with some slightly shy news vendors

interviews and I had photo sessions for newspapers and magazines. I was lucky enough to appear on the front cover of *Picture Post*, the leading magazine of its time with a high reputation for photo-journalism. I also made the front cover of *Picturegoer*, which was the leading British film magazine. I had lunches in London's most fashionable restaurants and I could have gone to a party every night if I had wanted to. It was all so hectic and exhilarating, my feet hardly touched the ground.

Naturally, my parents were deliriously happy about my success. I proudly bought my first car, a sporty little Hillman and called her 'Little Mo', after Maureen Connelly, the American tennis star who won Wimbledon so often and who died in the sixties of cancer so tragically young. 'Little Mo' was black with a red top and I loved her. At that time, to own a car at my age was thrilling, but it was also becoming a necessity because of the busy schedule I had to keep. Things were certainly buzzing!

The Mayor of Harrow invited me to open a Children's Club. I took the chance to have a go on their bowling alley.

I Play the Palladium and Work with Peter Sellers!

At the end of 1954, my first big stage break came. I was chosen to play the part of Marjorie Dawe in pantomime at the famous London Palladium. It was *Mother Goose* and my co-stars were to be Max Bygraves and Peter Sellers. It was every variety artist's dream to play the Palladium. It was similar to the American dream of playing the Palace in New York. At the time, the Palladium was at the peak of its fame. All the top names from both sides of the Atlantic would headline there, so I felt very privileged indeed to be starring in the their annual pantomime which ran for a six-week season. My first couple of years in the profession since I had left Aida Foster had been incredibly successful: I had launched my film career, I was well-known on radio and television, and now I was in the Palladium pantomime in a leading role. My good fortune seemed never-ending.

In the dressing room of the Palladium, while appearing in *Mother Goose*, signing my seven year contract with Alexander Korda. My father was required to sign on my behalf, as I was not yet 21.

A week later. Celebrating my eighteenth birthday backstage, with my brother Johnny.

Peter Sellers had become famous by then for being one of the original Goons in the famous radio show, *The Goons*. One time I was sitting in the studio audience watching them record one of the shows. I will never forget how funny those eccentric, colourful artists were. Although there was a script, they ad-libbed so much that you never knew what was going to happen next. Neither did they, I think. The studio audience ached from laughing so much.

I enjoyed the season at the Palladium. Playing to capacity audiences in the world's greatest variety theatre was thrilling, even if it was hard work and involved on occasions doing the show thrice daily. Once again, it was working in front of a live audience and I was honing my comic skills and my sense of timing. Of course, I could learn every performance from Max Bygraves and Peter Sellers, who both had masterly timing.

However, even in those early days in his career, Peter Sellers could be a handful as far as shows of temperament were concerned. I liked Peter, but he had his extremely insecure and needy side. He never seemed satisfied with his own performance and when he threw a tantrum, it was best to steer clear of him, leave him alone and wait for him to calm down. I don't think he ever meant to be hurtful to anyone, but when he was in one of his moods, he did hurt people. Afterwards, he would be terribly contrite and apologise all round. It was difficult for me to be angry with him because I saw him as a vulnerable, unbalanced child.

I worked with Peter again on the 1957 film *The Naked Truth*. Between the Palladium panto and making this film, he had become much more successful and famous and this had merely added to the pressures on him. He still was temperamental, even more so, and at times he was almost impossible to work with. At other times, of course, he could be charming and very, very funny. He was a real Jekyll-and-Hyde character. These were the days when he was still quite plump and before his first heart attack which nearly killed him. It was during the making of *The Naked Truth* when we were shooting a scene on a Thames barge that I announced my engagement to Colin Lenton Rowe, whom I had met and fallen in love with. During

54

a break in the shooting, the cast and crew toasted our engagement with champagne and Peter joined in with the rest. That was one of his good days.

Much had changed for Peter when years later Colin and I ran into him and his wife at that time, Britt Ekland, on the French Riviera. He had had his heart attack, he was slimmed down and he seemed very happy with Britt, who was absolutely gorgeous, of course. We met them at the famous Hotel Eden Roc in Cap d'Entibes and Peter greeted us as long lost friends. We all went out to dinner the next evening to a fine restaurant in Hauts de Cagnes, which Colin and I had gone to during our honeymoon and which, therefore, had special associations for us. I remember we had roasted pigeons cooked on an open fire. French cooking at its very best.

Peter made us all laugh during dinner and we decided to go up into the mountains to a club in Valbonne. I have never much liked alcohol and I certainly have never been able to take too much drink. I had already had some wine with the meal and when we got to the club, I had a cocktail. Peter was continuing to be the life and soul of the party, but inevitably his fame and his talent attracted hangers-on. The club was full of wealthy people who wanted to be near star names and so six strangers joined us. One of the banes of showbusiness fame is the number of hangers-on that such success can attract. Peter was extremely famous by then and everybody wanted to know him and, he, of course, loved an admiring audience.

I liked the look of the drink Peter was having and I asked him what it was. 'A mint julep', he said. 'I'll have one of those', I said blithely and so one was ordered. I drank it down fast and I then mixed it with other drinks. It was very foolish.

Another aspect of showbusiness fame is that there are always predatory people around who want to grab you or your husband or wife. Now my husband Colin was an attractive man, not with film star looks but with a natural masculine attractiveness that I and many other women loved. Colin had left the table and had been at the bar talking to this attractive woman who was clearly trying to take him over. My hackles rose. She was one of those predatory hangers-on who was clearly after my husband partly out of competition with me. As far I was concerned the evening was over for me. I went up to them and asked Colin if he was coming back to the table. But he didn't and then he started dancing smoochily with this lady, who was all over him. I danced too and in my irritation, I ordered yet another mint julep. Well, that did it! I felt extremely ill and had to make a dash for the rather sumptuous ladies room.

I lay there in a booth as sick as the proverbial dog. I don't know how long I was there for, because I had lost the place completely. I had never been so drunk in my life and never would be again. After a while, I heard Britt Ekland's voice outside the door: 'Shirley, unlock the door.' 'Oh, Britt,' I moaned, 'I'm so ill.' And I was. I felt like death. I'll always be grateful to Britt for her kindness that night.

I managed to unlock the door and Britt was attending solicitously to me when Colin, with a rather sheepish look on his face, walked in holding a tall glass of water in his hand. I took it from him and I went to throw it all over him. Unfortunately, because of the state I was in, I merely succeeded in throwing it all over myself. So there I stood, not only tottering with the ravages of drink but soaking wet as well.

By now it was 3.30 in the morning. Britt, Peter and Colin helped me to our car and Colin drove us back to the apartment that we were renting in Juan-les-Pins. To add more grief to the night's disasters, the German family who had been looking after our son Grant for us, told us that he had been crying a lot and so they had taken him up into their flat. This only made me feel worse and even more guilty.

I suffered from alcoholic poisoning that night and most of the next day. About five the next afternoon, I got up, put on a bikini and took a gentle swim. I gradually returned to my normal self. Colin and I talked it out together. It is a fact that in showbusiness, it is quite often the case that a man or a woman will make a play for the wife or the husband of the well-known personality. Whenever some predatory woman moved in on Colin, I would see red. I confess I have a jealous nature and was very possessive over my husband.

These kinds of things happen in the best of marriages and I had one of the best, believe me. Looking back on all the years we spent together, Colin and I hit two really bad patches in our marriage when we did not seem to be communicating or sharing. But I am a very 'rooty' person and I had an absolute terror of divorce. Perhaps not having had a father in the home for all those years during the war has reinforced my need for stability and permanence. I am not in favour of single parenthood, for example. I believe that raising children requires a male and a female parent.

I'm not a flippant person about relationships. When I married my husband, as far as I was concerned it was for life, so I did everything in my power to protect and nurture our relationship. Colin was a volatile, passionate man under the guise of a quiet exterior. We had our difficulties as the account of our night out with Peter Sellers illustrates, but we worked at it and came through to enjoy years of happiness and closeness. But the story of the night I got drunk also illustrates some of the dangers of the showbusiness life. There are predatory people out there!

One postscript to this saga involving Peter Sellers. I saw him at some premiere and we were talking about the days when we were in that Palladium pantomime together. We remembered how someone had arranged for the four stars, myself, Peter, Max Bygraves and the actress playing the Principal Boy to have a group photo taken of the four of us with our mothers. It appeared in the press as a kind of human interest item.

Shortly after the premiere, Peter rang me. His mother, whom, as most people know, he was very close to, had recently died and he wanted to get a copy of that old photo. 'I desperately want this photo,' he pleaded. 'I must have it,' he added almost obsessively. He sounded so sad and needy that I immediately sent him the only copy of the photo that I had, expecting he would have a print made from it and would return it. He never did, which in some ways was typical of Peter. He was a hugely talented man, but the price he had to pay for his fame and success was high. However, despite all the hideous tantrums and the wounding remarks he would make to people, and the ruthless exploitation he made of his star power, I still think of Peter as being fundamentally vulnerable and a childlike person. I was glad I had the opportunity to work twice with one of the leading comic actors of his generation.

Some Thoughts on Love

Writing about that particularly bad night during my marriage to Colin has made me think of the nature of love. How often that word 'love' is wrongly used. How ironic it is that we have to live almost a lifetime before we really understand the true meaning of love in all its many aspects. When I think now of my teenage years, I know for sure that what I thought then was love was really just infatuation, merely a young girl learning about herself and the opposite sex. Personally, I found my first few crushes on the opposite sex full of very mixed emotions. I'm beginning to giggle now as I think about those early nervous kisses and fumbles and hard things being rubbed against me and never knowing quite what to do about it all. I suppose what I needed at the time was a tender and experienced lover.

But I have fallen victim to the snares of false love, like everyone else in the world, I suppose. As I was approaching my eighteenth birthday, for example, I fell madly in love, or so I thought at the time. The man I fell in love with was in showbusiness, a major star, but he was married and he had children. I truly believed at the time that we had a future together. But that's what love does to you, it robs you of judgement, it makes you irrational. And I was very young!

Still, I've never forgotten those short but very exciting weeks when we seemed to be in love. It is very intense at that age and the joys and the pains of love linger. I was living in a dream world, I thought our love would go on forever.

One awful day, my father confronted me. 'What's going on between you and this man?' he asked angrily. My dad was an old-fashioned father and I guess he was feeling very protective towards me. I tried to defend my right to live my own life, but he finally made me admit that I was having an affair with this married man, who was

57

known to my father only because he was a big star.

There and then, he said we were going round to the man's house to find out what his intentions were. My father was very angry, I had never seen him so angry before. I seemed to have no choice in the matter. He was determined to have his confrontation.

It was, of course, a humiliating position for me to be in. Imagine my feelings as my father rang the doorbell of my lover's house and imagine my lover's feelings as he was confronted with me accompanied by a righteously steaming father!

I presumed his wife knew nothing of our affair so when, in his living-room, my father was demanding to know what her husband's intentions were towards me, it must have come as a very unpleasant shock to her to find that he had been having an affair with an actress much younger than he was. If it was a shock to her, she managed to disguise it and behaved with great dignity.

My lover, in front of his wife, told my father that, though he loved me, he would never leave his wife and children. Something about his sincerity or the strength of feeling he expressed both for me and his family must have softened my dad's heart, because before long the four of us were all embracing each other and shedding a tear. The consensus was these things happened and as long as nobody had been really hurt, then it wasn't too tragic. We even had a cup of tea together, as far as I can remember.

Of course, the aftermath for me wasn't that cheerful. You cannot come out of a love affair at that age without it hurting. But the whole business taught me a lesson. It had been a case of puppy love with me, not real love at all. To this day, I'm not too proud of my part in this episode in my life. I could have helped to wreck a happy marriage, which I'm glad to say I didn't, because the two of them, my ex-lover and his wife, are still married to this day. But it was a necessary stage in my growing up and perhaps that was an important part of it for me. Although my teenage years were very successful, I longed to be truly adult and perhaps that affair with this married man seemed to be a part of my growing up.

Young people today are much more knowledgeable about sex than I was as a teenager, perhaps too much so, do you think? I often wonder nowadays where the gift of innocence has gone. I fear it has disappeared forever in the society we live in now. The purest side of every human being is diluted nowadays, mainly due to the influence of so much media fantasy. You may think it a little odd that I who have been involved with the entertainment world on and off all my life should voice such an opinion. Everyone is affected one way or another by television and films, and because of the media, we now live in a desensitised world, which is a great pity.

Society has changed radically over the past fifty years or so and when I look around at the entertainment world business in particular, certain sections of it have clearly gone over the top. Satire on television, for example has no restraint. Young, and not-so-young- comics and presenters, think they have the right to say anything about anybody just as long as they get a cheap laugh and appear clever to the audience. Nothing, or no one, is sacred any more.

Then there is sex. Whoopee! No, but I'm being serious. Sex has become so overexposed in the media that it has lost its specialness, which is tremendously sad. Good, loving sex is one of the most wonderful sensations that any two people can experience together, but it is a private intimate union and not to be represented cheaply and automatically for titillation. Most of you reading this book must know what I am trying to say and I have no doubt that some of you will empathize.

Korda and More Movies

During the run of *Mother Goose* at the Palladium, I signed a seven-year contract with the legendary film producer, Alexander Korda. Among the films he had produced were *The Private Life of Henry VIII* with Charles Laughton, *Things To Come*, *The Four Feathers*, *The Thief of Baghdad*, *That Hamilton Woman* and *Anna Karenina* with Vivien Leigh. He had been seen as the saviour of the British film industry and had built Denham Studios. A Hungarian who had permanently settled in England, Korda was world-famous, having produced films in France, Germany and Hollywood, as well as in Britain. The famous actresses he had 'handled' included Vivien Leigh and Claire Bloom. Therefore, when he offered me a long-term contract, I had no hesitation at all in signing. It seemed I was giving my future over into the capable hands of one of the most famous film producers in the world and to be chosen by him to be part of his exclusive stable of stars seemed like incredible good fortune to me. I signed the contract backstage at the Palladium on my eighteenth birthday, with my father present as I was under 21. It was a very exciting moment.

But it was not to be. Alexander Korda died a few month later and I was never to appear in a Korda film. He was one of the greats in British film, a truly legendary name, and it would have been very exciting to have been associated with a man of his stature in the industry. It was all the more tragic because Korda was only 63 when he died and he could have had many more years of active filmmaking ahead of him if fate had dealt a different hand. I was extremely flattered when he signed me up because he was not a producer who threw long-term contracts around.

The Rank Organization bought up my contract when Korda died and that created some problems for me. Rank ran a kind of 'Rank Charm School' at that time, which nurtured 'starlets' and made sure they knew about presenting themselves whilst making appearances at premieres and other junkets, but not making that many appearances in actual films. Well, I had done all that and had already appeared in numerous movies, so I had absolutely no intention of being put through that particular mill. I just refused to co-operate with the 'Charm School' thing and got on with my career.

I had been cast in another British comedy, *The Love Match* with Arthur Askey, a veteran of the music-halls, radio, television and British films. He was an old pro, Arthur was, and he was also extremely kind and thoughtful. *The Love Match* was a northern comedy and Thora Hird played my mother with Arthur as the father. In my film career, I have had as mothers Joan Hickson, Peggy Mount and Thora Hird, a formidable trio, but they were all excellent actresses in their different ways and I learned from all three. Anthea Askey, Arthur Askey's real-life daughter, wanted to play the daughter, but I got the part and she played the girl-next-door. It was a fairly broad comedy involving football, ballroom dancing, railway engines, missing holiday funds and that standard joke of this kind of working-class comedy, the lodger. Robb Wilton, the legendary music hall star, did a turn as an eccentric magistrate and among the supporting actors were William Franklyn and Maurice Kaufmann, who was married to Honor Blackman. The 'love match' of the title was myself and a jack-in-the-box northern comedian, Danny Ross, whose main forte was to fall over and come upright again like a coiled spring. We win our way through to the final of a local ballroom dancing competition, but my character sprains her ankle during the final and so I was not able to show much of my dancing talent on screen. I did get to wear a glamorous ballroom gown, however. I had to talk broad northern and I am pleased to say that when I saw the film again recently, I thought my northern accent held up quite well! It was quite a large part for a seventeen-year-old and once again I was working with the cream of British comedy actors. And so I chalked up my second speaking film role

1956 was a momentous year for me – and for the world. In rapid succession during that momentous year I met my future husband, the Suez invasion took place and the Russians moved into Hungary to quell an uprising. *Charley Moon, Sailor Beware* and *Three Men in a Boat. Charley Moon* was, in essence, a musical, I made three more comedies: comedy, although I did not get much of a chance to show off my singing and dancing talents. Max Bygraves starred in the title role and I played Angel Dream, a musical performer whom Charley gets involved with when he decides to go on the stage after doing his National Service and forsaking the village life he had grown up in. It is quite a simple story about how the hero comes to realise where his heart lies and how he eventually turns down the glitter of showbusiness success and chooses to return to the rural idyll and his childhood sweetheart. I play a rather spoilt young woman, who turns out to be rather calculating. My one 'musical number' has me starting to sing 'I'm head over heels in love', but, sadly, I never get to finish it as my heel breaks off one of my dancing shoes, my hairpiece falls off and the microphone is not on. Disaster and a nightmare scenario for any musical performer! I blame *Charley Moon* and that is the end of a beautiful relationship. But I do wish I had been allowed to perform the number for real.

Max Bygraves sings 'Out of Town' in the film and that became something of a hit for him and there is one big production number called

Three Men in a Boat with Jimmy Edwards. I played Sophie, a prim coquette!

'Golden Boy'. The script and lyrics were by Leslie Bricusse who would team up later with Anthony Newley to create *Stop the World, I Want to Get Off*. He also recently created *Dr Doolittle* for the London stage, one of his many contributions to the musical theatre. I went out a few times with Leslie, just after he'd left university. He was very enthusiastic about writing and showbusiness in general. I would say he was completely star-struck and terribly ambitious. I liked him and we have bumped into each other over the years in the south of France where he has a house. But as for dating, there was no chemistry between us, well, not as far as I was concerned. He later married Eve, a voluptuous brunette actress, who, funnily enough, is a distant cousin of mine by marriage. The director of the film was Guy Hamilton, who

Publicity still for Charley Moon, starring Max Bygraves.

A photograph taken during the *Mother Goose* panto-mime at the Palladium. The stars with their mothers.

would, of course, later direct me in *Goldfinger*. Dennis Price was again in the cast, playing a fruity old trouper who has a double act with *Charley Moon* before Charley becomes a star. It is amazing when I think about it how much of a repertory company British comedy was in those days - I seemed to be working with the same people all the time, not that I am complaining because most of them were very talented. Other interesting cast members of *Charley Moon* were Florence Desmond, who was a famous British dancer and impersonator but who did not make very many films, Bill Fraser, the curmudgeonly character actor, and Eric Sykes in an early small role as a heckler who gives Charley a hard time when he's doing his act. *Charley Moon* presents a picture of rural England that is full of eccentric vicars, thatched cottages, old mills beautiful meadows and cosy village life with its Townswomen's Guild. The film looked good in Technicolor and there is a gentle, nostalgic note to it that is quite charming. One odd coincidence: I had played in *Mother Goose* with Max Bygraves

With Anthony Steele in the bar of the theatre while rehersing for the Royal Variety Performance, 1954.

shortly before at the Palladium; in the film I am again in pantomime with him, this time in *Cinderella*.

Sailor Beware was a very different kind of comedy. There was nothing very gentle about it. It is basically a slice of working-class life with the battle-axe mother-in-law at the heart of it. Peggy Mount, that redoubtable performer, played my mother who disliked the idea of my marrying a sailor (Ronald Lewis). She schemes to keep hold of me by persuading my character to put a deposit down on a house a few doors away from the family home and this without telling my fiancee. When my beloved finds out, he leaves me standing at the altar, but returns later to explain his actions. The awful mother-in-law seems to turn over a new leaf, but the scene at the end of the film when she walks away from the church berating her downtrodden husband shows us that she will always be the same.

Sailor Beware is full of familiar characters: the henpecked husband (Cyril Smith) who tries to blot out his wife's incessant demands and complaints by keeping ferrets in the garden shed, the crackpot, supposedly psychic aunt (Esma Cannon) and the nosy neighbour, Thora Hird. It was based on a successful stage play and it did quite well at the box-office in this country. I must also mention the late Gordon Jackson who played Ronald Lewis's pal in the movie. He was an exceptionally pleasant man who was not at all 'actorish' and as unpretentious a guy as you will find in the business. I was so pleased for him when he became really famous later through the television series *Upstairs Downstairs* and *The Professionals*. Sadly, like so many of the actors I starred with in those British comedies of the fifties, he is no longer with us.

The third comedy I made that year, *Three Men in a Boat* was based on Jerome K. Jerome's famous comic novel. It was again shot in colour and one of the best things about doing the movie was being able to wear those lovely period dresses and lovely hats. The three male leads were played by Laurence Harvey, David Tomlinson and Jimmy Edwards, while the three young women they get involved with were played by Lisa Gastoni, Jill Ireland and myself. I was paired with Jimmy Edwards in the story. It concerned the misadventures of the trio on a boating holiday. There is a coy scene where I am having a bath and Jimmy climbs the ladder to the bedroom window and peeps in. Oh, how innocent it all seems now. Again, it is a very English movie with scenes set at a cricket match and Henley Regatta. Character actors of a different generation, Robertson Hare, Miles Malleson and A.E. Matthews were also in the movie, which was directed by Ken Annakin who would later make *Those Magnificent Men in their Flying Machines* and *Monte Carlo or Bust*.

I enjoyed making *Three Men in a Boat* very much. It was mostly made on location on the Thames near Henley during the summer months. Miraculously, the sun shone for most of the time when we really needed it to. It is a well-known maxim in filmmaking circles that if you go on location and you really need the sun to shine, it always pours down in torrents, but this time we were very lucky and the weather was wonderful. The film benefits from it, too, as it looks gorgeous, and the summer sunshine helps to evoke the Edwardian period it is supposed to be set in.

There were many funny incidents by the river with all the summer boats cruising on holiday and us filming in between them, passing through all the different locks on that stretch of the Thames. I had come to realise by that time that filmmaking was a very collective, creative occupation; it was like a big family getting together, trying not to quarrel and to produce something memorable between them. Indeed, a lot of showbusiness has that quality about it. The main trap is the unavoidable truism it's only make-believe; when the day is over, or the curtain has come down, you all have to go your separate ways. Sometimes that's difficult to cope with. Perhaps, like a lot of people, I've always had difficulty with endings.

Live television beckoned again and this time I was to land a dramatic role playing opposite Kenneth Haigh, who was shortly to become famous as the first actor to play Jimmy Porter in John Osborne's landmark play, *Look Back in Anger*. I had to have several interviews with the producer, Chloe Gibson, before I finally got the part, an important one for me because I could prove I could take on a serious role as well playing comedy, providing some glamour and singing and dancing. Finally, the choice came down to me or Sylvia Sims, and I was chosen. So-called kitchen sink dramas, of which *Look Back in Anger* was the prime example, were just beginning to come into vogue. It was a two-hander, it was live and the roles were demanding. Both Kenneth and I were very nervous about doing it, but the transmission went well.

Kenneth Haigh and I liked each other and we became good friends for a while. He was a very gentle and sensitive person who lived at that time the typical life of a struggling actor. After appearing in *Look Back in Anger* and films such as *Life at the Top* as well as starring in series on television, he was no longer a struggling actor, however. He had become a star.

It was through this relationship with Kenneth that I learnt how vulnerable and insecure men could be. This came as a surprise to me, as my father had invariably been such a hearty and happy-go-lucky person. Kenneth, like a many actors of his generation, was seeing a psychoanalyst, so out of kinship and curiosity, and because of a certain emotional vulnerability of my own, I too had sessions with the same analyst. I found my time with her very interesting and revealing about myself. It left me with a fascination about why people behave in the way they do. It was the beginning for me of trying to understand the unconscious side of all of us fragile human beings. Strangely, I never told my parents about these sessions with the analyst, as they had always appeared such sunny and happy people. I thought they would be upset if they knew, because they don't believe in delving into the subconscious and they might have thought there was something wrong with me, when in fact I just wanted to find out more about myself and why I reacted in certain ways to events in my life.

Playing for Royalty and Cabaret

'*The Night of a Hundred Stars*' was an annual show that the Palladium hosted and the Queen and Prince Philip attended. It was always a glittering occasion in the showbusiness year and around this period in my life I was lucky enough to be chosen to join the cast for two of the shows. The days when all the stars got together to rehearse were very thrilling. I was mixing with the very top names in British, American and European showbusiness. Some famous names worked in the chorus or took small parts in comedy sketches. It did not really matter because we were all there under the same roof preparing for one special performance in front of the Queen and the Prince. The first show I did I had the immense pleasure of appearing in a sketch with Bob Hope and Maurice Chevalier. Both were giant names in the business so it was a real honour to share the stage with them. The second show I was in I did a sketch with Charlie Drake. I had worked with Charlie before on a television programme for teens called *Teleclub*. It was one of the first television programmes produced to attract a teenage audience. Charlie at that time had a slapstick act with a straight man, but shortly afterwards he made his meteoric rise to stardom on his own. So here on this auspicious occasion, I was doing another comedy sketch with dear old Charlie. I also did a sketch with the droll Frankie Howard. Frankie was a very highly-strung, emotional character.

When the curtain came down on one of the shows, about thirty of the artists who had appeared were presented to the Queen and Prince Philip. I was lucky enough to be among the chosen few and I was overwhelmed with pleasure to have the chance to meet the Queen face to face. As all the stars were lined up backstage in readiness for the presentation, there was such an incredible air of anticipation and excitement. I could feel it right down to my toes. I was standing between the great Nat King Cole and Sammy Davis Jnr. I was nervous, but those two were actually trembling to their very core. I think this moment was a

Royal Variety Performance, 1954. Aged seventeen, I played a 'bell-girl' in a sketch with the mighty Bob Hope and Maurice Chevalier.

tremendous one for them, just as it was for me. Showbusiness is amazing: one moment you can be down on your luck, unemployed and feeling a total failure, then the next moment Lady Luck comes up trumps for you and presents you with rare and wonderful opportunities. At the very end of the show when all the stars joined hands and faced the Royal Box to sing 'God Save the Queen', it was a highly emotional moment and it was hard for some us to hold back the tears. Suddenly, all the hard work and sweat everybody puts in to present a show like that hits home and the emotion wells up inside you. The whole cast and audience are spellbound by the magic of the occasion.

Meanwhile, I had, with some help, put together a solo singing act and was appearing in cabaret and in summer season. My act consisted of a twenty-minute singing and dancing routine. It took a lot of rehearsal until I felt I was ready to do this, but once I had done it, I gained a great deal of satisfaction from it. When I look back on this period of my life now, I just don't know how I managed to cram everything in. But youth has such energy and I set myself these goals and I went out and did it.

The peak of my singing career was when I was at the Prince of Wales Theatre in London. I was closing the first half of the variety show with my song-and-dance act, whilst Slim Whitman, the American country-and-western singer closed the second half. I remember standing in Piccadilly in the street opposite the Prince of Wales and looking up at my name in lights. I thought to myself, 'Shirley, is this really happening to you?' It was like a showbusiness fairy tale with a plot straight out a Hollywood musical.

Around this time, too, I was featured in a comic strip series that appeared in the *TV Fun*, the comic that had taken over from the old *Radio Fun*. The cartoon story was called 'Shirley Eaton - the Modern Miss in Merry Moments'. What a giggle! I am shown as 'the Modern Miss' enduring various escapades with the worthy purpose of helping people out. The strip appeared in the comic during 1958 and it was also included in the 1959 *TV Fun Annual*. I suppose I felt quite flattered that they used me as a representative Modern Miss, but from the vantage point of the nineties, it just seems a bit of a laugh. Still, it was further exposure and more evidence that I was becoming very well-known to the public.

The following Christmas I played Principal Boy in Aladdin in the pantomime at Worthing. The cast had only Christmas Day itself free, so after the curtain came down on Christmas Eve, I got into my little car and drove eagerly to spend the day with my parents. I arrived at two o'clock in the morning and as I walked up the path to our front door, I saw all the lights glittering from a big Christmas tree my mother had arranged in the hall. It was quiet and still and as she heard me approaching, she opened the door and there, waddling across the hallway, was my Christmas present -

A Rank studio portrait.

a tiny, black fluffy poodle puppy. A dog of my own! We had always had dogs in our family, but this was mine. I called her Selma.

More Movies

I was nineteen but I didn't much like being that age. I felt I was neither a girl nor quite a woman. I was longing to be in my twenties, thinking that then, magically, I would finally be grown up. What a naive soul I was! But it was around this time that I met the man who was to become my husband.

It was 1956, on Saturday, June the 2nd and just before midnight. I remember the time exactly because I am a very romantic kind of person. I was driving home from

London in my little black Hillman Minx with a cheeky red top. I had just left a party because on that particular night I wasn't enjoying myself.

As I drove with the warm night air cooling my face, I stopped at one of the traffic lights in St John's Wood. Suddenly I noticed a young man in a pale blue Ford Zephyr convertible close behind me. He was staring at me with a cheeky grin on his face - I smiled back at him. The lights turned green and I made a left towards the A41 which would lead me back to Kenton, where I was still living with my parents. I glanced in my rear window and. to my amusement, I saw that the pale blue car was still right on my tail. I put my foot down hard on the accelerator and drove very fast for about twenty minutes, thinking all the time, 'The cheeky devil! What does he think he's doing?' Curiously, I wasn't afraid. I was even laughing to myself. In those days, perhaps we weren't as full of fear as we are today about strangers. When I had almost arrived home, I stopped my car at the end of the street and watched the young man get out of his car and walk towards me.

I opened the car window as he came right up to me, leaned on the door and, with a perfectly charming smile, asked me where I lived. 'Just a few houses up the street', I replied. Even I, romantic soul that I am, can't recall every word we exchanged that night, but I do remember that before we said goodnight and he walked back to his car, I'd invited him to tea on the following day, a Sunday. How quaintly old-fashioned that seems nowadays - inviting a young man to a Sunday afternoon tea with my parents!

Little did I know, as I let myself quietly into the house that night, that I had just met the man who would become the love of my life!

Colin arrived at four o'clock the next afternoon as arranged. My parents, myself and Colin spent a pleasant couple of hours having tea and talking. I had told my mother that I had been introduced to him at a party, as I didn't think she would have approved of a meeting at a traffic light! After that historic afternoon tea, I saw Colin practically every day.

I was appearing in summer season during that summer, so Colin would travel up to see me at weekends. That meant we didn't have to be apart for long. We also wrote to each other constantly and telephoned each night. Colin was a very special man, you see. He made me feel secure and I felt an overwhelming love for him.

The first three months of getting to know each other were like a whole new world for me. I was ecstatic with happiness. We had begun a joyous journey of sensual, spiritual and mental stimulation, a journey that was to last until his death.

The memory of that first summer we shared remains eternally vivid in my mind. By late August, we had decided that we wanted to get married, even though it had been only a comparatively short time since we had met. So one evening Colin came to my house and we both told my parents of our plans. Colin went into another room and formally asked my father's permission to marry his daughter (remember those days?) The atmosphere between us all became very highly-charged! To say the least, my parents were not pleased. They thought I was far too young at nineteen to make such a commitment, forgetting, unfortunately, their own teenage romance that had led to my being born. My mother was also worried about my career, which she had been such a big part of. I think she thought she would lose all that she and I had had striven for since I was a child. Of course, I didn't see it that way. I loved both my parents very much and always would do. However, I couldn't understand their attitude and it hurt me very deeply.

However, by the end of that evening, we all agreed to a compromise. They were asking us to wait for a year. I couldn't marry without their permission because I was under twenty-one (that was the law in those days). But I did want their blessing. We had always been very emotionally close to one another. So Colin and I came to terms with the fact of having to wait a year before we got married.

Just before I made *Charley Moon*, I was appearing in a Bournemouth theatre performing my twenty-minute singing act. Colin had come for the weekend. In between shows, he sat in my dressing-room. He had been out front and said how much he loved me singing *How Deep Is the Ocean*. Then from his pocket he slowly took out a little box. I looked at him inquisitively as he gave me the most beautiful engagement ring. It was band of gold with diamonds running all round it - an Eternity ring. That evening became our private engagement party.

A few months later, we had our official party at his mother's house in Muswell Hill where he lived. His mother and I became very close down through the years. Colin had no connection with showbusiness - he ran his late father's building contractor's firm. He rarely visited the film studios where I was working, but late that summer he did visit Shepperton Studios where I was making *Three Men in a Boat*. At last, he was going to see me filming. Ken Annakin, the director, was very hospitable and Jimmy

Bridesmaid at my best friend Maureen's wedding, August 1956. The press turned up in numbers - a rehearsal for my own wedding twelve months later!

Edwards, one of my co-stars, made lots of jokes about us. Colin had a thoroughly enjoyable day meeting all the actors and technicians. I was so pleased he'd had a taste of what my life was like when I was filming.

During that year, as I waited like the dutiful daughter to be married, my career was striding forward and my love for Colin only grew and grew. Life was extremely full and happy. I made three films. I didn't know then that I wouldn't have time to appear in any more stage variety shows because of the pressure of making so many films until I quit thirteen years later. (I'll tell you how I came to make that decision in a later chapter). There seemed not enough weeks in each year to do everything I wanted to do.

The Wedding

Colin and I had planned a quiet wedding. We had chosen the fifth of August, 1957, an August Bank Holiday. My parents had come to realise that Colin was the man for me and that he was not just some teenage crush, as they had imagined. So my mother began the serious preparations for the great day.

The wedding was to be held at the Saint Mary the Virgin Church in Kenton. We were to have a somewhat unusual ceremony with two vicars performing the wedding service: Colin's family vicar from St James Church in Muswell Hill and 'my' vicar from Kenton. It was to be, hopefully, a complete romantic white wedding like the ones young girls dreamed of in those days (and some still do, I'm led to believe).

We had been very careful not to let the press know where and when the wedding was taking place. As a present, Julie Harris, the top film costume designer, whom I had worked with on several films, had created my wedding gown. It was made of ivory silk and chiffon, with a delicately pearl-embroidered bodice. The famous theatrical costumiers Berman's made it for me according to Julie's design. It was fabulous! I felt extremely privileged and happy. I'd been in and out of Berman's for fittings for dresses both for my stage work and films. Julie and Berman's were like family to me and they seemed almost as excited about the wedding as I was.

My twentieth birthday had occurred in January of that year. It seemed that so much had happened in those twenty years. It nearly took my breath away when I thought about it. I was, as they say, riding on a crest of a wave. Just before the wedding, I starred in another film: *The Naked Truth* with Peter Sellers and Terry Thomas.

When the eve of the wedding finally arrived, our house was like Paddington Station with people coming and going and the bridesmaids arriving to stay the night. The whole house was a riot of activity. I felt very excited and nervous: the great day was almost here.

As I opened my eyes on my wedding day, my first thought was, It's come! At last, the day of our wedding is here! I turned over in my bed to look towards the window and there was the early morning sunshine streaming in. The sky was the colour of a ripe peach. A great calm came over me as the pre-wedding nerves of the previous day disappeared. I was good and ready for what was to come. The house was still quiet and I lay very still in my bed, thinking happy thoughts of anticipation.

My six-year-old brother Johnny was to be a page boy. He was a

I planned my wedding as a quiet family occasion. This picture of Colin and I was taken in the garden of the hotel where we held the reception. You would never tell that thousands of well-wishers had thronged the church entrance an hour before.

somewhat highly-strung little boy and I hoped he would behave himself. Just as I was thinking about him, he came bursting into my room, jumped on my bed and asked if I wanted a cup of tea. That was his excuse for coming in so early. He snuggled down beside me for a while and we had a cuddle. Soon the whole household was awake and the house was bursting with excitement again. Colin's two sisters and a school friend of mine were to be the bridesmaids and my oldest friend, Maureen, was Matron of Honour (Maureen having married a year before). Two cousins were to be the tiny bridesmaids. Altogether, I would have seven people following me down the aisle.

Everything went to plan, thanks mostly to my mother, who's always been great at organizing. I remained calm throughout the morning. However, I had a little glitch with my father in the car on the way to the church. There I was in dreamland, as you might say, when he turned to me just as we were arriving at the church and said 'It's not too late to change your mind, you know.' I could have hit him, I'm ashamed to say. I thought to myself that I wouldn't have left it until that that moment if I'd had any doubts about what I was going to do. However, I hid my real feelings, stayed calm and said I was fine. I've found out many times over the past years that almost all fathers say the same thing to their daughters as my father did on the way to the church.

As we got out of the car, I noticed hundreds of people surrounding the church. In fact, the crowd was estimated later at two thousand people. My heart sank - I had

Singing in Cliff Richard's TV spectacular. Cliff had just broken through to pop stardom at the age of sixteen - I felt quite the grown-up!

really wanted a quiet wedding! There were press photographers everywhere and people shouting 'Good luck, Shirley, good luck!' Of course, it was sweet of them. In fact, the ushers, aided by other guests, had a hard job holding them all back so that I could make my way down the path to the church doors. Even so, people in the crush still accidentally trod on the train of my wedding dress. As I finally managed to enter the church, I was flustered and hot. But once inside that haven, I began to cool down because the atmosphere was so quiet and calming. My father put a reassuring arm around me. We both took a deep breath, then began to walk down the aisle.

The only time on that wonderful day when I almost lost control was when I heard the pure, sweet voices of the choir boys singing as I walked towards Colin. I really had to hang on then.

After the ceremony, Colin and the ushers helped me fight our way through the crowds again. They were all smiling enthusiastically and throwing confetti over us, shouting out their wishes for us to have lots of happiness in our future together. We waved goodbye to everyone, then got into the car without having the usual wedding photographs taken, as there was absolutely no space outside the church.

Later in the gardens of the hotel in Harrow-on-the-Hill, where the reception was held, the classic wedding photos were taken. That afternoon passed like a dream and then it was time to leave for our honeymoon. After all the hugs and kisses and emotional goodbyes were over, we climbed into Colin's blue car with its trailing tin cans and 'Just Married!' signs and started our drive to the south of France. At last, we were together! Our life together had begun. It had been a wonderfully romantic and glamorous day in my life and heralded the start of a marriage that would sustain and enrich us both for many years.

4
Carry Ons and Saints

Before I appeared in the first *Carry On* movie, I had made two more films, *Date with Disaster* and *The Naked Truth*. *Date with Disaster* was a smallscale thriller that costarred me with the American actor Tom Drake, who had been Judy Garland's beau, 'the boy next door', in that wonderful musical *Meet Me in St Louis*. The film also had Maurice Kaufmann and William Hartnell in it. I play the girl friend of Tom Drake, who is an honest car salesman, whose partners plan a robbery, using as a getaway car one of the cars he has previously 'sold'. The police suspect him of the robbery, I get kidnapped when the baddies make a desperate escape bid, but all ends happily. It was a film made under what was known as the 'quota system' in those days, whereby, for every American film that was released here, money would be provided for smallscale British productions. To boost their box office appeal, these 'B' movies often used imported American stars, hence Tom Drake's part in it. *Date with Disaster* was a modest thriller, but it was another starring role and this time a dramatic part.

The Naked Truth was fun to make. As well as Peter Sellers, it starred the wonderful Terry-Thomas playing a lord of the realm being blackmailed for some indiscretions by Dennis Price, who threatens to expose him in a scandal rag of which he is the sole proprietor. I play a model with a dubious past who is also blackmailed by Dennis. Peter is a bogus television performer, Wee Sandy MacGregor, who is a slum landlord on the side, a fact that doesn't match his homely, loveable image on television. We all

Peter Sellers and I acting the fool for the press on the backlot during the filming of *The Naked Truth*.

gang up together to get rid of the Dennis Price character. It is one of the British comedies of the fifties that stands up well. It was directed by Mario Zampi, an Italian who had settled in Britain and who had previously made the great Alistair Sim hit, *Laughter in Paradise*.

Once again, it was great to be acting with some of the cream of British film comedy talent. Dennis Price was a very accomplished actor who had graced some of the best of the Ealing Studios comedies such as *Kind Hearts and Coronets* and

whom I made numerous movies with. It is very sad to think that he eventually killed himself in 1973. Why do so many comedians or actors who specialise in comedy parts end up like that? Is it just the old cliche of the clown's face hiding the broken heart? I read something that Dennis had said about himself as an actor: 'I am a second-rate feature actor. I am not a star and never was. I lack the essential spark' Dennis Price was not second-rate, but clearly he had a problem with self-esteem. It is such a pity because he was a very talented man.

On location on the Thames filming *The Naked Truth*. A surprise celebration from the cast for my forthcoming marriage. Terry-Thomas, Peter Sellers, Michael Pertwee, myself and Dennis Price.

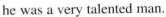

I have a rather unique distinction in British showbusiness: I appeared in the first of the thirty-one *Carry On* movies and I was also in the very first episode of *The Saint* with Roger Moore. Indeed, I did three early *Carry Ons* and three episodes of *The Saint*, two in its first series and one near the end of its production life. Both became hugely successful series in their different ways and have acquired genuine cult status, so I count myself lucky to be associated with them both.

It had been producer Betty Box who

had given me my chance in movies by casting me in *Doctor in the House* and now my association with Betty was to help in my being cast in *Carry On Sergeant*. Betty was married to Peter Rogers who was to become the legendary producer behind the *Carry On* series. The director of the movie was Gerald Thomas, who was to direct so many of the series.

When the cast and crew gathered at Pinewood Studios to start filming, none of us had any idea that *Carry On Sergeant* would launch such a

A sophisticated studio portrait for *The Naked Truth*.

successful series that would spawn 31 movies (to date). At that time, there was a television programme called *The Army Game* which was hugely popular on the new ITV station. It starred William Hartnell as a Sergeant Major and Peter Rogers had the idea of capitalising on the shows and Hartnell's popularity by making a cheaply produced army comedy for cinema release along the same lines as the series.

Let there be no illusions about the low budget nature of that first *Carry On*. It was shot quickly and with no frills with location shooting at Aldershot and interiors shot at Pinewood Studios, where I gather it was looked upon as a rather down-market, low-brow quickie that would probably do very little business. I myself thought of it as another British comedy potboiler, which might provide a stepping-stone in my film

career to better things. No one really knows in showbusiness or in the film making world what will succeed with the public in a really big way, and, of course, the *Carry Ons* were to provide box office receipts beyond Peter Rogers' wildest dreams.

Nevertheless, I was delighted to be cast as Mary Sage, the newly-married spouse of Charlie Sage

With Peter Sellers at the premiere for *The Naked Truth*.

Doctor at Large. In my dressing room, during the second film in the *Doctor* series.

(Bob Monkhouse). Because of some mixup about deferment, my film husband finds that he has to report for his National Service basic training instead of spending his wedding night and honeymoon with me. That was the basic dramatic situation and the rest revolves round our attempts to consummate the marriage and for the sergeant of the title (William Hartnell) to win a bet that his squad will pass out as the best of the new intake of National Servicemen. Considering the opportunities this plot line might have given for blatant double entendres, the film comes over as surprisingly innocent, even for a British film of the late fifties. But then the early *Carry Ons* were very different from the later ones.

The cast list of *Carry On Sergeant* now reads like a Who's Who of British film comedy, but it should be remembered that at that time a lot of these actors were just beginning to be well-known. No one other than William Hartnell was really famous, as they became later through appearing regularly in the series. Stars like Kenneth Williams, Kenneth Connor, Hattie Jaques, Eric Barker, Charles Hawtrey and Terry Scott were fairly well-known at that time, but their true fame arrived when they started acting in the *Carry Ons*. In addition to those stalwarts of the series, there were Dora Bryan as an inevitable barmaid, Bill Owen ('Compo' in

Publicity shot with real nurses for *Doctor at Large*.

The Last of the Summer Wine) as Hartnell's sidekick, Terence Longden as an upper-class recruit, Gerald Campion and Norman Rossington. It was good company to be in and I was delighted that my name appeared in the opening credits just below that of William Hartnell.

Bob Monkhouse and I provided the straight romantic interest, while Kenneth Connor and Dora Bryan play out a comic equivalent of our romance. I wangle a job in the NAAFI to be near my husband and finally Bob manages to squeeze a week's leave out of the pompous Captain Potts (Eric Barker) and the mission is accomplished, so to speak. I then help Dora Bryan's efforts to get together with the hypochondriac Kenneth Connors, who is always reporting to the medical officer Hattie Jacques in the hope of being invalided out of the army.

The comedy sequences during which a despairing William Hartnell and Bill Owen attempt to turn these no-hoper National Servicemen into the best squad in Aldershot really belong to Kenneth Connor. It is interesting to see how much this first *Carry On* depends on eccentric characterization and interaction between the various personalities dreamed up by scriptwriter Norman Hudis. Yes, there are double entendres, but they are very mild indeed. The main comedy comes from pinpointing the individual craziness of these bumbling recruits: Connors with his imagined illnesses, Kenneth Williams all sneering superiority, Charles Hawtrey, the mincing pansy, the rather patronising upper-class Terence Longden and the long-suffering but golden-hearted sergeant William Hartnell.

Hartnell was absolutely brilliant in the role, but was there ever such a split between an actor and part as in this case? In the film, and for those of you who can remember *The*

I always seemed to be playing doctors and nurses at this time! This still is from *Doctor at Large*.

Army Game, Hartnell appears to be the tough, no-nonsense army man par excellence, a guy who is wedded to the forces' way of life and delights in this rough man's world. It is an extraordinary fact, however, that in reality Hartnell was invalided out of the army after he himself was called up because he had a nervous breakdown during his basic training, similar to the training he puts his squad through in the film. He was told to get back to the theatre by the kind of sergeant he played in the television series and in the first *Carry On*. Odd, isn't it, how acting gives actors opportunities to play people diametrically opposed to themselves? Perhaps William Hartnell was so convincing as the tough sergeant becàuse he was trying to rid himself of that ghost from his past, some part of him wanted to be that rough diamond sergeant impatient with those who couldn't measure up to the demands of army training. Actors use what they can from their own lives to fill out a role and it looks like Hartnell used his unfortunate experience in the army, which he talked freely about and did not attempt to conceal, to flesh out his Sergeant Grimshawe.

This was the first of four occasions when I worked closely with Bob Monkhouse. In 1961, I would make two comedies with him, *A Weekend with Lulu* and *Dentist on the Job*, and in 1963 I would act with him on stage during the long run of *Come Blow Your Horn*, the Neil Simon hit, at the Prince of Wales Theatre just off Piccadilly Circus. Yet for all the times I worked with Bob, I felt I never got to know him. Bob is perhaps unknowable. He was nothing but very pleasant to me. Yet I have the impression that he is always putting on an act, he is always on stage, making an appearance, almost impersonating himself, or at least the public image of him that he projects. You want to say to him, 'Will the real Bob Monkhouse please stand up?' Bob hides from the world by doing his Bob Monkhouse thing.

If Bob Monkhouse was something of an enigma, I found Kenneth Connor the very opposite. He was a very sincere, open, warm and unphoney man. I don't like phoney actors, the members of our profession who are always giving themselves airs, the 'luvvies' that become the easy target for the satirists in *Private Eye*. Kenneth was the exact opposite of the phoney luvvie. He was very good at what he did and a lovely fellow. Like so many of the oldtimers of the *Carry Ons*, Kenneth is no longer with us.

Carry On Sergeant is a prime example of filming-on-the-cheap. It was completed in something like three to four weeks and believe me, there were no glamorous star trailers available for those of us with star billing. My role in the three *Carry Ons* was to provide some girlnextdoor glamour. Robert Ross in his book on the *Carry On* series writes interestingly about my part in what he calls the 'canon': 'Shirley Eaton's contribution remains important to the *Carry On* canon, setting up the glamorous blonde leading lady which would run throughout the majority of the series, developing from Eaton's sexually naive, eyeflash-fluttering darling to the more forthright and vitally comic figures of Liz Fraser and Barbara Windsor.' I think that's fair comment. Certainly, the *Carry Ons* changed down through the years and this change was perhaps illustrated by the casting of the glamorous actresses they used as the series became ever broader and double entendre piled on double entendre. Liz Fraser and Barbara Windsor, both of whom I admire greatly, are not Shirley Eaton, and vice versa; the differences between us I leave for other people to define. Let's just express it like this: I would have found it difficult to fit into the later *Carry Ons* with their emphasis on bums-and-tits, bodily functions and really outrageous campery with Kenneth Williams leading the way. But then notions of glamour have changed since those early days of the *Carry Ons*. Glamour now seems to be synonymous with blatant sexuality and I don't think that's a change for the better.

I guess what I am also saying is that the *Carry On* series lost something of value after the first six of the series. Norman Hudis wrote the screenplays for *Sergeant, Carry On Nurse, Carry On Teacher*, *Carry On Constable, Carry On Regardless and Carry On Cruising*. Thereafter, Talbot Rothwell was the major screen-writing influence. The series became cruder, more basic, more and more like the most obvious of seaside postcard jokes, which is fine, except that it all went too far, in my opinion, and veered towards tastelessness. But that's exactly why so many *Carry On* fans loved the series in the first place because of those tasteless, groanmaking old

The premiere of *Carry On* Sargeant. Colin and I had no way of knowing the series would run to 31 films.

jokes that schoolboys down through the ages have revelled in.

For example, the way women were represented in the later *Carry Ons* became more 'tarty', the female body became the object of ridicule as though breasts and bums were inherently funny, as well as being fanciable. Maybe that's how the average British male handles his attraction to the opposite sex. Because he is scared basically of sex, he has to turn it into a dirty joke and women's bodies into a subject for laughter. Still, I don't want to give ammunition to the politically correct people who throw stones at the *Carry On* series because it's so sexist and all that. You can be far too po-faced about it all. I had this conversation with Liz Fraser when I met up with her at the celebration at Pinewood Studios on 26 April 1998, to mark the fortieth anniversary of *Carry On Sergeant*. We agreed that the politically correct people were out of their tiny minds. The

trouble with politically correct attitudes is that they are authoritarian, telling you what to, and what not to, find funny. I don't want to join the grimfaced puritans in attacking something as harmless as the *Carry Ons*, not at all, but I just want to say my preference was for the earlier movies in the series, and I hope I'm not saying that because I was in three of them!

I would imagine that there are two main types of *Carry On* fans: there are those that prefer the gentler, Ealing-type comedies of character (the first six) and there are those fans who prefer the post-Norman Hudis *Carry Ons* in which Kenneth Williams does his outrageous camp act and Sid James, well, is Sid James. After I was married to Colin, Sid James and his wife used to come

Cornell Lucas was my favourite photographer. I really enjoyed working with him, and together we produced some of the most stunning photographs ever taken of me.

to parties at our house. Sid was much like he was on screen, a rough diamond, but pleasant with it.

I will be describing the fortieth anniversary celebration of the first *Carry On* at the end of this section, but let me just mention here that I met Norman Hudis at that gathering. He is a lovely, gentle man, and I can quite see how those first six screenplays emanated from him. I think the comparison with Ealing comedy is apt. Ealing comedies generally dealt with more middle-class characters and settings than those first six *Carry Ons*, which, although they represent a cross-section of British classes, are basically working-class, but Ealing comedy shares with the early *Carry Ons* a gentle humour, a regard for the importance of the individual and an allowance for the eccentric, and the idea of people coming together to accomplish something against the odds. I mean, at the end of *Carry On Sergeant*, the team of no-hoper recruits suddenly turn into this crack squad, winning the bet for the sergeant who is about to retire and they even club together to give him a retirement present. Such sentiment is noticeable by its absence in the later *Carry Ons*.

Carry On Nurse

The fantastic success of *Carry On Sergeant* (it made most of its production costs back on its first weekend of release) led inevitably to a sequel being put together and I was cast as Nurse Dorothy Denton in *Carry On Nurse*, which was released in 1959 and would prove to be the most successful film at the British box office of that year. Joining me from the cast of *Sergeant* were Kenneth Williams, Kenneth Connor,

A close-up.[Cornell Lucas]

Terence Longden, Hattie Jaques, Bill Owen, Charles Hawtrey and Norman Rossington. Newcomers to the series included Leslie Phillips, playing his RAF-type cad, Wilfred Hyde White, playing an awkward cuss of a patient intent on placing his bets on the horses (seemingly an obsession in his own life and one that led to well-publicised debts), wonderful Joanie Sims as an L-plated nurse, Joan Hickson who had played my mother in *Doctor in the House*, June Whitfield, who plays Kenneth Connor's wife, Irene Handl, doing her inimitable act, Susan Stephen, Susan Shaw and Jill Ireland.

On the subject of glamour, Susan Shaw was a glamorous star of British films of the forties and early fifties before her career seemed to fizzle out. She was in *Holiday Camp* (1947) as the daughter of the famous Huggett family (lead by Jack Warner and Kathleen Harrison) and she also starred with Jean Kent (another glamorous British star) in The Woman in Question. Her other films included *Train of Events*, *The Intruder* with Jack Hawkins and *The Good Die Young* which starred John Ireland and Laurence Harvey. Susan Shaw was an attractive blonde lady who usually played working-class women in her films; her real name was Patsy Sloots and she was a product of the Rank Charm School whose tuition I had already rejected when Rank bought up my contract after the death of Alexander Korda. I think Susan was an example of a really attractive British actress whom no one quite knew how to use in British films. I mention her here for that reason, as well as for the fact that she died in 1979, absolutely penniless and by that time unknown and forgotten. Indeed, the Rank Organisation paid for the funeral expenses, so destitute had she become. That is a very sad story and another cautionary tale about the ups-and-downs of this showbusiness we toil in. The rewards of success can be very high, but when your luck changes and people forget you, or you run into some personal problems that interfere with your concentration on your career, then the fall from the top can be very fast indeed and quite devastating.

A Marilyn Monroe smoulder! [Cornell Lucas]

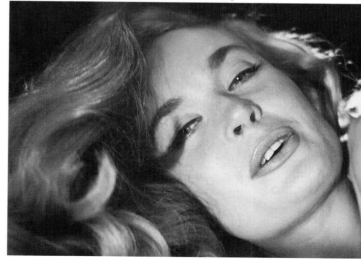

Jill Ireland I had, of course, known since we made *Three Men in a Boat* together. She was married to David McCallum, whom I would later work with on *Around the World Under the Sea*. They seemed very happy together, but their marriage went the way of many

A sassy look! [Cornell Lucas]

A boudoir portrait. Anticipation is the greatest of all pleasures! [Cornell Lucas]

showbusiness marriages and ended in divorce, which I found very sad, although both found happiness in second marriages. Jill married the Hollywood star, Charles Bronson, and appeared in several of his movies. Sadly, her story ended tragically as well after a long and courageous battle against cancer. We never know what life has in store for us, and perhaps it's just as well, looking at the cast list of *Carry On* Nurse. Susan and Jill met early deaths. Kenneth Williams apparently committed suicide and Charles Hawtrey became more and more of a recluse towards the end of his life. I would describe Charles as a will-of-the-wisp character. He was very highly-strung, a thin, reedy man, who obviously had his own demons to battle with. It could not have been easy in the fifties and sixties for a man of Charles's inclinations to survive in a hostile world.

Hattie Jacques had a bigger part in Nurse than she had in *Sergeant* and deservedly so. She was a very funny woman and absolutely adorable. She wasn't glamorous, of course, but she had an overwhelmingly warm quality about her and everybody liked her. She had a very happy marriage to John LeMesurier, that brilliant comic actor who was in many British films and then found real fame in *Dad's Army*. John was very good-looking and some people might have been surprised that he chose Hattie as his wife, but she proved that attractiveness is not necessarily to do with measurements and conventional ideas of beauty.

Carry On Nurse is judged to be almost the best of the series in the opinion of many fans. Certainly, it has some excellent people in it and the script is one of Norman Hudis's best. My romantic partner this time was Terence Longden, who made several *Carry Ons* always as the rather languid upper-class type. I think *Carry On* Nurse is rather good about petty snobbery especially in the character played by Brian Oulton who wants to conceal that he and his wife live on a council estate. In the later *Carry On*

84

films, there wasn't the same interest in that kind of gentle social observation, more's the pity.

The movie was obviously trying to feed off the success of the *Doctor* movies and offer a less middle-class picture of hospital life. In fact, it is largely seen from the point of view of the patients, while I waltz around in a starched nurse's uniform looking coyly at Terence Longden. Everybody remembers the final daffodil gag, when Wilfred Hyde White's temperature is taken by inserting a daffodil in a particular part of his body, although, this being 1959, you don't actually see any naked bottoms.

In between *Carry On Sergeant* and *Carry On Nurse*, I managed to squeeze in two more films: *Further Up the Creek* with Lionel Jeffries and David Tomlinson again, and *Life Is A Circus*. *Further Up the Creek* was the sequel to the highly successful *Up the Creek* and was directed by Val Guest. It also starred Frankie Howerd and Thora Hird. The story concerns a particular frigate in the Royal Navy, which the Admiralty decides to sell, much to the dismay of members of the crew who have been operating a profitable bookmaking business from on board. Realising that their bookie days are numbered, they decide to operate one more scam. They advertise a luxury cruise aboard the frigate and manage to snare nine unsuspecting customers, including the character I play. David Tomlinson is the unwitting captain who finds himself trying to hide the scam from his navy bosses and also inadvertently influences the course of a revolution in the country to which the frigate sails on the cruise. It is all good, knockabout stuff. The *Monthly Film Bulletin* in their review commented that 'Shirley Eaton beams her way good-humour-edly through a non-existent role.' That about sums it up.

A teasing look, but don't get too close! [Cornell Lucas]

Life Is A Circus had all of the Crazy Gang in it, plus Michael Holliday, who was a very popular singer of that time. Perhaps those of you who are a bit younger might not realise how much of a showbusiness institution the Crazy Gang were. By

1958, they were nearing the end of their long careers, which had been mainly on stage in musical revues and variety. Bud Flanagan and Chesney Allen of *Underneath the Arches* fame were perhaps the best-known of the team. This movie is the closest thing to a screen musical that I ever did. I do a simple dance in a funfair setting as Michael Holliday sings to me, and later on I also have a dance with Bud Flanagan. During the closing credits I have a share of a duet with Michael again. It was something, but perhaps not enough to display what I could do in singing and dancing. The story was a simple one of a circus which is run by the Crazy Gang against the odds and which is threatened by a takeover by a bigger outfit. Joseph Tomelty, that fine Irish character actor, played my dad and Lionel Jeffries who seemed to be popping up in all my films played a genie in a lamp who grants the Crazy Gang their wishes. It was all harmless fun and the title number 'Life Is a Circus' sung by the Crazy Gang and Michael is quite catchy. Bud Flanagan was an adorable man and it was great to work with showbusiness legends like the Gang. Lionel Jeffries is not only a fine actor, but also a very down-to-earth, unshowbusiness type of guy, which I like.

It was a bit of a challenge swinging on a trapeze in some of the circus sequences, because it was really quite high. Of course, a trained trapeze artist stand-in did all the difficult bits, but the little I did I found scary but fun. People have often asked me how I have kept so slim and fit-looking. Well, I have never followed a fitness regime and I have always eaten exactly what I wanted. I seem to be able to burn up any excess calories with my outflow of energy. I have always liked swimming, walking and gardening, which I guess has also helped. I had never been much of a drinker of alcohol, but I gave up altogether when I was forty, because my husband had given up drinking after he had had an operation on his gums.

I also made *In the Wake of a Stranger* during 1959, which costarred Tony Wright, who was a beefcake kind of actor whom Rank had tried to make a star of. In addition to Tony, Harry H. Corbett, who later found fame in *Steptoe and Son*, was in the cast playing a villain. There was also that large cockney actor, Danny Green, who played the 'thug' in *The Ladykillers*. The plot concerns a seaman's attempts to piece together the events surrounding his discovery of a corpse when he was on a drunken spree. The characters played by Corbett and Willoughby Goddard try to frame him for the murder and I play a schoolteacher, Joyce Edwards, who gets involved with him and tries to help him. Yes, and you guessed it: we fall in love! The action is set in Liverpool and one of the other actors in the movie is Alun Owen, who would shortly become a famous playwright for both the stage and television. One review called the film 'a murky crime thriller'. Yes, it was dark!

Motherhood

It was during the filming of *Carry On Nurse* that I learned I was pregnant. Colin and I were absolutely delighted at the news and my first son, Grant Lenton Rowe, was born on the twenty-third of June, 1959. My world was almost complete: I had a successful career, a very happy marriage and now I had achieved another ambition. I had become a mother. It changed my outlook on life; the girl had turned into a real woman and I felt wonderful!

I have often thought life is like a marathon race. You don't have to win, but you must give your all in the effort to arrive at the finishing line. I've sometimes been told, and especially by my mother, that I'm not ambitious enough. That isn't the way I see it. It depends on how you evaluate your life. My career was very important to me and I tried my best at everything I did, and still do, by the way! But what has always been my main goal was to have a successful family life. It far outweighed anything else I could possibly achieve.

So now I was a mother and being a good mother is the most demanding and satisfying career any woman can possibly try to achieve. Children are the only worthwhile legacy we have. My husband and I tried to give as much love and emotional security to our sons as we could. They were the main reason I decided to stop working at the age of 32 when my career as an actress was at its height. I do not regret it for one moment. Now they are grown men with families of their own.

After *Carry On*, Nurse became such a huge success in Britain, my agent rang me to ask if I would agree to go to New York to help publicize it in America, as it was due for release there. I was twenty-three years old, I had made twelve films, had a wonderful husband, a baby son and everything in my life was striding along wonderfully and now I was being asked if I wanted to go to New York to publicize my latest film. I said yes.

The English publicist was sitting with me in the first-class cabin of the aeroplane. We were drinking champagne and munching caviar. He had never been to New York before either, so it was a bit of an adventure for both of us. It was sunset as our plane circled to land at the airport. My memory of all the skyscrapers we saw from the cabin window was that they looked incredibly beautiful bathed in the pink and orange light of the evening. It was my first impression of America and one that I have never forgotten.

On the first day of the trip I met several of the American publicists I was going to be seeing throughout the week. I also gave a couple of newspaper interviews. That evening there was going to be a sneak preview of *Carry On Nurse* out of town, as they say in America. As our entourage entered the cinema quietly and sat at the back, nobody noticed us. The lights went down and a trailer was on the screen. When the titles for

Carry On Nurse (with my name at the top of the credits) appeared, we all sat there anxiously wondering if the film would have the same impact on American audiences as it had had on British ones. We need not have worried. The audience absolutely loved the film. They were rolling about with laughter. The publicist whispered to me, 'This is it! It's going to be a great success here in the States! I can tell by their reactions.' Clearly, the *Carry On* humour travelled across national boundaries.

The week that followed passed so quickly. Every day was full of television interviews on the breakfast, midday and evening shows. There were interviews at Sardi's, the famous showbusiness restaurant in the very heart of Broadway. We also went to other well-known theatre restaurants in Manhattan. What a whirl it was, this my first experience of America.

To cap it all, Bob Hope asked me to be on his television show. This was another first for me, although I had worked briefly before with Bob in London. It was an eye-opening experience in several ways. I had never seen 'idiot boards' before. When I went into the television studios and Bob and I were about to start rehearsing the sketch we were doing, there leaning against the wall were huge placards with words in giant letters on them. This was the dialogue for the sketch we were about to do. It was Bob who called them 'his idiot boards'. We were never stuck for the next line, because all we had to do was glance just off-camera and there it was in big letters. It happens in movie studios as well, I understand. Marlon Brando, for example, on occasions has had his lines pasted up all over the set. So that mannerism of Brando's where he looks off to the left or the right of the person he's playing opposite has nothing to do with the acting technique known as The Method, he's just checking what his next line is! As for Bob Hope's idiot boards, I have to confess they made live transmissions less nervewracking.

That summer it was hot, very, very hot. The sun seemed to burn through you and the humidity was almost unbearable. However, as I left the city of skyscrapers, I was in high spirits. I had helped, in my own small way, in the process of turning *Carry On Nurse* into a hit in the States. I wondered how long it would be before I returned to that great city.

Carry On Constable

I was only in a couple of scenes in the fourth of the *Carry Ons*: I am discovered in the shower by Leslie Phillips and photographed discreetly from the back. The creative team behind the series had obviously decided to play down the straight romantic interest this time around. This *Carry On* is, of course, notable for the first appearance of Sid James in the series. From then on, he was to become the lynch pin of the *Carry Ons* and

I have to say this helped to create the more leering tone and generally cruder humour. I liked Sid, but there is no doubt that his comic appeal depended on that 'ho-ho-ho' kind of stuff.

Leslie Phillips, who plays one of the bumbling constables in a story that is a kind of parody of Dixon of Dock Green, is quoted in Robert Ross's book as saying this about his participation in the *Carry Ons*: 'One will always have happy memories of the three *Carry Ons* that I made in the early days they were fun and very badly paid. The people I worked with were a joy, but it was a long time ago! One has thankfully moved on.'

I think that more or less expresses what I feel myself about the three *Carry Ons* I was in. It was a pleasant experience working with all those highly talented people, but it would be wrong to suggest there weren't tensions among them as well. Especially after the huge success of the first film, actors realized that appearing in a *Carry On* would do their careers no harm at all and so they were very anxious to grab as much screen time and to make a real impact as possible. There was a strong sense of competition among them. One way of putting it would be they sparked off each other. When you have volatile characters like Kenneth Williams and Charles Hawtrey around, there was bound to be a good deal of larger-than-life antics. Actors are generally egotistical, looking out for the size of their parts, if you'll pardon the expression (goodness, now I'm sounding like a *Carry On* script!)

The Carry On Reunion

As I have mentioned already, the British Comedy Society organized, in April, 1998, a celebration to mark the fortieth anniversary of the first *Carry On* film. It could only take place at Pinewood Studios where all the movies were shot. Sadly, numerous members of the team had died including Sid James, Hattie Jaques, William Hartnell, Kenneth Connor, Eric Barker, Peter Butterworth, Esma Cannon, Charles Hawtrey, Frankie Howerd, Jon Pertwee, Ted Ray, Kenneth Williams and director Gerald Thomas. But able to be present were Barbara Windsor, Bernard Cribbins, Jack Douglas, Fenella Fielding, Lance Percival, Leslie Phillips, Liz Fraser, the producer Peter Rogers and myself. I realized how the years had passed since those early days when so many famous names associated with the series had passed on.

But it was not an occasion for sadness, but a celebration, although tears were shed by quite a few people. Peter Rogers paid a moving tribute to his close associate Gerald Thomas and was almost overcome with the emotions he felt. A plaque in honour of Kenneth Williams was unveiled by Barbara Windsor, who very amusingly said in her speech that Kenneth was probably looking down at her from heaven and saying, 'Look at her, silly little cow, what does she think she's doing?'. Barbara was very much the star of the occasion because of her success playing Peggy, the owner of the 'The Vic' in EastEnders, who has two tearaway sons. Barbara is absolutely brilliant in the part and deserves this renewed fame she gets from appearing in the soap opera. Mind you, I did my fair share of signing autographs for fans that day, as did all the surviving members of the *Carry On* team. Not that I was ever a member of that team, although perhaps I had more than honorary status.

Leslie Phillips unveiled a statuette of Charles Hawtrey that had been specially commissioned and Jack Douglas did the same for the Sid James plaque. Then the whole cast joined in unveiling a plaque in tribute to the whole *Carry On* series. It was that kind of day!

Tom O'Connor acted as auctioneer in an auction of *Carry On* memorabilia, the proceeds of which were to go to charity, which good cause prompted me to pay over the odds for some stills, comprising one still from each of the 31 *Carry On* movies. It was a lovely day out and revived a lot of memories. It was great meeting up with so many old faces, although there were some notable absentees as well.

The Saint

I made three appearances in *The Saint* series as guest star to Roger Moore's Saint: *The Talented Husband* (the very first episode transmitted on 4 October 1962), *The Effete Angler* later in the same year, and then in a colour episode from 1969, which happens to be my favourite of the three, *Invitation to Danger*. I had done the film *What A Carve Up* for the producers of *The Saint* series, Monty Berman and Robert Baker, so when the first episode of *The Saint* came along, they cast me as an undercover insurance investigator, Adrien Halbern, who was looking into the suspicious deaths of the wives of a theatrical producer, played by that excellent actor, Derek Farr.

No one realized when we were making that first ever episode of *The Saint* that the series would eventually stretch to 118 hour-long episodes made over a sevenyear period. We did know that it was going to be a big budget (for television at that time) series and that it had every chance of success with Lew Grade's name behind it and Roger Moore, who had become well-known through appearing in Maverick in the States, playing the lead. Most importantly there was a ready-made audience out there who knew the original Saint novels by Leslie Charteris. With all these things going for it, and the high level production values injected into the episodes, perhaps it isn't so surprising that the series became such a long-running hit on both sides of the Atlantic and, indeed, almost all over the world.

I had met Roger Moore before I worked with him on *The Saint*. When he was making the television series *Ivanhoe*, he came onto the set of one of the movies I was making. I remember he was wearing green tights and he is one of the few men around who can wear those and get away with it. Until I recently met Pierce Brosnan, I considered Roger the prettiest man I had ever known. That is not to say I was immediately bowled over by him, although, as is normal between two attractive people, there was some kind of chemistry between us. I am not usually attracted to very handsome men of that type.

The best thing about Roger is his self-deprecating humour. A star of his magnitude, who is lionized on all sides and no doubt had women throwing themselves at him all the time, could easily get a very inflated idea of himself, but Roger never took himself too seriously, which may have worked against him somewhat at times. For example, there is his well-known humorous self-analysis of his acting style that is so often quoted about him: 'Raise left eyebrow, raise right eyebrow.' Well, that is all very amusing and self-deflating and people love him for it, but that anecdote has been quoted so often as defining the Moore acting technique that it has perhaps prevented Roger receiving the credit due to him as a professional actor.

And believe me, despite all the practical jokes on set and the self-deprecating remarks, Roger was, and is, a very professional and skilled actor. Someone calculated that making 118 episodes of *The Saint* was equivalent to making 59 feature films over the course of seven years, which is a colossal workload. My experience of Roger is that he always came prepared to the set, more or less knowing his lines, and even if he did not know them word-for-word, he was experienced enough to get a very close approximation to the script so that no one was thrown.

He was also absolutely a master at keeping everyone on set happy. In those days in the film studios (*The Saint* was shot on film, not on telecine, in order to help sell the series to the American networks) the technicians unions were very powerful and could prove very awkward when the issue of finishing shots at the end of the day were concerned. Roger worked at creating a good relationship with the crews and they would do anything for him. When you are the leading actor in a series like *The Saint*, and Roger also coproduced a lot of the episodes as well as directing some of them, there is an onus on you to keep everybody sweet and the way you behave to people, from stars to grips, sets the tone for the whole project. Roger takes a lot of credit from the fact that *The Saint* was a happy series to work on.

His practical jokes were legendary, however. Who was the actress who came up against Roger in one scene and felt something very large and hard pressing into her, only to find that her costar had pushed a hair dryer down the front of his trousers? Not me, I am perhaps lucky to say, but that was typical of the kind of boyish jape that

Roger got up to relieve the tensions and keep everybody laughing while getting down to the very serious task of producing a high-quality television series.

I came back to work on the first ever episode of *The Saint* after a short break from my career after I had my son, Grant. It was just another job for me, but I was looking forward to working with Roger, of course. He was a sweetheart to work with. He was just beginning his relationship with Luisa Mattioli at that time, whom he would marry in 1968. Luisa and Roger became friends of my husband Colin and I. We would meet in the south of France and eat, drink and be merry. It was a great shock to us both when Luisa and Roger split up because they had been together for almost as long as Colin and I. Apart from the upset it causes the two people concerned, when a marriage of a couple of close friends breaks up, it has an unsettling effect on your own life. The two people you have known as a couple are now no longer together and it is difficult to stay friends with both. I am still firm friends with Luisa and see her from time to time, which does not mean to say I don't feel friendship towards Roger any more. It's just that a split like that separates not only the couple but the friends that they had in common. As I say, I have always had a great dread of divorce and I count myself very lucky that I escaped that particular trauma in my life.

Glamour was an essential ingredient of *The Saint* series, so I feel flattered that they invited me to appear in three episodes. The women had to be pretty and when you look at the roster of actresses that appeared during the series in starring roles, you can see what they meant: Nyree Dawn Porter, Sylvia Sims, Stephanie Beacham, Ann Bell, Suzanne Lloyd, June Ritchie, Dawn Adams, Justine Lord, Annette Andre, Honor Blackman, Eunice Gayson, Catherine Woodville, Mary Peach and many others. *The Saint* himself was meant to be a gentleman so the kind of female glamour the series represented was 'classy'. Indeed, Simon Templar played by some kind of Queensberry Rules and was an upper-class kind of English chappie. Actually, as is well-known, Roger came from fairly humble origins, but he carried off the gentleman adventurer very well. He has also been quoted as saying, 'Don't call me an actor, I'm not an actor.' Roger, don't be silly, you're an actor, just like the rest of us and a damn good one at times.

In that first ever Saint episode, Patricia Roc was one of the guest stars. On the subject of glamour, Patricia had been one of the truly glamorous stars of British movies of the forties and fifties, appearing in *Madonna of the Seven Moons, The Wicked Lady, The Brothers, Jassy, The Perfect Woman* and numerous others. Those Gainsborough melodramas she appeared in presented both male and female stars in a glamorous light. Indeed, the movie she made with Margaret Lockwood and James Mason, *The Wicked Lady*, caused quite a stir because of the supposed lowness of the necklines Patricia and Margaret wore. The Americans, in particular, got all steamed up about the amount of bosom the two British stars were showing and insisted they wore modesty veils for the American version of the movie. If you look at the movie now, and it was a gigantic box office success in its day, probably because of all the hooha that was generated over those necklines, it seems incredibly tame. Judged by what contemporary actresses have to expose, Patricia Roc and Margaret Lockwood, two of the most glamorous stars of their day, were showing very little. But they didn't have to: glamour isn't about exposure, it's about beauty and taste and style. Patricia Roc had a lot of it and still had by the time she was in the Saint episode with me.

That sophisticated man-of-the-world image of Simon Templar/Roger Moore came, of course, from the original stories by Leslie Charteris. I met Leslie a few times, mainly in the south of France and you could easily detect in his personality and style how he came to create this debonair fictional character. There was a lot of himself in ST, although naturally those aspects were enhanced and exaggerated for the purpose of entertainment.

In the second episode I did, *The Effete Angler*, I was given the chance to move away a bit from my usual girl-next-door role into a character that was more dramatic and sinister. I play Gloria Uckrose, the scheming wife of a smuggler in Miami, Florida. Florida! Some hopes! The budgets for *The Saint* might have been large by television standards at that time, but there was very little money for location shooting. Any exotic locations either had to be concocted in the ABC studios or in some humble suburban location in England. *The Saint* series might provide the illusion of international intrigue and travel, but hardly anyone including Roger Moore ever ventured further than Twickenham in making the series. Apart from the money that exotic location shooting would have entailed, there was the issue of speed: these episodes were shot in ten days. Five to six minutes of film had to be in the can by the end of each day. To the uninitiated that might not sound very much, but when you consider that on the average feature film you are lucky if you have 90 seconds film by the end of a day's shoot, you can understand that there was no time for dawdling. Everybody had to know their job and be prepared. This put added pressure on the actors who knew that if they caused endless retakes because of fluffs, then they were upsetting the tightly timed schedule.

I remember that when I was making *The Effete Angler* episode, I had this speech that I kept fluffing. Some stars might have got very impatient and made me feel small, but not Roger Moore, who happened to be directing that particular episode. He knew what to do. He allowed me to take a break, have a cup of tea, relax and then try again, and, of course, it worked. Are you listening Henry Hathaway, wherever you are? Kindness and patience works, even when you are making films.

In *The Effete Angler* I enjoyed the chance to look glamorous in swimming costumes and in a bath scene. I was playing a bit of a vamp, which I loved, and Roger has this immortal line at the end of the episode when he was asked how he had managed to remain pure despite my vamping: 'In the face of irresistible temptation, I really behaved like a saint.' Perhaps he hasn't always behaved like a saint in his own personal life, but I still have a very soft spot for him.

The third episode I did, *Invitation to Danger* was shot on colour film, so I enjoyed that more, because I was allowed to look even more glamorous! People have said to that I usually looked very confident on film. Well, in *Invitation to Danger* I played a very self-confident lady who follows Simon Templar out of a casino. I enjoyed playing a woman who was not goody-two-shoes, which during my career I tended to be cast as. I'm not like that in real life, honest! In this episode, I was the duplicitous Reb Denning who at one point pretends to be a CIA agent. The plot involved a stolen Top Secret file and money lifted from a fancy casino. I get to shoot the character played by Julian Glover and to say the line, 'Do I now belong to the League of Grateful Women whose lives have been saved by Simon Templar?' It was refreshing to play a baddie and end up, by implication, in prison for my crimes. You can get tired of playing nothing but 'good' girls.

I liked doing *The Saint* because it was a glamorous series. I am not surprised that it is still such a cult programme, even though the 'revival' series in the seventies with Ian Ogilvy did not really work, nor the 1997 film version with Val Kilmer (an American actor playing the very English Simon Templar they had to be joking!). *The Saint* belonged to its time and reflected the sixties, just as *The Avengers*, in a different way, did. Whether they could make a new series of *The Saint* as we go into the new millennium is questionable. Glamour, that old fashioned type of glamour that I have talked about, seems out of style. We now live in a cheaper, more tabloid age where the sensational seems to take precedence over almost everything. Moderation is out, excess is in. For example, I recently watched Kate Winslet, one of the stars of the blockbuster *Titanic*, being interviewed on the Clive Anderson talk show. Now there's a wholesome-looking young woman/actress. She came across as delightfully natural and unspoilt. She talked about the movie, of course, and the films she had made since, but the the subject changed and Clive Anderson asked her how she felt about appearing nude on screen, suggesting that every young actress nowadays seems to be obliged to show their all. Kate looked thoughtful for a moment, then replied, 'I was nervous the first time I was asked to take all my clothes off, but another actress told me I would feel liberated afterwards.' Then, smiling at Clive, she said, 'And that's exactly how I felt.' I thought to myself how the inherent modesty that most women possess has been discarded under the guise of art.

5

Life with all its complications

1961 was another very busy year as far as movies were concerned. I managed to squeeze in four, despite my comparatively new role as a mother. It is always problematical balancing your need for a successful career and the demands of family life. I think I got it about right in the decade that followed, with the wonderful cooperation of Colin, who was never an absent father. On the contrary, we shared parental responsibilities fifty-fifty. But the pressure would tell and this chapter is the story of my sixties until my decision to retire from showbusiness in 1968.

The first movie I made in 1961 was *Weekend with Lulu,* which also starred Bob Monkhouse, Leslie Phillips and Graham Stark. This was a Hammer movie, the producing company that would become famous for the series of horror classics that have millions of fans all round the world. The producer was Michael Carreras himself, who was Hammer's guiding light, especially in those early days. Hammer Films were located at Bray Studios, which in essence was a large country house where most of the classic Hammer horror movies were shot. I played a character called Deirdre and this time my screen mum was played by that fine character actress, Irene Handl. Other members of the cast included Alfred Marks, Kenneth Connor, Sid James, Sidney Tafler and pianist Russ Conway in a guest spot. The '*Lulu*' of the title is a caravan which is hauled around by an ice-cream van. I play the girl friend of the

A Weekend with Lulu with Bob Monkhouse and a visiting Russ Conway (right).

Leslie Phillips character, who owns the caravan. On a weekend caravan trip, somehow we accidentally take the ferry to France and then there ensue the usual French frolics when the British make a film about les anglais in that country: we get mixed up in the Tour de France, with an amorous French count, a seller of dirty postcards and the Madame of a brothel. Yes, ooh-la-la indeed! In the end when my boy friend is knocked out, the French gendarmes in their infinite Gallic wisdom assume the ice-cream van is an ambulance and obligingly rush it to a air freighter which spirits us back to dear old Blighty. One review described it as 'rowdy episodic British humour.'

Nearly A Nasty Accident once more had a cast of the usual suspects of British comedy: Jimmy Edwards, Kenneth Connor, Eric Barker and Jon Pertwee, none of whom, alas, are alive today. The gist of the story is that Kenneth Connor is a walking disaster area, round whom mayhem in all its forms breaks out. As he is in the RAF, this causes more than a few problems. I play a Wren, Jean Briggs, who has been posted to the squadron that the Group Captain played by Jimmy Edwards commands and which is thrown into a state of total panic by the misadventures of Kenneth's character. Nobody played the blundering fool better than Kenneth Connor and playing a ambitious RAF officer who was all mouth and bluster was right up Jimmy Edward's street. Jon Pertwee, who later would be one of the Dr Whos, chipped in with a cameo portrait of an old buffer, General Burtenshaw. Then came *Dentist on the Job*, a sort

Now we are three! In the back garden with Colin and Grant, our first son.

of *Carry On Dentist* type comedy once more with Bob Monkhouse, Kenneth Connor and Eric Barker. Graham Stark made a guest appearance as did Charles Hawtrey. Bob Monkhouse and Ronnie Stevens play two newly-qualified, ne'er-do-well dentists who are employed by Dreem Toothpaste to endorse their product with some professional authority. I play Jill Venner, who is an advertising model. My first scene in the movie is a very discreet bubble bath sequence which gets Bob's character all hot and bothered. Again, all very innocent, as are all the many double entendres of the script. I supply the glamour and get to dress up as a French maid later in the film. All good, clean British fun, as they say.

Nearly a Nasty Accident, with Kenneth Connor. My joy in working with Kenneth is clearly to be seen in this still.

I then made *What A Carve Up*, round which several interesting stories revolve. At the time I did not realise it was a spoof of the 1933 British horror movie *The Ghoul* which starred Boris Karloff and had been the British cinema's attempt to cash in on the huge success of the Universal Studios horror cycle of movies. The original film had been based on a novel by Dr Frank King and the press book that was issued at the time of its release referred to Karloff as *The King of the Eeries* because of his recent success in *The Mummy* and *The Old Dark House*. Another interesting aspect of the *The Ghoul* is that the great British actor Ralph Richardson made his screen debut in it, playing a villainous vicar. The film was 'lost' for many years before it resurfaced on video in the nineties.

What A Carve Up was known in America as *No Place like Homicide*. The script was co-authored by Ray Cooney (with Tony Hilton). Cooney would go on to be a famously successful writer of farces for the stage. Its setting is a haunted house, Blackshaw Towers, to which the character played by Kenneth Connor is summoned to hear the reading of his uncle's will. Other members of the cast included Sidney James, Michael Gwynn, Dennis Price, Donald Pleasence and Michael Gough, who play Connor's scheming upper-class relations or crazed family servants. I played a young nurse who for a time is suspected of being the maniac killer who is bumping off all the others. I am also Kenneth Connor's girl friend in the movie until Adam Faith in a small role turns up and takes me away from him.

What A Carve Up became the inspiration for the brilliant novel of the same name by Jonathan Coe whom I now count as a friend and a mentor of my own writing. Jonathan had first seen the movie on television in the late sixties and it had made a deep impression on him. His main character in his novel is writer Michael Owen , who as a young lad had been fixated by a scene in the film in which I discreetly undress in the same room as Kenneth Connor who is tempted to ogle my semi-naked body (only from the back!). Jonathan's novel mixes real characters like me and other actors with the characters of his fiction. For example, in one scene, one of the baddie Winshaw family visits the set of *What A Carve Up*! at Twickenham Studios and tries to spy on me undressing, until Sid James as Sid James steps in and evicts him. There are references to numerous other films in the novel which is part parody, part mystery and actually very political and angry about the injustices that people with too much power and money inflict on the rest of us. 'I', that is, the real and fictional Shirley Eaton crop up in several sections of the book. When it was translated into German, they choose the title *Allein mit Shirley*, which means *Alone with Shirley*. My photograph also adorns the cover of the book.

Jonathan's publisher sent me a copy of the manuscript before it was published to see what my reaction would be to being featured in this way in the novel. Initially, I have to admit, I wasn't too pleased because there was something slightly 'off' about the scene of the young man by himself watching me half-naked on the video, but when I got used to Jonathan's freewheeling, wideranging, effervescent style, I began to like the book very much indeed. It was a very well-written novel and I am a great fan of all Jonathan's work and, as I say, he has become a good friend. It is strange this business of moviemaking. Films and scenes in them come back to haunt you years after you made them. *Goldfinger* is a case in point, of course, but who would have thought that a minor British comedy such as *What A Carve Up* and a scene that I played in would, over thirty years later, become an important part of a novel that won so many plaudits from the critics and established Jonathan Coe as one of our leading novelists?

The Theatre Again and Then Mickey Spillane

Come Blow Your Horn by Neil Simon was playing at the Prince of Wales Theatre in

98

London's West End. It had been a great success on Broadway and now it was replicating that success in London so I was pleased when I was asked to join the cast, taking over from Nyree Dawn Porter. Initially, Bob Monkhouse was playing opposite me, but then Peter Murray took over Bob's role. Yes, Peter Murray, better known perhaps as Pete Murray, the disc jockey. He had quite a successful acting career before he turned to disc jockeying. Anyway, he was an absolute sweetheart to work with.

Michael Crawford was also in the cast. He was more or less just at the beginning of his career and he was showing every sign of becoming the big star that he is now and has been for the last thirty years. A very talented man and a very nice guy.

Other members of the *Come Blow Your Horn* cast included David Kossoff and Libby Morris. I stayed nine months with the play and by the end of my stint I was almost tearing my hair out with the tedium of it all. For some of the time, I was also making *The Girl Hunters* during the day so I had set myself a demanding schedule. But that wasn't the cause of my boredom. Nine months playing the same part seven times a week is just too much. Long runs in the theatre is something I don't like because it is very difficult to retain any freshness in playing your part and you don't really look forward to going to the theatre and repeating the same thing you've been doing for weeks on end. I know other actors don't react in the same way and don't seem to mind long runs, in fact, they welcome them because it gives them financial security for a while, but I can't take them. Long runs are one of the reasons I much prefer the cinema to theatre. When you're making a film, there are tedious stretches when it seems to take forever to set up a shot and you seem to be hanging around all day just for a few minutes in front of the camera, but I don't mind that so much as I do the tedious repetition that comes with a successful show in the West End. With the best will in the world, you find yourself as an actor operating on automatic pilot and that can't be a good thing either for audiences or for the actor concerned. I just love the intimacy of the camera most of all.

When Christmas arrived that year, I gave Colin a rather different present from the usual kind of thing. He loved chess so I bought him a

Life is a Circus with The Crazy Gang and Lionel Jeffries. I played a saloon gal in a sketch within the film.

beaut-iful chess set and asked the stage manager of *Come Blow Your Horn* to teach me how to play the game. So for weeks, when I was waiting off-stage to go on, this guy would teach me how to play chess and by Christmas I was able to play. Colin was delighted with his special present that Christmas and more so because I had taken the trouble to learn how to play, an accomplishment he never thought I would master.

Just three weeks after that Christmas, the American film producer Robert Fellows came to see the show. He was looking for a girl to play opposite Mickey Spillane in an adaptation of one of Mickey's own stories, *The Girl Hunters*. Mickey, of course, was going to be playing Mike Hammer, the famous tough guy private eye that he had created and featured in a number of his hardboiled thrillers. Both Fellows and Mickey watched me on stage that night and came round back stage after the performance to say hello and there and then offered me the role. I was thrilled because it was to be a dramatic role, a pleasant change for me after all those comedies. I had no hesitation in accepting their offer.

The Girl Hunters was to be my first American-produced movie, although it was to be made in England with English technicians and with a mainly American cast. The only hitch was that they wanted to start filming in three weeks time and I had still four months left of my nine-month contract for the play. Experienced actors had told me never to accept filming work during the day when you were in a theatre show in the evening, but I decided to go ahead and do it. I think it was one way of preventing myself from dying of boredom during that long run. I worked on the film for four weeks. At the end of the day's shooting, all I wanted to do was go home to my family, but that was impossible. The show had to go on and I had committed myself to it. At first I drove myself to the theatre from the studios, but after a while, as fatigue caught up with me, I hired a driver. In the back of the car, I used to snatch an hour's sleep so that I could face the evening performance.

Mickey Spillane I found to be a very interesting person. He was a mixture of Mike Hammer and the real Mickey. In the film he was surprisingly good at playing Hammer, considering that he had never seriously acted before. The trick was that he really believed in Hammer as a character and there was so much of him in Mike Hammer anyway. One reviewer described him as 'thickset with the face of a pugilist and the walk of a sprightly gorilla' and that he 'bites out his lines as other men bite off cigars.'

Mickey is an earthy man, amazingly good at practical things. He is a tough guy, but he is also a strong family man. There is something of the poetic cynic about the guy and he has certainly an element of sweetness in his character, despite his tough novels. At any rate, I felt I was working with a legend on *The Girl Hunters*. I don't know how

Love scene with Mickey Spillane in *The Girl Hunters*. He plays his own hero Mike Hammer, I play a wealthy widow with hidden motives.

many copies of his books have been sold since he started writing, but it must run to several millions and he continues to write to this very day. In fact, we still keep in touch and he sends me copies of his books. 'I'm not an author', Mickey likes saying, 'I'm a writer.' He makes that distinction and I think I know what he means. He sees himself as a professional, a craftsman who has perfected a particular genre of crime fiction, and he does his best to make his books as entertaining and well-written as he can.

In the film I play a sophisticated American lady, Laura Knapp, the widow of a recently murdered American Senator. My accent had to be American, of course, and I think I managed that quite effectively. Hammer is employed by the American Secret Service to investigate the murder. He falls for me, but he discovers that I am involved with an international gang led by someone called The Dragon, who is really at the forefront of a plot by the communists to seize control of the world. When Hammer confronts me with the accusation that I have conspired with The Dragon to murder my Senator husband, I threaten him with a shotgun. Unfortunately, in the process I manage to blow my own head off. This is one of the few times in my movie career when I come to a sticky end, but I welcomed the chance to play someone who was just a beautiful bitch.

One evening during this hellish schedule I had set for myself, I had a frantic phone-call ten minutes before I was due to go on stage for a performance of *Come Blow Your Horn*. It was from my new nanny and she was hysterical. She confessed that she had just given our four-year-old son a severe hiding. She had completely lost her temper, but she was full of remorse. My heart sank. I tried to calm her, but I was ready to burst into tears myself. Oh, God, why was I there at the theatre waiting to give a

This Is Your Life. I was invited to appear as a guest when Hattie Jacques came under Eamon Andrews' microscope.

performance I no longer wanted to give? Why was I not at home with Grant and Colin? How I got through that evening's performance, I shall never know. Colin came to get me at the theatre that night. I told him what had happened and he was very upset. However, when we arrived home and found our son fast asleep, we felt relieved and tried to put the whole incident behind us.

However, one result was that I decided I would never work in the theatre again. The nanny left. I didn't want another live-in girl and by a wonderful stroke of luck, I found a neighbour who was willing to babysit. Little did I know at the time that this sprightly woman would come to mean so much to all our family. We called her Luffy.

On holiday on our cruiser Kep with Colin and Grant.

When *The Girl Hunters* was released in the USA, I went to Los Angeles and New York with Mickey Spillane to publicize the film. We had a very hectic schedule as always on those kinds of trips. While I was in LA, my agent telephoned me to say he had arranged a meeting for me with the

The Girl Hunters. The climax!

producer and director of a new comedy film starring Jack Lemmon with a view to my playing opposite him in the movie. I was thrilled. I'd always been a great admirer of Jack Lemmon and the very thought of working with him sent the adrenaline racing. Everyone was very enthusiastic about the idea. A screen test was quickly organized at the studio and Jack Lemmon himself would do it with me. The day before the test, I was taken out shopping with the costume designer. We rushed from one high-class clothes shop to another, until we found exactly what we were looking for. I was so excited about the test. If it went well, it would be my very first film in Hollywood. However, I only had a day to learn the script, in between all the interviews for television and magazines publicizing *The Girl Hunters*. I must say I was feeling pretty pressurized. The night before the test I lay in bed with the script in my hands, trying to remember my dialogue, and it just wouldn't sink in! I tried not to worry, but I didn't get a wink of sleep until the early hours of the morning.

I arrived at the studio the following day feeling very apprehensive. The director was very welcoming and introduced me to Jack Lemmon. The three of us sat and talked for a while. I couldn't take my eyes off Jack. He seemed so relaxed and kind, just as I had imagined he would be. Then we went on the set to play the scene.

Well! We did take after take, but I just could not remember my lines and I felt a total fool! Jack was absolutely wonderful and tried to make me relax. Finally, we got the scene shot in small sections. I knew I had given a bad performance and I was furious with myself. When I left the studios, I felt depressed. I couldn't discuss my disastrous morning with Mickey because he had left Los Angeles. On my way back to the hotel, I kept saying to myself, 'It's not the end of the world, it's only a film!', but that didn't help. However, I pulled myself together and clearly understood the reason for my failure: I was overtired and overnervous. Needless to say, I didn't get the part. I blew it! I don't remember if the film was made or not. As far as I was concerned, I tried to put the whole episode behind me. I suppose that kind of situation has to happen at least once in the lifetime of an actor's career.

Rhino!

The ravishing Ava Gardner, one of the old-time Hollywood stars I had particularly admired when I was growing up, had made one of her most famous films *Mogambo* on location in Kenya. Now in 1963 I had accepted the female lead role in an adventure film called *Rhino!*, which was to be shot in Africa, and after the sadness of leaving Colin and Grant in England, I found myself on a aeroplane travelling to Johannesburg. My mind drifted away to the adventures that lay ahead. I day-dreamed, as I glanced out of the window at the powdered clouds, which were like tumbled blankets of snow, with infinity above, clear and shaded blue. I had often thought maybe one day I would like to make a film in Africa and the fantasy had now turned into reality with my part in this new film.

Harry Guardino and I share a scene in *Rhino*.

The producer Ivan Tors, who was best known as the creator of *Flipper*, the television series, and the American and African cast and crew all met in a Joburg hotel. After spending a few days there to finalize the schedule, we boarded a chartered aircraft for our destination, Umpholosi in Natal in the middle of Zululand. Finding myself among all these different nationalities in a strange land was an exhilarating experience. Ivan had already told us about the small game reserve that we would working and living in. The game warden was Ian Player, whose more famous brother was the golfer Gary Player.

As our small plane touched down on a dusty field in this magic place, I saw mile upon mile of yellow, sun-drenched land. My first reaction was how vast and overwhelming it was and as my feet touched the ground, I knew I was in a world totally different to anything I had experienced before. Africa rushed at me like a tidal wave and my spirits soared. I had never before experienced this level of spiritual awareness. It was as if the spirit of Africa had entered my soul.

We lived in little round huts called 'rondarvals' made of white cement walls and thatched roofs. Not much glamour there (I wonder if Ava Gardner had it any better when she was shooting *Mogambo*), because living conditions were very spartan: a couple of beds, a table and two chairs. The primitive outside toilets and showers were a luxury. Behind the huts was a long native cookhouse where all our meals were prepared. I made spaghetti bolognese for everyone one evening with the African cook looking on with amused interest, learning how to make it as he watched.

The little encampment rested on the crest of a hill. The view that spread out before us was haunting and breathtaking, especially at sunset. The splendour, the beauty and the sheer peace of it all was spellbinding. We often used to hear the roar of a lion, but we never actually saw one. However, the first day we arrived we went in a jeep with Ian Player to meet the original inhabitants of this particular area the white rhino. The

105

A natural look captured between takes on location in Zululand for *Rhino*.

jeep stopped when Ian spotted two. He said, 'Quietly follow me.' My knees were trembling, but I just had to see these wild and wonderful ancient creatures. My heart was pounding as we approached them from downwind. My body was quivering as I took it slowly step by step. Finally, Ian, who was, incidentally, the founder of the World Wilderness Foundation, signalled for us to stop as we were close enough to see them properly, but not too near as to disturb them. I held his arm for reassurance. He understood without words what I was feeling, as he had seen it many times with people who experienced this kind of world for the first time.

Ian Player, backed up by his team of rangers, helped us finish the shoot, for without them we would not have been able to make the film. Rhino! was a movie about the work to save the white rhino from extinction. That task has now been accom-plished, and, although our film was fiction, it was based on fact. Harry Guardino and Robert Culp were my co-stars. Guardino, who often played tough guys in American films such as *Pork Chop Hill*, *Madigan* and *Dirty Harry*, plays an unscrupulous big-game hunter who has been offered a lot of money for two rare white rhinos. Culp, whose best known film is probably *Bob and Carol and Ted and Alice*, plays a scientist who is devoted to saving African animals and especially wants to preserve the rhinos. I play Guardino's girl friend, a local district nurse. Guardino and Culp join forces because the former needs the doctor's drugs and tranquillizers to capture the animals, but he steals the doctor's equipment. Culp forces me to lead him to Guardino's hiding place, there is a fight and eventually the doctor saves Guardino's life from a snake bite. The rhinos are eventually captured but for the purpose of preserving the species.

On one of my days off, I was invited to join Ian and his men on one of their usual rounds. I had, by now, got used to looking in my boots for scorpions and keeping a watchful eye out for snakes. I was feeling more at home in this totally different environment from London and England. Every day, there seemed to be something new to discover. On this particular day we were rounding up impala, a species of African deer. There were two jeeps racing and bumping madly over the rough terrain, when suddenly there was a shout and both jeeps stopped. Ian had been standing up in one of them when it went over a particularly large clump of bush with the result he fell and broke his collar bone. Much to his disquiet, someone had to put his arm in a sling. I sat next to him in the jeep and although he was in great pain, he never said a word. We had to get him back to his house so he could see a doctor. I felt very close in spirit to this man of Africa. On the way back we were still being thrown about because of the rough ground, but he just sat there, quiet and strong. Trying to help, I gave him an aspirin from my satchel. His gentle courage was very impressive. Most of the men who work as rangers are very unusual people. They have great physical courage mixed with a quiet respect and love for all of nature.

When we moved to another location, I saw the incredible sight of buffalo stampeding. One straggler who was badly crippled was shot quickly by a ranger to put an end to his misery, because the animal would ultimately have died of starvation. Then we saw the regal, gentle giraffe, timid but also curious about us, not at all threatened by our presence. We did some filming and then returned to Umpholosi. It was a Sunday when no filming was scheduled so the whole company decided to go for a day's relaxation and to picnic by the river. The spot we found was a beautiful, shaded glade right on the river's edge. The sun was hot. Soft tissues of cloud were passing overhead, the trees were full of monkeys, chattering and screeching at our intrusion, watching us with their bright, age-old eyes and eventually reconciling themselves to our presence.

We ate, laughed, took photographs and were generally enjoying ourselves when some bright spark suggested we swim across the river to cool down. I am not what you would call a strong swimmer and my desire to take part was not strengthened when we were told there were crocodiles in the river. Not knowing whether to believe that or not, I decided I could not resist the challenge and, indeed, most of us took the plunge. When you are living so close to raw nature, you find you do things you never thought you would be capable of. At any rate, I survived the swim, although I did keep an eye open for those crocodiles.

The location shooting did have its dangers at other times as well. Once I was in a boat and the river was full of hippos. Their large, heavy-lidded eyes kept popping up above the surface. I was astonished, fascinated and a bit scared. Hippos can be dangerous and they can easily overturn a small boat, so we did not stay long in their vicinity.

There was one sequence in *Rhino!* that involved two hundred Zulus. A local man, who seemed able to deliver anything we needed, persuaded many tribal people from distant corrals to join us. These people were true primitives, as yet unspoiled by western influences. On the second day, we needed them to dance one of their ritual dances. Late in the morning they began to drink their own special brew of alcohol and gradually as the day wore on, they became more and more uninhibited. They had slaughtered one of their sacred cows for the occasion while we watched from the sidelines. The heat, the dust and the flowing blood all added to the feeling of ancient ritual. For a few hours I was totally mesmerised by it. I learned much about the local people's customs and etiquette.

They were as fascinated by us as we were by them. The children were especially interesting. Often as we were having our lunch break, eating our boxed lunches, a group of youngsters with their appealing faces would come and sit beside us. When I gave an orange to the youngest child, she automatically passed it to the eldest. Then it was shared by all. Their sense of family unity and tribal tradition was all-important to them. When I thought of England and our way of life, I saw how rushed and superficial our western life was.

Another time I went on a hunt to catch a wild white *rhino* for shipping to another part of Africa where they were becoming extinct. The ranger tracked it down, shot it with a tranquilliser, then, difficult as it is to move a heavily drugged *rhino* weighing several tons, he and the others completed the procedure with the utmost care for the animal's welfare. One of the *rhino*s they caught was a female. She was tagged and named after me (Um Eaton). I feel very privileged to know that one of these great animals is called after me.

My spell on location in Africa felt like a lifetime because I had experienced and seen so much. I shall never forget that Godgiven country, the beautiful scenery, the wonderful wild species and the hospitable people. Being transported into this other world for a short period was one of the great bonuses of being in the movie business.

When the shoot was finished, I flew straight to the south of France where Colin and Grant had already started their holiday. From the African bush to the sophistication of the French Riviera! What an adjustment I had to make because, in some ways, the spirit of Africa was still burning inside of me. I did not want to let it go. It took time for me to unwind. I always find that when a film is completed, I am exhausted but the adrenaline still runs high. I very much enjoyed the times between films just being a woman at home. I loved the variety in my life even though being a complete mate to your husband and caring for your children properly is a far more difficult challenge than most careers can ever be. Careers come and go, but being a parent lasts your lifetime.

Two postscripts to my African experience. During the Cote D'Azur holiday, with the encouragement of Annie, a close French friend and a talented painter, I took up painting on a course at an art school. I believe that the motive behind my starting to paint came from all the new dimensions that had crept into my untapped senses because of what I had experienced in Africa. I felt I was expanding in all directions. I painted pictures of animals, mythical Greek warriors, all sorts of portraits, any subject that caught my imagination. I had a photograph of an African child whom I had met while I was there. When I looked at it, I felt all the beauty of Africa and the awe I felt coursing through me. Somehow, onto that plain white canvas, I recreated that child and the

Saying goodbye to Grant at the airport, as I leave for a whirlwind tour of the USA to promote *Goldfinger*.

feeling of African heat. The imaginative teacher encouraged me by saying, 'That's really good, for a start.' I often think of that teacher and the help he gave me, for without his enthusiasm I would probably not have continued to learn to paint.

I was forcefully reminded of the stark contrast between the simplicities of Africa and the downside of living in a big city like London when I returned to England. I came home one day after collecting Grant from school to find that our house had been burgled. Every bit of furniture was turned over, the bed was a mess, clothes were strewn everywhere, cupboard doors were wide open and the drawers tossed anywhere. I telephoned the police, I telephoned Colin, then I felt really frightened. In my state of anxiety, I imagined the burglars might still be in the house. I had an overwhelming desire to get out of the house, but I was scared to go downstairs. I armed myself with a heavy glass ornament and managed to get Grant and myself next door and into our

Dancing with Graham Hill at the SOS Ball at Grosvenor House, December 1965. You can't see from the picture, but at the time I was heavily pregnant with my second son Jason. Graham's sense of humour was legendary, and he took dancing with 'Shirley plus one' in his stride.

neighbour's house. They sat us down and gave us a cup of tea. They told me they had seen two men come into the driveway in a van, dressed as painters, but they thought nothing of it, as we had been having the house painted and workmen had been coming and going over the past few weeks.

The police arrived. I then had to go back into the house to find out exactly what had been taken. My jewellery had gone and many other things that meant a lot to me. All that I had left was what I was wearing that day. When Colin came home, we realized that many sentimental objects, things that were special to our life together, had disappeared from our lives. I didn't want any more jewellery given to me after that experience. For months afterwards, I felt uneasy about the house. Every time I went out, I wondered if I would find the place in the same turmoil again when I returned. It isn't just the objects that are stolen that is so upsetting. It is the creepy feeling that strangers have been prying into our home and privacy that hurt and disgusted me. The spiritual effect of Africa seemed that more distant when I, with this cruel experience, came slap up against some of the harsh realities of urban living

Bond, Tramps, Christie and Hollywood

I have already written about the *Goldfinger* part of my life at the beginning of this book. It was when I came back from shooting *Rhino* in Africa that I was summoned, in my brand new tan, to see Harry Saltzman. Perhaps the deep tan did help me become Jill Masterson, so the African experience paid off in more ways than one. And being cast in *Goldfinger* more than made up for the fact that I had been burgled.

Life was very full. I had a husband and child I loved, my career was going well, and we had lots of friends whom we spent time with when we could. Two of those friends at that time in the sixties were Jackie Collins and her late husband Oscar Lerman. Jackie and Oscar were sitting at our dining room table enjoying a meal I had cooked for them and another couple of friends. Jackie' second book had just been published and her husband had recently opened a nightclub in London called Tramps, which had established itself quickly among showbusiness people and other social fireflies as the place to be. Colin's birthday was coming up soon, so I thought it would be a good idea to present him with a membership card as a birthday gift.

We went to Tramps occasionally with friends for a while after that. One night I had been dancing until I was ready to drop when I looked around for Colin. I could just see him distantly across the dance floor, still happily dancing with a friend, so I wandered off to get myself a drink at the bar. The club, as I say, was often filled with celebrities. I perched myself on a stool between several men. In the dim light, you were never quite sure who you would see there. I found myself facing Anthony Newley, whom I knew already, and I started chatting to him. Behind me, I felt the presence of another man. I turned round on my stool and saw that it was George Best, the great Irish footballer, who was very young at that time and probably at the height of his career and fame.

In the early sixties, George Best was the man of the moment, on and off the football pitch. In fact, they called him 'the fifth Beatle', not only because his talent matched the Fab Four's (in a different sphere, of course), but also because he had a great social life and young women flocked to be near him. Indeed,

An American look for an American location still.

everybody, it seemed, wanted something from George Best. I have mentioned the danger of hangers-on in the showbusiness world, and George Best, although he was a footballer, was, in essence, a showbusiness star. I could understand why he was the

target for so many women. He had a somewhat shy Irish charm and was incredibly good-looking. Even though he wasn't very tall, a sexual aura emanated from him.

I turned round to speak to him and although he didn't say very much, those gorgeous Irish eyes glowed at me even in that smoky club atmosphere. We didn't dance together because friends whisked me away to join a table where Peter Sellers was sitting. We stayed late at the club with our friends, dancing

The Naked Brigade. Ken Scott, Mary Cropolopolis and myself.

The Naked Brigade. The dramatic role is reflected in this rather intense studio portrait.

until we were exhausted and we left feeling drained but happy.

My memories of nights like that at Tramps vividly brings back some aspects of the 'swinging Sixties' in London. The Sixties was a time that set sexual freedoms above everything else, and as most people realize now, changed attitudes towards sex and family life for the following decades. Indeed, we speak of the Sixties as a turning point in social behaviour. It certainly was that and more.

Inhibitions, especially sexual inhibitions, were set free to fly wherever they could find satisfaction. But that caused problems for people even in the freewheeling Sixties, because people are people and they have their jealousies and their possessiveness. Quite often at clubs like Tramps you would witness all sorts of dramas between couples when too much alcohol had been imbibed and too many flirtations between attractive men and women had got out of hand. Very often a man would leave the club with a different woman he arrived with, and, of course, vice versa. The atmosphere, after all, was intensely sensual, it was set up to be that way. There was the music, the sexy dancing, the young stars of the showbusiness world all eyeing each other, it was inevitable that there would be clashes of one kind or another. Perhaps in the years that followed, the pendulum has swung too far towards the sexual freedoms that started in the Sixties. We are all now so desensitized in so many ways.

My next film was *The Naked Brigade*, a AmericanGreek coprod-uction. It was a war movie which was shot on location in Greece. It co-starred Ken Scott, who plays a Greek lieutenant. It is set in Crete in 1941 and I play Diana Forsyth who arrives on the island to persuade my father to return to England before the Germans invade. In an attack, my father is killed and I am rescued by a group of female guerrillas who take me to their mountain retreat. We all take part in blowing up a German munitions ship and although there is an attraction between myself and the Greek lieutenant, at the end of the movie, I leave Crete by submarine.

Most of my memories to do with the making of *The Naked Brigade* were of heat, flies and jellyfish! I had never been to Greece before and hadn't appreciated how hot it could become there. When you are on location working, and by definition not vacationing, the heat seems even greater, although I must say it was a wonderfully dry heat in Greece, not the exhausting wet humidity other countries endure.

We did a lot of filming way out in the countryside in places not often visited by tourists. When our lunch break came, we'd have to find the nearest café. No five-star catering was available! We'd sit under a kind of porch and try to eat the uneatable, with the flies joining in just to give the food an extra flavour!

During one of the days when we were not filming, Ken Scott and I went to visit the Acropolis. It was fantastic and I was overwhelmed by what is left of the huge ancient monument. It was breathtaking and we took many photographs. We also went to the ruins of Delphi, the original capital of Greece, where there is a famous statue of a man. I remember thinking how short he was, compared to the relative giants of contemporary youth. I bought myself a local artefact because whenever I was on location I would treat myself to something that would remind me later of the country.

Those were the fun days. Back to work now. We (Ken Scott, and the Greek actress who was costarring with us and myself) had to shoot a scene at night in the port of Athens. The scene had to be shot with us all swimming in the water - the fithy port water! However, we all took a deep breath and silently slipped from the quay into the black murky sea. We were meant to be silent, as the script dictated. Well, just a few yards from the quay, the Greek actress gave out the most piercing scream and, splashing about, looked back at me as I was a few feet behind her. 'Look out!' she yelled. 'Look out, look out, there are jellyfish everywhere.' The director frantically shouted, 'Cut! Cut!'. By this time we were both clinging on to one another, but the

more we panicked, the more stings we received. My legs felt as though they were on fire! Both the assistant directors jumped fully clothed into the port to help us out.

After getting two hysterical actresses out of the water and inspecting the red weals that had erupted all over our bodies, they called a doctor, as both of us were in a state of collapse. However, the doctor reassured the director and ourselves that we would be fine by the morning. We shot that scene again the following week, but not in

Ten Little Indians. I pull a gun to defend myself against an unseen assailant.

the port of Athens!

The location for my next film, *Ten Little Indians*, adapted from an Agatha Christie play, was not perhaps as exotic as Greece, but in its own way Dublin is just as fascinating. The film company rented an old mansion for the interior shots, although the 'castle' is meant to be perched on top of a snowcovered peak at the end of a cable car line. Grant, my son, went down with a bad case of measles just before I had to leave for filming. He had got over the worst by the time of my flight, but I still found it very difficult to leave because I was very worried. However, he got over the illness and was able to fly over to Dublin with Colin during the shoot. The weather was very bad as they approached Dublin Airport and the plane made three unsuccessful attempts to land. Grant handled his worry about that by asking his Dad, 'What would happen if the plane landed upside down?' Fortunately, it didn't and we were reunited as a family.

Ten Little Indians has a plot that is not entirely dissimilar to the story of *What A Carve Up* except that the reason for gathering all those people in an isolated mansion in Indians_ is because of their past crimes and in *Carve Up*, it is for the reading of a will, but it is a staple plot element of thrillers to find some excuse to assemble a cast of individuals together and then one by one bump them off with the killer being left to the last. Indeed, another link with Jonathan Coe's novel *What A Carve Up* is forged with this movie because Jonathan used the name of the 'Judge' character in Indians, Owen, for the name of his leading character in the novel. In Indians the Judge's name is U. N. Owen as in Unknown and he is played by Wilfred Hyde White. He turns out to be the man behind the scheme of bringing all these people with guilty pasts together in a house they cannot escape from because of its position on top of a mountain and because it is snowbound.

I played Ann Clyde, who has been lured to the mountain top because I have been appointed secretary to the mysterious Mr Owen, who is not present apparently when his 'guests' assemble. I provide the love interest with Hugh O'Brian, who is pretending to be his own best friend who has died in mysterious circumstances. I found Hugh O'Brian to be a very vain man. He was used to women chasing him and he flirted a lot, but he certainly was not my type of guy.

Another cast member was the Israeli actress, Daliah Lavi, who was a very striking glamour girl. She was like a long-legged, untamed thoroughbred and she had been in the Israeli army. However, she was very temperamental and used to shout at the makeup people, 'Where is my ice? I want my ice now.' This was not ice for her drinks but for her face, which she would apply to improve her skin. She had just fallen in love with a stunt man who had just completed a picture with Burton and Taylor. In the film, she has, as they say nowadays, very big hair, which makes her look rather grotesque. She probably was less than pleased when she disappeared from the picture as the fifth victim of the revenging killer, having been dispatched by lethal injection.

Fabian, the American pop singer of the time, was also in the picture and he had the misfortune to be bumped off first when he swallows a poisoned drink. Scripts like *Ten Little Indians* establish a kind of pecking order for the actors the quicker your character is killed, the lesser your role, so I was lucky that I was the one, with Hugh O'Brian, who survives to the end. My 'crime' has been murder, but it turns out that I have taken the rap for my sister who is in a mental institution.

The cast also included these fine, old English actors: Stanley Holloway, who had recently been such a big hit in the stage version of *My Fair Lady* as Eliza Doolittle's dustman father, a role he was to repeat in the 1964 Hollywood film of the Lerner and Loewe musical; Leo Genn, that veteran of many a British war movie and Hollywood epic (remember him as the patrician Roman who ridicules Nero in *Quo Vadis?*); then there were the two actors whom I seemed to be in a lot of films with, Dennis Price and Wilfred Hyde White.

There was one feature of *Ten Little Indians* that is especially noteworthy. Towards the end of the movie, a voice-over announces there is now going to be a 'Whodunnit break' of sixty seconds during which the members of the cinema audience should make up their mind who the murderer is. 'Turn to the person next to you and discuss who the murderer might be', the voiceover encourages and then there followed a quick montage of shots of the murders and of those characters who were still surviving. I don't know how many people in cinemas across the world turned to the person next to them and solemnly discussed who they thought was the guilty party, but it was a novel idea, although it was a ploy that the American director, William Castle, one of the kings of cheap horror movie-making, had pioneered. Castle also dared the public to see his films with gimmicks like give-away insurance policies to insure against death by fright when viewing one of his movies, seats that supposedly gave

With Brian Kelly and Lloyd Bridges on the set of *Around The World Under the Sea.*

audiences 'tingles' and mobile skeletons. Castle produced his films as well and often introduced them in the Alfred Hitchcock manner. *Ten Little Indians* did not go as far as Castle in the gimmickry stakes, but by breaking into the movie in the way it did, it was taking a risk by threatening the audience's suspension of disbelief.

The climax of the film has me pretending to shoot Hugh O'Brian's character dead in order for the murderer to show his hand. The Judge (Wilfred Hyde White), whom we have been led to believe has been murdered himself, turns up alive and is in the process of taking a poisoned drink because he has accomplished his task of meting out justice when Hugh O'Brian reappears and explains his shooting has been a putup job . All very Agatha Christie, but it works, and the movie still retains entertainment value when it crops up, as it does, on television.

In the summer of 1965, I flew to Miami to make *Around the World Under the Sea*, where it was to be made on location and in a studio there. MGM was the producing company with Ivan Tors as the producer. I was pleased to be working with Ivan again after my experience on *Rhino!*. Miami is where he had made his successful children's television series, *Flipper*, starring Brian Kelly, who was to star also in *Around the World Under the Sea*. The cast also included those veterans of many a Hollywood movie, Lloyd Bridges, the father of Jeff and Beau Bridges, and who died recently at the age of 85, and Keenan Wynn. In addition there was David McCallum, an old pal, and Marshall Thompson. David McCallum had met Jill Ireland around the time Jill and I were making *Three Men in a Boat*. I remember one day when all three of us were having lunch in the Pinewood Studios restaurant. The looks they were giving each other across the table surely meant they were in love and shortly afterwards they married.

Jill came to Miami to be with David during the shooting (this was before their marital breakup). Indeed, most of the cast had their families with them, which made for a great atmosphere. Colin and Grant had came out to join me a few days after I arrived, which helped to make it one of the most enjoyable films I worked on. Of course, Colin and Grant were on holiday while I was working. Grant was an adventurous six-year-old and needed entertaining so we hoped that on my days off from filming we would be able to see whatever there was to see in Miami. In fact, Marshall Thompson and his wife took Grant to Disneyland for the day and he couldn't stop talking about it for weeks (Grant, that is, not Marshall!) Ivan Tors was his usual kindly self and Lloyd Bridges and Keenan Wynn were great to work with. I loved Keenan's sense of humour and gravellike voice, while Lloyd Bridges came across as a typical American hunk with an eye for the girls.

Brian Kelly came from Boston. His Celtic appearance which combined sensitivity and masculine magnetism was very attractive. I also found his sense of fun and his penchant for not taking himself too seriously very appealing. He had not worked with

With David Macallum in a boat in Miami during *Around The World Under The Sea*.

an English actress before and I think the attraction was mutual. I guess we had an on-screen kind of magic which overflowed to off-screen times and we became good friends. When Colin met him, he instantly liked him as well.

One evening Brian said he would like to show us some of the Miami night life. The evening was balmy and romantic. The three of us got into his car and went from one club to another, laughing, drinking and dancing with an air of abandonment. Although Colin and I had done the same thing several times in London, this particular evening was special with the three of us enjoying each other's company and behaving with childlike pleasure.

In the wee small hours of the morning we were heading back to our hotel in Brian's convertible along a stretch of highway when he decided to drive dangerously fast. The wind rushed past us as we laughed and then I looked back and there strewn across the highway were the contents of Brian's suitcase, jeans, tee shirts, socks etcetera, fluttering and dotted like a line of washing that had gone through a wind machine. We stopped the car, got out and started to pick up the clothes, but we gave up in the end because we were laughing so much. They just didn't seem that important.

The next day was a Sunday, or should I say it was already Sunday, and Ivan had

Grant with THE fish. It was bigger than him!

hired a boat for all the cast to relax on for the day. It was leaving the Keys at 8 a.m. so Colin, Brian and I just had time to shower, collect Grant from the hotel and then go to the boat. It was a marvellous day. I remember the sea was so inviting with its pure turquoise colour. I floated about like a mermaid, enjoying everything. It was idyllic.

Brian and I had been asked to do a photo session at the manmade lagoon where the dolphin that 'played' *Flipper* was kept. I had never been close to a dolphin before so I was looking forward to the experience. Actually several *Flipper*s were used during the television series, as the work load was thought to be too much for one dolphin. Dolphins get nervous exhaustion just like us human performers.

Beside the lagoon there was a big round tank with this beautiful creature swimming around. Brian was kneeling at the side of the tank and started to make signals to the dolphin. Each sign he made, the dolphin obeyed. I was mesmerized. I forgot all about the photographer and just wanted to enjoy the fascinating creature I was watching. After a while, Brian noticed how enchanted I was and asked if I would like to get into

Brian introducing me to *Flipper*!

the tank and swim with the dolphin. I accepted immediately. Who could pass up the chance to swim with Flipper? I disappeared to change into my bikini and when I came back, Brian was already in the tank and he beckoned me to his side. I was quivering with excitement and a little nervous at the prospect of being in the water with this huge wonderful dolphin. However, I slipped into the water, made a signal and the dolphin came gliding up to me, letting me hold onto his dorsal fin. He slowly pulled me through the water. What a sensation! I shall never forget it. I have swum with Flipper!

Ivan Tors took a great interest in Grant. He was soon to be shooting more episodes of *Flipper*. He asked Colin and me if we would consider allowing Grant to play the younger brother in the series the following year. Grant had an innocent, freckled face and a pleasant nature, so, although we could understand Ian's suggestion that our son be in the new series, we said no. Although I was flattered by the idea of Grant being in a television series, we said no because I didn't want our innocent son to be immersed in the stresses and strains of a fantasy world. Real life, after all, is difficult enough for youngsters to cope with. He was just six years old! I felt we had to protect him. I wanted him to have a real childhood, because we only have one shot at it. I honestly feel that the decision for someone to become an actor should not be made by the parents. If a young person really wants to go along the hard path of becoming an actor, they must make the decision themselves, when they are old enough to know exactly what they are letting themselves in for. Then, if they have talent and determination, they will find their own way (with a little luck), which, in the long run, will prove more rewarding.

Just before the filming was finished on our last Sunday before we left Miami, Colin and Brian hired a deep sea fishing boat for the day. Grant loved being on the sea as much as Colin and none of us had been deep sea fishing before. The crew showed us how to use the fishing lines etcetera, and we sat in those wonderful chairs you see in the movies as we waited patiently for the fish to bite. Of course, we were hoping to catch a marlin, but that kind of thing only happens in Hemingway novels.

The sun was piercingly hot and the breeze helped to cool us, as we took turns in sitting in the chairs. At first, we had several bites, but each time the fish escaped. There was an atmosphere of anticipation about the day as we sailed around. Grant was as fascinated at the prospect of catching a really big fish as we were. He was very quiet, never became bored and liked to listen to the crew weaving tales about deepsea fishing and the adventures of the boat.

Suddenly there was a pull on Grant's line. We all got very excited. The crew were telling him what to do, but after a time one of them had to take the line from him because he was getting exhausted with the effort of it all. We were all peering over the side of the boat willing it to be a marlin, but out came a very big fish indeed: a dolphin! Not a *Flipper* kind of dolphin, but a dolphin fish, which apparently is delicious to eat. Grant jumped about in his excitement. When it was finally quite dead, we held it against him and it was almost as big as he was. On our way back to the shore, Colin caught two more dolphin fish smaller than Grant's and three tuna fish as well. I caught nothing. When we moored the boat, we thanked the crew for a wonderful day and gave them the tuna to use as bait for another trip.

Brian suggested we give the dolphin fish to Keenan Wynn and his wife as they had rented a house and loved cooking. The next day on set Keenan told us that they had tasted delicious.

Brian remained a good friend to Colin and me for several years after making the movie. He came to our home in London and also visited us in the south of France when we were on holiday. On one of his visits to London, while he was dining with us at home, he mentioned to Colin he wanted to visit Rome. The next week I was waving them both goodbye and thinking I must be mad. About two years later we heard he had a horrendous motorcycle accident in the States. We were greatly saddened by the news and frustrated as we were never able to find out exactly what had happened to him.

As for the movie itself, I played a scientist, Dr Maggie Hanford, the only woman among five male scientists on a cramped 'hydronaut', which was meant to be an advanced submarine vessel powered by atomic fuel which was being used for research into establishing a warning system for imminent earthquakes. Naturally, the plot involved the tensions the female presence causes among the competing males, although there never seems any doubt that I will end up in Brian Kelly's arms. I am so much of a distraction that the male crew let their minds wander and almost crash the vessel into barrier reefs. There are all kinds of adventures involving a giant conger eel attack on the hydronaut, an underwater volcano and being caught on its shelf and climbing out of what remains of the submarine to swim to the surface. The main interest of the movie has to be the underwater filming, however, which was shot in the Great Barrier Reefs of Australia and in the Bahamas.

It was a really fun movie to do and I will always remember the sense of camaraderie there was among the cast. After all the goodbyes were said, Colin, Grant and I left for a ten-day holiday in the Bahamas. I can see them now in my mind's eye: rows and rows of green bushes with pineapples springing from the branches. Wherever you looked there were fields and fields full of ripe pineapples. We asked our taxi driver to take us to places of interest. Our driver, a native Bahamian, wore a black suit with a bright green shirt and yellow tie and a smile that made us think of sunshine. When it was lunchtime, he took us to a tiny house where a large family was already eating. The mother got us and gave us all sorts of wonderful dishes, five in all, followed by, yes, pineapple. The hospitality was just stupendous. The island of New Providence at that time was relatively unspoilt. We loved it and spent our days away from the hustle and bustle of the city and the big hotels.

The birth of my second child

The trees were rushing by, the fields were green and frosty. Little houses stood in rows like strings of beads. The rhythmic sound of the train was gently hypnotizing me. Grant had his nose pressed to the window watching everything pass by so magically. Colin was quietly reading. Selma, our dog, was curled up asleep on my feet on the carriage floor. I was sitting a little uncomfortably midst this peaceful scene. There was a new child pressing against my ribs. I was wondering, 'Is it a boy or girl? It must be a girl. This pregnancy has been so different from my first.'

We were on our way to Cornwall to spend Christmas with my parents. After selling their furniture shop, they had bought a house in a very quiet part of that beautiful county. Their new life was to be in Fowey, that picturesque little village by the sea, that has strong associations with Daphne du Maurier, the author of *Rebecca* and other novels that had been turned into famous films. It was exciting to be going to see my parents in their new home. They had transformed the house into a large, very comfortable guest house and this new venture was a challenge to them. Johnny, my brother, often helped them by waiting on tables. But for this Christmas and the family gathering, there were to be no guests, no work, just all of us relaxing together.

With the refreshing cold sea breeze helping to relax us after the rigours of city life, we explored the little village nestling at the head of the estuary leading to the sea. We walked up the cliffs through a path in the woods which wound its way upwards until we were granted a splendid view of the coastline. It was certainly a beautiful place to live and I felt a sense of contentment for my parents.

After Christmas was over and we made our emotional goodbyes at the station, we once more set off on the long train journey home. We felt fresh after our break; the sea air had been bracing and there had been all the nostalgic feelings associated with a family Christmas. The new year (1966) was about to begin. The baby was due at the end of February. There was so much to look forward to.

But life has surprises in store for all of us. Just two days after we arrived back home, I became ill with influenza. The doctor came. I told him I had begun to have labour pains. They were faint, but they were there. I was confined to complete bed rest in the hope that the contractions would cease. It was far too early for the birth. But Nature has its own schedule and a week later my waters broke. On the third of January, labour began in earnest, which was seven weeks early!

It was six o'clock on a cold wintry evening. Colin was not at home; he was still in London taking an intensive French language course. I telephoned Luffy, the lady who helped me look after Grant, and said, 'I must get to the hospital!'. Her husband drove me there, doubtless hoping I wouldn't produce there and then on the back seat of his car. Colin joined me at the hospital. We were both anxious about the well-being of the baby. He sat next to bed, as usual loving and supportive, but as I lay there in a dazed state of labour, my thoughts drifted back to the birth of our first son. I had thought then, 'Never again!', but here I was going through the same hellish but wondrous experience again. This time my labour only lasted six hours. However, the birth itself was extremely fraught because it was a breech birth, that means, he was coming out feet first, which was traumatic for me and dangerous for the baby.

Just after midnight and with the birth imminent, I was heavily sedated. A little while later, I became conscious again. It was all over. My first words were, 'Is the baby alright?'. Colin answered yes. We had another baby son. I fell into a relieved sleep.

Our new son was put into an incubator. My heart turned over because I could not yet hold him in my arms. I stood there crying, looking at him, just looking at him. He was perfect with reddish hair, like Grant. He was ever so tiny but alive! What a miracle the birth of a child is!

The following day when I spoke to the pediatrician, he said the baby was doing fine, but by the third day serious complications had started to develop, so he was taken to a specialist premature baby unit in another hospital. Colin and I were desolate. We lived through the next two days as though we were in the middle of a nightmare. We dreaded what another new day would bring. But the tide turned. On the fifth day, our son came back to the maternity hospital a much healthier boy. He had won his second battle, but was still very frail. I could not breast feed him because he was too weak to suckle from my breasts. The doctor, however, wanted him to have breast milk as it was more nourishing, so I drew mine off and they gave it to him little by little.

I returned home after a week, as the doctor and nurses had by then complete control over our baby's welfare. I visited him every day so they could draw my milk and I could just look at him. Because of the stress I was under, my milk began to dry up, so another mother gave her milk to our son.

We had called him Jason. As the weeks passed, Jason became stronger and stronger. Finally after six weeks, he weighed six-and-a-half pounds and I was able to take him home. Those six weeks will be forever etched in my mind.

Thereafter, we had to take him for regular check-ups to measure his development. The pediatrician told us it would take until he was about twelve months old before we could be certain that he did not have any brain damage from all the complications.

When Grant saw his baby brother arriving home, he was fascinated by how small he was. By then Grant was six-and-a-half years old and accustomed to being the only child. He looked up at me and asked, 'When will he be old enough for me to play with

122

him?'. I laughed and said, 'Soon, you'll see, soon.' I loved Grant so much. I really tried very hard not to make him feel put out by this new, demanding little presence. For the first few weeks after Jason came home, while he was still having a feed in the middle of the night, Grant would hear us and come toddling in, his hair all tousled and with his sleepy loving face, and he would curl up on the floor with his head on my lap to share the moment with Jason and me. As he got used to having a baby brother, he stopped waking in the night and spent a lot of time playing big brother to Jason during the day. He was very protective towards him. Now with our family of two sons, Colin and I were content. I didn't want to work until I felt Jason's health was stable and for me to get used to being a mother of two sons.

Hollywood

About ten months later I was offered my first work in Hollywood. It was to be a film made for American television but which would be released in cinemas in Europe. MGM was to be the producing company, yes, the great MGM studio that had at its zenith in the thirties and forties boasted it had more stars than there were in heaven. Well, it wasn't quite like that any more.

I was able to leave Jason in the very tender care of Luffy. I did this with more than a few pangs, but I knew our new baby and Grant would be in very good hands with Luffy and of course, Colin was a very attentive and caring father.

The new film was called *The Scorpio Letters* and it co-starred Alex Cord, who plays an American agent hired by British intelligence to find out who has murdered one of their agents and why. I play Phoebe, who works for a rival intelligence agency. It turns out that we are up against a ring of blackmailers headed by the mysterious Scorpio, who is a former French Resistance leader and whose gang have all belonged to the same Resistance group. The film has been described as 'imitation Bond', but the trouble was that, as one critic wrote, 'the criminal organization to be destroyed is as about as threatening as a set of toy poodles.'

The MGM studios are in Culver City in Los Angeles, not technically Hollywood. Hollywood, as someone once said, is more a state of mind than a location. The studio gave me a beautiful Mustang car during my stay and I had to get used to driving along the five-lane Los Angeles freeway system. That was just too much and so I asked for a driver as well, which, thankfully, they agreed to. I like driving at times, but driving in Los Angeles forget it!

The MGM studio was run along factory lines. You had to have a chit for everything and schedules were scrupulously overseen. Even in the heyday of the studio, the daily

Eight on the Lam. How on Earth did they persuade me to wear that hat!

schedule of great stars, who were literally making millions for the moguls, was minutely logged and checked. So there would be a form which an assistant director would fill in each day for, say, Clark Gable's day from the moment he arrived in the makeup room, to the time he arrived on set, to the time he had lunch and how long he took for it, and then how many camera setups there were, how much footage was shot and what time (to the exact minute) the work for the day ended. That's how MGM kept tabs on how their money was being spent and at the peak of the studio's success, such factory-type organization clearly paid dividends. But time had caught up with the studio and it now had very few contracted stars or directors, which gave an opportunity to actresses like me to make films there.

One day during the lunchbreak, I went to the studio canteen with some of the people I was working with. As I walked in, I saw Henry Fonda sitting with a man at another table. Now I had always been a huge fan of his, so I took my courage in my hands and walked over to his table, excused myself and said who I was and how I felt I had to come over and say how much I had always admired him. You see, we actors are all fans of one another and I was just like any other fan when I had the opportunity to meet the legendary Henry Fonda. He was absolutely charming and asked what I was doing at MGM. I told him I was making *The Scorpio Letters* and he showed some interest in that. In fact, he couldn't have been more pleasant to me and I have always remembered how gracious his manner was.

I kind of fell in love, you might say, with Henry Fonda when I was in my teens. His screen image fascinated me. I hardly took notice of the films he was in or the fact that he was such a gifted actor. It was him I was intrigued with and the gentle, complicated mystery of his personality, as I perceived it. As I sat watching him on screen in those dark auditoriums, he seemed to glow. To me he was sheer magic, a fantasy lover, a father and a friend all mingled together. One of my alltime favourite films is the movie he made just before his death with his daughter Jane and Katherine Hepburn, *On Golden Pond*. He thoroughly deserved that late Oscar for his performance in that movie, which clearly meant a lot to him and his daughter.

The MGM studio canteen which was called 'the commissary' for some reason was certainly a place to encounter famous stars. During another lunchbreak Bob Hope was sitting at another table with his entourage and when we saw one another, we exchanged waves of greeting. Then later Bob came across to the table. 'Hi, Shirley,' he said, 'it seems a long time since we've seen each other.' I had worked with Bob on the Royal Command Performance I have already mentioned. 'What are you doing here at MGM?' I filled him on the details of the film I was making and then he said, 'I'm just about to start shooting a film here. How would you like to be my leading lady?'. Naturally, I was delighted to be asked by a star of the stature of Bob Hope to be in his film and in such an informal way. When you think how actors usually have to sweat blood to land roles in movies and here was Bob Hope almost casually mentioning in the MGM studio canteen that he'd like me to be his co-star in his next movie, well, I had to think I was a very lucky woman. The details of the contract had to be worked out, but basically when I said yes right away to Bob's suggestion, the deal was made.

So, when I finished filming *The Scorpio Letters* I had another three weeks work in Hollywood as I worked on Bob's film *Eight on the Lam* which was a family comedy. Bob plays a widower with seven children and I play a teacher who becomes involved with Bob and the kids after they go 'on the lam' after a misunderstanding over some missing money at the bank where Bob's character is meant to work. That screwball comedienne Phyllis Diller was also in the cast as were Jonathan Winters and Jill St John. I provide the love interest for Bob and we do a little dance in a launderette sequence. It was good to work with Bob on this movie because he is such a warm, humorous man who is really professional when he's working and indulges in no shows of temperament. I think he appreciated my professionalism as well and my looks.

Back home in England after completing Eight on the Lam, Colin and I had to take Jason for regular checkups to make sure he hadn't suffered any brain damage because of the kind of birth he had. To our huge relief, he was given the all-clear. Jason was declared a perfectly healthy baby boy.

Strangely enough, when it became absolutely certain that Jason was a healthy baby, I went into decline myself. Probably the year of waiting to see if he was going to turn out to be normal had taken its toll. During that year I suffered post-natal depression, a condition which is now regarded with much more understanding than at that time. However, I was one of the lucky ones. My husband, although not able to understand my moods completely, gave me tremendous support. His strength and love helped me through one of the most difficult periods of my life.

Sumuru. All alone with my band of women!

Sumuru and That Girl from Rio

Producer Harry Alan Towers offered me the leading role in *Sumuru* which was to be based on a story and characters by Sax Rohmer. It was a fantasy action film about a woman called *Sumuru* plotting to take over the world for female domination. I was playing a kind of female Fu Manchu. I had long black hair, a wig actually. No way was I going to dye my own blonde hair black! I wore sexy dresses and I relished playing a role that was almost all bad for a change. Frankie Avalon, George Nader, Wilfred Hyde White and Klaus Kinski were my co-stars.

Sumuru was shot in Hong Kong. It was summer time and very hot and humid. The studio was like an oven. Many of the scenes in the film where I looked glamorous and confident were, in truth, just the opposite. It was hellish working in those conditions. All the time perspiration was running down my body underneath my beautiful dresses. It's amazing we ever got the film shot! When the day's filming was over, I couldn't wait to get back to the comfort of the airconditioned hotel to have a cool shower, eat, then glance at the next day's scenes in the script before sleeping.

One weekend the Chinese movie mogul who owned the studio invited several people from the cast and the director to dinner. We entered his palatial home, feeling a little overawed by its size. It was furnished very ornately with expensive paintings and ornaments everywhere, but what struck me most was the atmosphere. It was cold, so cold, and I don't mean the temperature of the house, but the feeling. However, when it came to having dinner, we were all ushered by his staff into a gigantic dining room. We sat down at a huge round table with great quantities of delicious-looking food set upon a revolving 'lazy Susan' in the centre of the table. I looked down at my place setting, then glanced across the whole table and noticed there wasn't a fork in sight, just beautifully carved chop sticks. I'd never used them before and I was terrified of making a fool of myself. Our host, with his expressionless face, gracefully turned the revolving table towards me and asked me to help myself. As luck would have it, bad luck, that is, the dish directly in front of me was laden with tiny buttered mushrooms! I cannot think of anything more difficult to pick up with chop sticks than slippery buttered mushrooms, especially if you've never done it before. So, as I hesitated, our host saw my embarrassment and my eyes met his. I thought to myself he is going to ask his staff for some forks. But, no, he just sat placidly and watched me struggle. By the end of the meal, I had learnt the hard way about how to manage chop sticks. I have never forgotten how ever since.

When *Sumuru* was released in Britain, Colin and I went to see it with Shirley and Leslie Porter (it was before they had been honoured with titles). We were good friends. We all laughed at that Shirley Eaton up there on the screen pretending to be the beautiful evil woman who hated men. Leslie thought I was wonderful in the role.

Shirley's family and ours had been friends for a long time, way before she became involved with Westminster Council. To me, a friend is a friend. All I know about the troubles she has had is the woman I know as a good friend. Politics is a nasty game, even at its best, as we are all aware of. Whatever people may say, I think she is a very gutsy woman and in some quarters that quality is not appreciated. Could the hostility she aroused also have been because she was a woman in a powerful

Sumuru. I enjoyed the opportunity to play a ruthless villainess.

position, because she is Jewish and because she is rich?

Sumuru was, according to one critic, 'a lighthearted spoof which ambles along pleasantly enough.' The same critic added 'Shirley Eaton makes as attractively menacing a villainess as ever held a whip.' At any rate, *Sumuru* was successful enough to spawn a sequel, *That Girl from Rio* (aka *The Million Eyes of Sumuru* and *The Seven Men of Sumuru*), which was shot in Rio de Janeiro in Brazil. Rio was a beautiful and exciting city to be working in, but everything was clouded emotionally for me. I had been away from home many times before making films on location and I had generally enjoyed it, but that was before I became the mother of two sons. When I had only one son, I seemed to be able to continue working without too much stress, but after our second son came into our lives, it was a different story.

That Girl from Rio resurrected the part of *Sumuru*, Empress of a women's organization out to conquer the world. My co-stars were Richard Wyler and George Sanders. It is not nearly as good a film as *Sumuru*, but despite that, perhaps because of the cult status of the director Jesus Franco, the movie itself has become a cult. But I was unhappy most of the time during the filming and I knew I had a big decision to make about my life. At last, filming ended and I was on my way home to England on the plane.

As we took off through the misty clouds into the clear blue sky, I thought, 'Well, Shirley! You've got plenty of time on this long flight back to England to sort out what you really want out of life.' I had indeed nineteen hours of flight ahead of me and that would give me a wonderful opportunity to concentrate my mind. I had been thoroughly miserable during the making of *That Girl from Rio* and I had missed Colin and the children desperately. I hated being away from them all. Yes, I enjoyed the stimulus of visiting different continents, but, oh, the emotional upheaval just wasn't worth it. I had been away so often. Now I was sick and tired of being torn apart and dividing myself between two kinds of lives. Something had to give. I could not cope any more. Although Colin had been able to join me during the making of the two movies I had made in America, that was not the norm. After all, he had his building business to run in London and Grant was now at school. I had to make a decision! As the plane transported me at great speed through no-man's land, I lay back comfortably in my seat and knew what I had to do. I there and then decided I had to stop working.

When I arrived back in England, I felt a huge sense of relief because I had finally made the decision that had been stewing in my mind for so long and especially since Jason had been born. I have a horror of separations, all kinds of separations.

Although I had made up my mind to give up my career after twenty years of working in various branches of showbusiness but especially movies, I could not let go just like that. I had to give myself time to adjust. I told Colin of my decision. He said, 'You must do as you think best.' As usual, he understood what I had been going through and why I had come to this decision.

At this time, I changed my agent and I chose a woman as my new representative, hoping that she would understand my predicament. And she did. When offers of work came in, I always put obstacles in the way, so gradually I was saying no to everything and very slowly

With Grant, Colin and Jason at Le Ferme, our favourite restaurant on Le Grande Corniche near Monte Carlo.

the offers stopped flowing in. The press found out I was thinking of retiring and would telephone to ask if it were true. As I hate to close doors and I thought perhaps I might go back to work again once my sons were grown up, I usually said that I was having a long holiday.

I settled very happily into being at home all the time. Jason was a lively little character, which meant there was never a dull moment when he was around, if you know what I mean! Grant was a weekly boarder at Highgate School and seemed to have adjusted to his new routine. As I wasn't working, I felt I had the chance to spread my wings in many different directions, which I'd never had time to do before. Sometimes, obviously, I felt the loss of my career with the independence, the people, the money it brought. But when I did feel stifled by domesticity, I had my painting to turn to for creative satisfaction.

A neighbour of ours who was teaching at a primary school in Radlett suggested that I have a look round the school with a view to sending Jason there later, so I telephoned the headmistress and made an appointment. It was early summer. Jason (who was two-and-a-half by then) and I jumped in the car with me and off we went. As the headmistress and I were talking while wandering round the school, Jason was following us, taking in everything as well. She showed us into the school play room, with little tots like Jason, all happily doing different things. Jason joined them and never gave me a backward glance. The next week he started school two mornings a week.

I took other steps to make my new 'freedom' interesting. With my friend Annie I attended Camden Art Centre twice a week for painting classes. Indeed, I had started to

hang my paintings in our house. One time, Jackie Collins and Oscar Lerman, her husband, whom I have already mentioned were friends of us both, came to dinner and when Oscar saw my paintings on the walls, he offered me an exhibition in the gallery he owned. I was delighted! Unfortunately, by the time I'd got twenty new paintings completed, Oscar had sold the gallery.

Jason was enjoying his mornings at play school. He liked being with all the other children, so I sent him three times a week, even though he was so young. I became friendly with the headmistress, who was a very kind and humorous woman. She asked me if I would like to teach art to three and five-year-olds. I said I would love to. For two years, I taught those little bundles of trouble. When I say I taught them, what I actually did was encourage them to feel happy slapping paint and a brush around, which was not a difficult task as they liked getting into a mess! It was interesting to see, even at their young age, those who had natural ability and those who hadn't. Both the kids and I enjoyed the classes. At the beginning of each lesson I would read them a story, usually from one of my own children's favourite books; this was to settle them down and when I finished with the reading, I'd ask them to paint something that they found interesting in the story. It was fascinating watching them paint. So often the little girls would paint houses and gardens, mothers and fathers. The boys would paint cars, boats or animals. They were learning from me, but I also found my time teaching there very educational.

Through both of us having sons at Highgate School, I met Jean Englander, who asked me round for coffee one morning. We found we had a lot in common, apart from being mothers of sons. Dotted all around her house were lovely watercolour paintings. She is a very creative, artistic person and was just to enroll for sculpture lessons at the same school I went to for painting lessons. She immediately suggested I joined her. I took to sculpture and after a while produced some interesting work, which was mostly heads that are now scattered (as are my paintings) around my family's and friends' houses.

In this new free existence I had, my life was very full. I was loving the security of family life and my own expansion into the arts. Finding new ways of expressing myself was marvellous. I was busy with every-thing that was really important to me.

Life Moves On

The rain was torrential. Grant was pleading, 'Please Mummy, we must go!' I was looking out of the dining room window, thinking that I didn't feel like driving to the

Working at home on a head of Colin after completing my studies at Art School.

other side of Hertfordshire in that filthy weather. Jason was tugging at me too. 'Please, please, let's go.' Parents will recognize the scene. The three of us got in the car in the pouring rain on a busy Saturday morning. We were bound for a dog kennel. Selma, who had arrived in my life all those years ago one Christmas, had died at the grand old age of fourteen and we were longing for another dog. After reading a book that told us all about the different breeds, the boys and I decided on a Welsh Springer Spaniel. When we finally arrived safely at the kennels, the owner was very brusque with us and said we could not choose which puppy we wanted as there was only one bitch in the litter. I had insisted we had a bitch because they are usually so good-tempered. We all stood in the heavy rain while the owner fished the puppy out. Our new friend was a tiny soaking wet thing, which Grant now held in his hands. He tucked her inside his anorak and we got back into the car. By the time we had got back home, she had dried out and to our amazement she looked very beautiful.

The boys helped me house train her. The garden was another matter as far as Centime and I were concerned. I loved the garden and worked in it every spare moment I had. We had had a corner of it turned into a herb garden little did I know that some dogs like the smell of thyme or rosemary as much as humans. For weeks Centime would dig up the thyme and rosemary bushes and come bursting into the kitchen with them. Eventually, she lost her boisterous puppy ways and became a wonderful family friend. I love dogs. They are so consistent with their affections.

In the summer of 1971, my graceful mother-in-law was suddenly taken gravely ill with heart disease. When I heard the news, I was devastated. Her caring but forthright doctor told us she would be dead within a month. She lived alone as Colin's father had died many years before. We lived the nearest to her out of her family, so Colin would visit her every morning on his way to the office and in the evening on his way home. His two sisters, with large families of their own, visited her as often as possible. She was in and out of hospital, but whenever she could, she preferred to stay in her own home alone. We tried to persuade her to have someone to live with her, but being the strongwilled, independent person she was, she absolutely refused. When her family could not visit her during the day, then a wonderful neighbour, Mrs Struthers, took her a meal and made sure she was all right. We were all truly thankful to that warmhearted woman. I often visited my mother-in-law during the day and invariably took her something she really fancied to eat. Each time I let myself in the front door, I had visions of finding her dead somewhere in the large house. Throughout her illness she was very brave, but as the time passed, the strain on all of us began to show. The effect of his mother's illness took a special toll on Colin. He was devoted to her, but slowly, as the weeks turned to months, he became more and more withdrawn. I tried to comfort him, but he was locked in his own grief and he wouldn't let me in. I did not understand at the time and became more and more depressed myself. Our marriage was crumbling and although we tried to pull it together in this awful crisis, we were not very successful.

Colin had been through it all before with the death of his father, but for me it was the first time I had come close to death and although I tried my best at the time, now, in retrospect, I think I failed him. We drifted apart into our own separate desolation. Our relationship was nearing breaking point. I felt as if I were drowning. I couldn't stand staying a moment longer in the house so I made a decision. I went to stay with my friend Pat in Ibiza for a week. After that break, I returned home with renewed courage.

After a while, and it had been over a year since we had been told that my mother-in-law could die at any moment, it all began to build up again: the tensions, the frustration, the grief. The week she died in hospital, I did not see her. The day she died, my sister-in-law had taken her back to her lovely house, which she had longed to see. When they returned to the hospital, her heart failed her and she passed away quickly. It was all over. At last she was at peace.

Colin and I managed to pick up the threads of our life again, but he was never quite the same person after her death. It had been a demanding time in both our lives and we had to look to our future together. Our marriage had been tested and it had survived, but not without more than a few alarms. But life seldom stands still for long. Changes were on the way and there was a new life ahead for us.

6

Glamour

As the Americans say, if you have it, flaunt it. Well, that's not quite my philosophy because I've never really flaunted it during my career in films, but, equally, I have never felt exploited as a sexual object. Why shouldn't any woman, or any man for that matter, make the best of the looks that fortune has granted her or him? I don't have a problem with that, although some present day feminists seem to have. Of course, there is out-and-out pornography, which is harmful and frequently violent, but that's not what we're discussing here. I'm discussing glamour, straight old fashioned glamour, and as I have been known as a 'glamour girl', I want to reflect on that theme now and write about some of the female stars that I consider to have that almost indefinable quality called 'star glamour'.

I consider myself lucky to have grown up pretty, because when I was a kid, I was a skinny little thing. But adolescence came and I blossomed and soon I could not help but notice that people thought of me as pretty. Of course, prettiness is one thing and glamour is another. Lots of girls are pretty but not really glamorous. What is that extra portion of allure that turns prettiness into authentic glamour? To begin with, you have to make the best of what you have been given. You have to be well-groomed and stay fit, although, as I have already said, I have never made a fetish of that. Above all, glamour has to do with personality and perhaps that's the ingredient that turns prettiness into glamour. Personality plus good looks. We all have known women who are pretty, even beautiful, but who somehow miss out on being really attractive because of a personality deficiency. True beauty has to be full of vitality and freshness and energy. Personality is perhaps that extra something.

I never felt I was really stretched during my film career in terms of the roles that were offered to me. English directors only saw my looks and they cast me accordingly as the glamorous girl-next-door or occasionally the femme fatale. They didn't really know what to do with me apart from putting me in comedy. Doesn't that say something about the British attitude to sex in general? If I'd been American or French, I'm sure my career would have turned out quite differently. But in British films, because I was successful at playing the type of part I was offered in all those comedies, they kept using me in the same kind of role. I got typecast because they fitted me into a category and I was seldom allowed to escape. However, at the time I was just very happy to get the work. I consider myself very lucky to have had the kind of career I had. I only wish that I had been offered more demanding roles.

Until I made *Goldfinger*, I was represented by Richard Stone, who had many of the top variety artists in Britain on his books. But Richard's variety orientation may explain why I tended to get parts in light British comedies rather than more dramatic parts. After *Goldfinger*, I made the change to being represented by Dennis Selenger of ICM because I felt he would be better placed to find me work in the international market. Richard Stone was a father figure to me and it was a wrench leaving him, but I felt I had to make the move. Dennis was associated with the William Morris Agency in America and this agency wanted to shape my American career, but it would have meant my uprooting myself and my family from Britain and that was not something I was prepared to do, so when that particular crunch came, there was no real debate. I would not do it because everything I held dear was in this country.

Perhaps if I had gone to Hollywood and stayed there, they might have used my talent more appropriately and accepted I was 'glamorous', whilst finding me meaty dramatic roles. After all, Hollywood had done that for many female stars, some of whom I have discussed in earlier chapters. Now I would like to say what I think about some of the glamorous stars, British, American and European, who have been famous for their looks, allied, for some but by no means all, to their personality and talent as actresses. Like any other movie fan, I have my preferences: some of these stars I admire and warm to, others leave me somewhat cold.

Marlene Dietrich

Marlene Dietrich was a Capricorn like me. I haven't mentioned before that I put a lot of faith in star signs. Dietrich, as she came to be known, was an icon of glamour. As she grew older, she seemed to miraculously retain that glamour and she was known as 'the glamorous grandmother' when she did those shows in her early

Marlene Dietrich

seventies wearing diaphanous gowns. Naturally, discreet stage lighting had a lot to with the glamour she projected. Harsh lighting can be very unforgiving and I guess Dietrich had the good sense to hire technicians who could make her look her best while she was on stage. There is absolutely no doubt that she had a huge following and still has, even though she died quite a number of years ago. Many of her fans are gay men and I don't pretend to understand why. Perhaps she had something androgynous about her and this may be part of the reason. It is well-documented that she had many lovers of both sexes.

There was something rather remote about Dietrich. She was certainly not the girlnextdoor type. Joseph von Sternberg, the famous Hollywood film director, helped create that Dietrich image in the 1930s in films such as *Morocco, Shanghai Express, The Scarlet Empress* and *Desire*. In those films, Sternberg used exquisite lighting effects, sumptuous sets and gorgeous costumes to help him create the screen goddess he was after. Although Dietrich's film career possibly peaked in the 1930s and then went into something of a decline, she went on being a legend for the rest of her life because she had that something extra about her, a special aura that fascinated people. I know that not everyone liked her, of course. Some people think she was cold and fairly limited in talent, but I think she certainly had glamour. She certainly set an example for older women in that she went on being glamorous into her old age. In our society, women are too often taught that you are over the hill by the time you are forty, which is, of course, absolute rubbish. Many women reach the peak of their attractiveness in their middle age and go on blooming in their 'third age'. And this without the help of skin lifts, cosmetic surgery, fanatical training schedules or pills. Growing old gracefully means accepting that your face and body change with the passing years, and that each period of life brings its own different kind of attractiveness. Autumn as a season can be just as beautiful as spring, if not more so, and even winter has its very own attractions. Youth has no monopoly over beauty or glamour, for that matter. Dietrich proved that.

Marilyn Monroe

When I was starting in films in the midfifties, Marilyn Monroe was at the very height of her fame. Indeed, let me tell you an anecdote about a connection, however slight, I had with this most famous and tragic of the screen goddesses. I was making a film at Pinewood Studios just after Marilyn had been working there on the movie she made with Laurence Olivier, *The Prince and the Showgirl*. Marilyn and I shared a taste for men's white towelling dressing gowns. I expect you have seen pictures of her in one. One day, I needed a dressing gown at the studio and one of the wardrobe women handed me this lovely white gown. 'Here you are, Shirley, have this one. This was the dressing gown that Marilyn Monroe used when she was making *Prince and the Showgirl*.'

You could imagine I felt quite thrilled about wearing Marilyn's gown. I wore it a lot during the making of my film and I guess you could say it suited me. However, my husband Colin liked that kind of dressing gown as well, so when filming ended and I was able to keep Marilyn's, I gave it to Colin to wear. He wore Marilyn's dressing gown until it was worn and then I don't know what happened to it. I guess it went the way of all old clothes. However, we thought it was fun at the time.

I think what I, and a lot of other people, liked about Monroe was her vulnerable quality. Interestingly, she was liked equally by both men and women. Men were attracted to her physically, but they also wanted to protect her. Women liked her vulnerability, her childlike quality, her gentleness, and generally they did not feel threatened by her. Her 'niceness' came across.

However, there were at least two Marilyn Monroes: the very public screen goddess and the private, hurting Marilyn, who probably never got over the traumas of her childhood. She never knew who her father was and her mother suffered from mental illness which meant she was institutionalized a lot of the time and Marilyn ended up in orphanages. No wonder that in later life she sought the approval and love of older men such as Joe DiMaggio and Arthur Miller. She craved security in her life, the kind of emotional security I managed to get for myself in my marriage, but she never achieved it and finally it destroyed her. I don't know whether her death was as a result of an accident, suicide or even murder, but what is absolutely certain is that she would not have died prematurely if she had found a lasting emotional bond with someone who would have provided a haven for her in her stormtossed existence.

Monroe was certainly sexually exploited by men. It seems very likely from all the evidence that she had to endure a good deal of couch casting in order to make her way in Hollywood. But despite this tawdriness, there was an enduring innocence about her, and a delicacy that withstood all that Hollywood could throw at her. It was the innocence of the child within her, the child who had never had enough love and who went on searching for it for the rest of her life. Matters just got out of hand with her and this led to her destruction. Marilyn was a Gemini and they tend to be self-consuming. Her inner demons finally caught up with her.

However, Monroe left us the legacy of her films and although they are by no means all classics, there is usually something about her performance in them that reminds us of that special quality and unique glamour she embodied. Laurence Olivier rather unkindly called her 'a professional amateur' and I am sure that at times she was murder to work with. Asked what it was like kissing Monroe in *Some Like It Hot*, Tony Curtis replied, 'Like kissing Hitler.' Many of the men who worked with her had an ambivalence about her. Take this quote by Billy Wilder, who directed Monroe in *Some Like It Hot*: 'I have never met anyone as utterly mean as Marilyn Monroe. Nor as utterly fabulous on the screen and that included Garbo.' The notoriously harsh director, Otto Preminger, said that directing Monroe was like directing *Lassie*. But the fact is they all wanted her in their movies and exploited her sexuality in them. You can see why they queued up for her services when you watch *The Seven Year Itch*, *Bus Stop*, *Some Like It Hot* and *The Misfits*. No one would call her the world's greatest actress, but she emanated glamour, sexiness and vitality.

Monroe had to battle to get herself parts that were not just variations on the 'dumb blonde' stereotype. The tragedy was that by the time she died, she had almost won that battle. Her husband, Arthur Miller, wrote her a strong dramatic role for her in *The Misfits* and I am sure that she would have gone to more strong dramatic roles if she had lived. However, would the world have allowed Marilyn Monroe to enter middle age and change from being that blooming, ripe sexy young woman into a more mature woman with her own different brand of glamour? Would she have become more and more of a joke, a parody of her younger self? It is possible, because the world as a whole wanted its Marilyn Monroe to be ever young, ever childlike. For her to have been able to have matured gracefully and accepted growing older, she would have had to learn to love herself more and replace her low self-esteem with the idea that she was a worthwhile person in her own right. The abandoned child she had been never disappeared. When she died, she had returned to being that child. Her life was in some ways a tragic waste of beauty and talent, but she is still remembered and loved by millions.

Other Fifties Blonde Bombshells

Diana Dors was often referred to as Britain's Marilyn Monroe, but, for me, she was too much like a barbie doll to deserve that tag. Don't get me wrong: I admired Diana, especially when she played strong dramatic roles as she did in *Yield to the Night*, a 1956 British movie that was roughly based on the story of Ruth Ellis, the last woman to be hanged in Britain. Indeed, I wish I had been offered some of the roles that came her way. Later in her career in the seventies and eighties she returned to the stage and received favourable notices from the critics. She died in 1984 of cancer, a sadly premature death for someone so full of life. She is still remembered as an archetypal British glamour girl, but her type of glamour was different from the kind I projected: Diana was the goodtime girl, while I was the coy girl-next-door. I think Diana had to try too hard to be sexy with her platinum blonde hair and uplift bras. If you are sexy, you don't have to work at it. Marilyn Monroe, for example, was very offended when Laurence Olivier, directing her during the filming of The Prince and the Showgirl, told her to 'act sexy'. Marilyn considered herself innately sensual and did not think she needed to 'act' it. She took Olivier's instruction as an insult and their relationship never recovered.

Diana Dors more resembled Jayne Mansfield than Marilyn, in my judgement. But I have to say I did not admire Mansfield. Dors could act, Jayne could not. All she had to offer was an immense bosom and a huge bum. In fact, she was a joke figure, a caricature woman, someone who carried no threat for most men because she was so risible. Whether Jayne Mansfield was acute enough to know that she was being used in this way, I do not know. Her main films (*The Girl Can't Help It*, *Will Success Spoil Rock Hunter?*, *Kiss Them for Me*, and *Too Hot to Handle*) all presented her a dumb sex object and I think she was demeaned by that. Inevitably, as the years passed and she got older, her career declined until just before her death she was appearing in absolute dross. The other thing that people remember about Jayne Mansfield is that she died when she was decapitated in a horrendous car crash. She was yet another fifties blonde bombshell who died in her mid-thirties. Thirty years earlier, the blonde bombshell of the thirties, Jean Harlow, had died at the age of 26. The casualty rate among Hollywood blondes was very high.

Kim Novak, however, had much more going for her than Mansfield. Now, Novak was beautiful and I have always thought there was something of Ava Gardner about her, although her colouring was quite different. With Novak, there was a mixture of innocence and sensuality. And there was something rather remote about her, a detachment, almost an embalmed look to her, which Alfred Hitchcock used to great effect in one of his greatest movies, *Vertigo*, when Kim plays a character who kind of returns from the dead. She was often rather stiff and self-conscious in her film acting, but in *Vertigo*, because of the nature of the story, she was ideally suited to play the object of James Stewart's fantasies. Kim Novak was not a great actress, but she leant real glamour to movies such as *Picnic* (remember that erotic dance scene she had with William Holden?), *The Man with the Golden Arm*, *Pal Joey*, *Bell, Book and Candle* and *Strangers When We Meet*. Finally, perhaps, Kim Novak was intriguing because she had us wondering: does this woman have hidden depths or is she just dumb?

Seemingly, Harry Cohn, who controlled her early career at Columbia Studios, gave her a hard time, treating her like a piece of meat. I once had the misfortune to have a meeting with Mr Cohn, notorious for being one of the rudest and disreputable of the old Hollywood moguls. I got the distinct feeling that there was something else on the agenda as far as Mr Cohn was concerned other than discussing possible film roles I might play. This did not happen to me very often, I am happy to say, but Mr Harry Cohn was not a pleasant man. Red Skelton, the famous American film comedian, perhaps deserves the last word on Cohn. When he was told that thousands of people had turned out for Cohn's funeral, Red said, 'It proves what they always say: give the public what they want to see and they'll come out for it.'

Another glamour girl of this period was the Swedish star, Anita Ekberg, who had a stormy and shortlived marriage to British actor Anthony Steel. Fellini used Ekberg memorably in La Dolce Vita as a kind of symbol of the eternal female, but he clearly saw her as some kind of fantasy figure rather than as a real human being. The fifties was the era for pneumatic blondes and Ekberg filled the bill, but like most of these inflated icons, she did not seem to last the pace and her career fizzled out. There is a real downside about being a film director's favourite fantasy: once you've done that, or had that done to you, where is there to go? There has to be some personality behind the glamour and the body to sustain interest, I really believe that.

Brigitte Bardot

Colin was mad about Brigitte Bardot, but then he was a great Francophile, as I was. She was dubbed the ultimate 'sex kitten', which was a stupid tag that she began to hate more and more. Curiously Bardot has not aged well and she sounds very bitter when she talks about her youthful fame and the way she was used in her films. She has been quoted as saying, 'For twenty years I was cornered and hounded like an animal. I didn't throw myself off my balcony only because I knew people would photograph me lying dead.' No doubt the level of media and fan attention Bardot suffered from was at times overwhelming, but she must have known at the time that the kind of films she was making and the image she cultivated might well produce that kind of frenzy.

Roger Vadim, her ex-husband and the director who directed her in some of her most famous films including *And God Created Woman*, said this about the Bardot persona: 'It was the first time on the screen that a woman was shown as really free on a sexual level, with none of the guilt attached to nudity or carnal pleasure.' That was it with Bardot: her nudity and sensuality came across as entirely natural and uncomplicated. It wasn't the kind of plastic American sexuality that Jayne Mansfield, for example, symbolized. It is revealing that the British film industry cast Bardot in one of the *Doctor* movies, *Doctor* at Sea. The way that British movies tried to deal with open sexuality such as Bardot's was to place it in a comedy context much safer that way, you see, fellas!

The French knew how to use Bardot in their films, however complaining she is now about the films she made. The Americans, in my experience, are the most appreciative of nations as far as women are concerned, but French women, of all nationalities, know how to make the most of themselves. In my opinion, and speaking very generally, French women are not as naturally beautiful as British women, but where they have it over us is how they present themselves in terms of clothes, makeup and general allure. That's what 'ooh-la-la!' really means.

Another French star who made a notable British film in the fifties was Simone Signoret, who created an impression in the 1957 *Room at the Top* co-starring with Laurence Harvey in the screen adaptation of John Braine's novel. That film caused quite a stir at the time because of its frank language and representation of sex. And, of course, now it seems very tame indeed, except that it remains a fascinating social document of its time. I know many people thought of Signoret as being sexy and glam, but for the life of me I could never see that. If anything, I thought she was always rather maternal in her looks, rather mumsy, in fact, which is fine, but 'mumsiness' is not usually perceived as glamorous. If I am candid, I would say that the best thing that ever happened to Simone Signoret was to be married to the handsome Yves Montand. Now he was sexy and glamorous and perhaps it was by association with her husband that she acquired the same reputation. But, then, as ever, glamour is in the eye of the beholder.

Joan Collins

Joan Collins is a little older than myself, but I guess that makes her roughly a contemporary of mine. Anyway, we are different types of actresses and project a different kind of glamour, Joan creating an image that is more sultry and overtly sexy than mine. I have known Joan since the fifties, although I would not claim to be a close friend. There is absolutely no doubt that she has worked very hard to get where she has. She is an international star, and she has become a byword for glamour, even though she is in her mid-sixties. Certainly, Joan is expert at presenting herself in the best light. Grooming, makeup and clothes are always top-notch and I have never seen her look anything but very glamorous when she is in the public eye.

When she started out in British films in the fifties, she projected a rather innocent sexuality of the 'teddy girl' sort in films such as *Cosh Boy*, *Our Girl Friday* and *The Good Die Young*. She was only about twenty when she was dubbed one of the leading glamour girls of British films. She even did a 'Diana Dors' when she played a dowdy role in a prison drama *Turn the Key Softly*.

But she clearly was fired with ambition and it was Hollywood she was aiming for. She survived some terrible films such as *Land of the Pharaohs*, *The Girl in the Red Velvet Swing* and *The Wayward Bus*, but she kept working even though some of her American films are long forgotten. Many Americans are bowled over by a glamorous woman speaking in what they consider to be a posh British accent and Joan filled this bill admirably. Then when her American screen career began to falter, she turned producer and built two steamy dramas round herself, *The Stud* and *The Bitch*, which were very successful. The screenplay for *The Stud* was written by Joan's sister, Jackie, which she adapted from her own novel, and the screenplay of *The Bitch* was adapted by Gerry O'Hara also from a story by Jackie, so these two box office hit movies were quite a Collins family affair.

I don't know whether it was her success in those sex driven movies that prompted the Americans to cast her as Alexis Carrington in the hugely successful series *Dynasty*, but some acute casting director or producer saw her as perfect to play the archetypal bitch and it certainly paid off for her and the makers of the series. At one point in the eighties, Joan must have been nearly the highest paid actor on American television. It was with this role of Alexis that she finally achieved world stardom, because, of course, *Dynasty* was shown in almost every country in the world and is still being shown in reruns.

But such success and megafame almost always has its price. I recall meeting Joan at the 1987 Monte Carlo Grand Prix. Colin was mad about Grand Prix racing and I enjoyed the occasion, although the noise of those machines was incredibly grating. We were watching the race from a balcony of the Loewe's Hotel. Joan was then at the very peak of her fame through her success in playing Alexis. We stood on a balcony looking down at the race as the cars wound their way round the streets of the town. 'Well, Joan,' I said, 'you have it all, everything you ever wanted, you've got it now.' Joan turned and looked at me and said quietly, 'Yes, but at what a price.'

She didn't say any more and I was left wondering what exactly she meant. I couldn't help thinking that she was referring to the ups-and-downs of her marital life. I know she's been married numerous times, but it couldn't have been easy keeping a marriage going with all the immense pressures she had to contend with. People have to make their choices in life all the time. Joan made hers and I made mine. I have no regrets for always putting my family first, but I do have a few about the dramatic parts that did not come my way. I have no doubt that Joan has her own regrets, but she has been hugely successful. And for many people she is the epitome of glamour and, of course, she has deserved her success because of her sheer determination, but, as she said herself, there's a price tag.

Grace Kelly

One glamorous actress I was sometimes likened to was Grace Kelly. She certainly was a beautiful lady and I was flattered by the comparison. The reason may have been, or so I have been told, that we both gave out mixed signals, which intrigued men. They never quite knew whether we were approachable or not! Seemingly, this has its own kind of seductive allure. Grace Kelly was well-publicised as being an ice-cool blonde - but nothing could be further from the truth, if we can believe the biographies that have been written about her. She was a real lady - a very passionate and sexy lady.

She was extremely fortunate to be cast in three of Alfred Hitchcock's movies, *Dial M for Murder*, *Rear Window* and *To Catch a Thief*, which is my favourite film of all the movies she made. When I see it occasionally on television now-adays, I have hauntingly beautiful memories of the location where it was shot - because I lived there and knew so well that lovely area in the south of France.

Kelly was cute in *High Society* and well-suited to the part, having been born into a wealthy family herself, and again in *The Swan* in which she played a princess, a role she was shortly to play in real life when she became the Princess of Monaco, having married Prince Rainier. Unfortunately, it seems she never really came to grips with being a princess and the stifling life of the royals of Monaco. You would imagine that

Grace Kelly had just about everything: fame, riches, status, beauty and even a kingdom to share, but no, she was unhappy and began to drink too much. Maybe the drinking contributed to her sad premature death in a car crash near Monaco in 1982. Who knows? Under certain circumstances, we are all fragile human beings.

Tippi Hedren was sometimes talked about as being something like Grace Kelly. She was one of those cool blondes, whereas I like to think of myself as a warm blonde! Alfred Hitchcock cast Tippi in two of his best-known movies, *The Birds* and *Marnie*. I think Hitchcock's attitudes to blonde ladies was complicated, to say the least, when you consider what he did to them on screen. Think of Janet Leigh's grisly end in *Psycho* and the birds tearing at Hedren's face and body in *The Birds*. Seemingly, one of the scenes where the birds are meant to attack Hedren's character got quite out of hand and she almost lost the sight of an eye. Yes, Hitchcock was a complex man. He was hugely talented, but I think you would have to say that he was working out some personal demons in some of his films as many other directors obviously do.

Incidentally, when I was in America on a publicity tour for one of my films, the William Morris Agency wanted to have me cast in *Marnie* in the Tippi Hedren role. Obviously it did not happen and I never actually met Hitchcock to discuss the possibility. But I was, I guess, the type of blonde actress he seemed to favour. Think of the other blondes he had used apart from Janet Leigh (whom, after all, I had doubled for in *Prince Valiant*) and Tippi Hedren. There was Kim Novak in *Vertigo*, Doris Day in *The Man Who Knew Too Much*, Grace Kelly in *Dial M for Murder* and *Rear Window*, Eve Marie Saint in *North by Northwest* and Vera Miles in *Psycho* and *The Wrong Man*. The man had a thing about blondes and I have to say I regret never being in one of his pictures. But I wonder what he would have put me through!

Jean Simmons and Deborah Kerr

One of the most beautiful of British actresses was Jean Simmons. I have already mentioned that Jean was at the Aida Foster School a good few years before me. When I went there, she was held up to us all as an example of what you could achieve. Fame came to Jean Simmons when she was very young when she was cast as the young Estelle in David Lean's 1946 film of *Great Expectations* and as the Indian princess in Michael Powell's classic movie about repressed sexuality, *Black Narcissus*. But it was probably Laurence Olivier's casting her as his Ophelia to his *Hamlet* in his 1948 film that established her as a future star. Not only was this young woman very beautiful, but she could act in Shakespeare as well and up against the leading actor of his generation. Hollywood beckoned and for a while they did not quite know what to do with this talented glamorous young British star. Jean got very frustrated with the roles that Howard Hughes' studio RKO offered her, but with movies such as *The Robe*, *Guys and Dolls*, *The Big Country*, *Elmer Gantry* and *Spartacus*, she hit the big time and became one of the leading actresses in Hollywood. Such success led to problems in her private life, however, and her marriages to, first, Stewart Granger and then writer-director Richard Brooks, ended in divorce. I wonder whether her immensely successful career was sufficient compensation for her unhappiness in her private life. Could it ever be? Anyway, Jean Simmons is one of the most talented and most beautiful film stars Britain has produced.

Deborah Kerr is another very beautiful and sophisticated British star. Born in Helensburgh, Scotland, Deborah Kerr is really a classic Scottish beauty with her auburn hair. It took some time for producers in Hollywood to realize that behind the classy exterior of this British actress there was a layer of sensuality that could come across on the screen. And come across it did, of course, in *From Here to Eternity* when she played the bitter adulterous wife who has a torrid affair with Burt Lancaster. Everyone remembers the clinches on the beach as the waves pounded the shore and Deborah and Burt, both in swimsuits, clung to each other in passionate embrace. Her earlier British screen career had her invariably cast in well-bred roles: Major Barbara (playing a Salvation Army girl), *The Life and Death of Colonel Blimp* and *Black Narcissus* (as a nun). It took Hollywood to uncover her innate sexiness. But it was always a subtle kind of sex she projected, nothing too blatant or earthy. She was a lady but sexy with it in *The End of the Affair*, *The Proud and the Profane*, *Tea and Sympathy*, *An Affair to Remember* and *Bonjour Tristesse*. Sometimes she reverted to her 'repressed' roles in films like *Separate Tables*, in which she played a mother-dominated dowdy spinster, *Heaven Knows*, *Mr Allison* (a nun again) and *The Innocents* playing a genteel governess. But she always brought beauty, a subtle sensuality and intelligence to her roles and she is an actress I have always admired and thought of as very glamorous in her own distinctive way.

Sophia Loren, Gina Lollobrigida and Anna Magnani

These three Italian actresses found stardom around the same time in the fifties, but they are very different from one another. When I first became aware of Loren, I was, like many people, starstruck by her incredible beauty, but I have come to feel there is something distant about her, something cold even. She is voluptuous and sensual-looking, but there is perhaps something withholding about her. She has proved she can act in movies such as *Two Women* and *The Key*. And certainly she is a strong

145

woman. Loren is a Virgo so her strength is not a surprise, but for me she lacks real passion as an actress and all that classical beauty is less impressive because she keeps a lot of herself back. But glamour? Yes, she has glamour and she has remained glamorous into her midsixties.

Gina Lollobrigida is a more obvious lady with her peaches-and-cream looks and curves, but there is no mystery to her and where there is no mystery, perhaps there can be no real glamour. Magnani was totally different from Lollobrigida and Loren. There was nothing remote about her, nothing manufactured or plastic. If she had glamour of a kind, and she had, it was an earthy, peasant glamour. She was all woman, passionate, large in body and heart, tempestuous. Actually, although she is seen as one of those quintessential Italian actresses, she was Egyptian-born. She made a name in Rossellini's *Open City*, an early neo-realist movie about the end of the war in Rome. When she went to Hollywood, I think they found it difficult to find adequate roles for her. She would not be constrained by Hollywood stereotypes and in *The Rose Tattoo* and *The Fugitive Kind*, she found vehicles that were almost worthy of her talents. Magnani was larger-than-life and although she was not everybody's idea of female beauty, she proves that personality and passion do play an important part in sex appeal. She was a 'stirring' actress and you had the impression that how she appeared on screen was a true representation of what she was like in real life.

Ingrid Bergman

Mentioning Rossellini in connection with Magnani brings Ingrid Bergman inevitably to mind, because it was for Rossellini that Bergman gave up her American career and husband and children. This brought the accusation that she was a homebreaker because Rossellini himself was married at the time. For a while, she was in essence exiled from America where her career had been flourishing. The opprobrium of a portion of the American media and public landed on her head. That is the downside of stardom and fame when the media and the public feel they have the right to comment on what is going on in your private life. Ingrid Bergman certainly suffered from this kind of intrusion, not only in terms of the personal angst it caused her but the damage it did to her career as well.

Bergman was a natural-looking Swedish beauty who summoned up images of the open air and fjords. Her first Hollywood movie was *Intermezzo* with Leslie Howard and she became an instant Hollywood star. Then, unforgettably, she was in *Casablanca* with Humphrey Bogart when she and Bogart did the noble thing and turned their backs on their love. In real life, Ingrid Bergman followed her heart and paid a price for it. *Casablanca* is a very romantic film and Bergman was always in love in her films, often in stories of tormented or thwarted love. Think of the torments she endured in *Gaslight* at the hands of Charles Boyer, the struggle she had with the amnesiac Gregory Peck in *Spellbound*, the scorn of Cary Grant in *Notorious*. There was something vulnerable about Bergman, almost a desire to suffer, tears always just below the surface. Her private life seemed to mirror some of her screen roles.

Hollywood did not forgive her for her affair with, and marriage to, Robert Rossellini until they divorced. Then, in 1956, Tinsel Town welcomed her back and she starred, and looked beautiful, in *Anastasia*, *Indiscreet* and *The Yellow Rolls Royce* among many other films. Ingrid Bergman was perhaps beautiful rather than glamorous and she was certainly not everybody's favourite star, but her place in film history is safe.

The Gamins

Audrey Hepburn has her devoted admirers and quite rightly too. She had an elfin charm that was at times very appealing, but I have to say she wasn't my kind of woman. That doesn't mean I didn't appreciate her particular kind of glamour, but that androgynous quality she had didn't appeal to me. I suppose I like women to be women and men to be men. I like womanly women and manly men. That doesn't mean I like stereotypical extremes of both sexes, but there is a point where 'boyishness' in a woman teeters on the edge of sexlessness. I think Audrey Hepburn appealed to men who wanted their women unthreatening so they could protect them.

Leslie Caron played the gamin in movies such as *An American in Paris*, *Lili* and *Gigi*. At times she was asked to overplay the girlishness in those films. However, there was some steel behind this girlish facade and this has emerged in Caron's more adult roles when she has been allowed to be a woman rather a retarded adolescent. She is a very elegant woman and if I say she is 'jolie laide', it is meant as a compliment, as the French mean it. She was a great dancer in her prime and made some wonderful musicals.

Katherine Hepburn, a star from an earlier generation, had a slightly 'masculine' air to her in roles such as *Sylvia Scarlett* and those comedies she made with Spencer Tracy in the forties. But she was an 'angular' star. Someone said of her that you could throw a hat at her and wherever it hit, it would stick. Yet she has charm and a kind of unusual beauty and grace. And personality! That's what really makes her attractive: that voice, that wit and that composure. Most people either love her or loathe her. At one point in her career, she was dubbed box office poison by exhibitors, but she has proved them wrong by lasting the pace and making movies well into her seventies. As I have said, *On Golden Pond* is one of my favourite movies, and she was great in that. With Katherine Hepburn, we have to forget all about stereotyped notions of beauty. A lot of men are attracted to 'sassiness' and Hepburn had that in spades. She was also very bright, very special and very independent. She lived for many years with Spencer Tracy, who was a devout Catholic and would not divorce his wife. It could not have been easy for Hepburn not to be publicly acknowledged as Tracy's partner, but she stuck with it, defying convention and going her own way as usual. One of my favourite films of hers is *The African Queen* where she plays a spinsterish type who takes control in wartime and gets grumbling Humphrey Bogart to act heroically. She was great with Bogart as she was with Tracy, and later with Henry Fonda.

Lauren Bacall has something of Katherine Hepburn's sassiness and, of course, she made her reputation being sassy to Humphrey Bogart in *The Big Sleep* and *To Have and Have Not*. Amazing to think that she was only in her teens when she made her first film with Bogart. He recognized real class when he saw it and promptly married the girl. They seemed to have had a close, loving relationship until his death in 1957. The promotional material for *To Have and Have Not* described Bacall as 'Slinky! Sultry! Sensational!' and for once the publicity people got it just about right. That sultriness and slinky sophistication were paraded in other movies such *Key Largo*, *How To Marry A Millionaire*, *Woman's World*, *Written on the Wind* and *Designing Woman*. Bacall was a model when she was discovered by director Howard Hawks and she has always known how to dress elegantly. And then there is that throaty, sexy voice of hers. She is now well into her seventies, but she is one of those actresses who have aged well, as she showed in her recent appearance in the Barbra Streisand movie, *The Mirror Has Two Faces*. Bacall has always had a mystique about her and appeals to both men and women.

The last tomboyish actress I want to mention in this section is Doris Day. The singing-and-dancing side of me loved those Doris Day musicals such as *Calamity Jane*, *The Pajama Game* and *Young at Heart*. But she was so tomboyish and virginal, so much the sexless girl-next-door, that a lot of her other movies left me cold. No one could really call her glamorous. She was much too sensible and sensuality is not something you associate with Doris Day. It is odd that those sex comedies that she and Rock Hudson made were such hits, because as we all know now, Hudson was gay and Doris Day was, well, sexless. So where did the sexual spark come from? It wasn't there at all, really.

Elizabeth Taylor

I guess Liz Taylor could fairly be described as the beauty of her age. She certainly was a very beautiful woman in her youth and in her prime, but clearly her career and fame have taken a toll on her. She seems always to be in the headlines either because she has just had another divorce or because she is once more at death's door.

Like me, Liz Taylor entered showbusiness at a young age. She was ten when she made *Lassie Come Home* and *Jane Eyre* and only twelve when she was in *National Velvet*. *Father of the Bride* was perhaps the first movie in which she was allowed to be a young woman rather than a girl and she was eighteen when she made that. She looked absolutely breathtakingly gorgeous in *A Place in the Sun* opposite the very handsome Montgomery Clift, whose life was also beset with problems and who eventually died a very premature death a few years after a horrendous car crash altered his beautiful features forever.

I think Liz Taylor has had to battle against prejudice about her acting abilities. Beautiful actresses, and some male stars as well, often are dismissed as merely decorative because they are so good-looking. Some critics cannot seem to take them seriously, but I think this is particularly unfair on stars like Taylor. If you consider her performances in *Giant*, *Cat on a Hot Tin Roof*, *Suddenly Last Summer*, *Who's Afraid of Virginia Woolf* and *Reflections in a Golden Eye*, then she has to be taken seriously as an actress.

The other thing that has worked against her is her eight or whatever marriages. It does seem an awful lot, I have to admit. However, she has said that she marries all her lovers, so knowing that, perhaps it doesn't seem that many!. Still, eight marriages mean eight divorces and you know what I think about divorce the thought of it has always terrified me. So it is hardly surprising that Liz Taylor has had her ups-and-downs emotionally. But she's a survivor and every time she's counted out, she seems to bounce back and find a renewed zest for life. It seems there were two real loves in her life: Mike Todd who died in a plane crash, leaving her devastated, and Richard Burton, the hellraiser whom she married twice and divorced twice. Both these men were not easy to live with and I admire her for taking them on. Liz Taylor has lived life to the full, gambled with her happiness and her health and still lives to tell the tale. I admire that, even though she has led a totally different kind of life from me. I needed, and still do, stability. But Liz has beauty and glamour and fame and riches. She has had it all and with it came pain, unhappiness, disillusion and grief. She has run the gamut of life.

Julie Christie

Julie Christie was born in 1940, so she is roughly a contemporary of mine, although because I started making movies when I was so young and Julie didn't make her first film till 1962, it may not appear that way. Julie is a lovely-looking woman and deserves her reputation for a particular kind of British glamour. She was very much a product of the sixties and that quality of being very much of her time perhaps detracted somewhat from her performances in period films such as *Doctor Zhivago* and *Far from the Madding Crowd*. Somehow she seemed out of place in the Ural Mountains of Russia or the Dorset countryside of the nineteenth century. Her milieu seemed to be the swinging London of the sixties, King's Road and all that. She won an Oscar, of course, for playing a quintessential young woman of the sixties in *Darling*. The first time she made a real impact on screen was in another John Schlesinger-directed film, *Billy Liar*, when the director had his camera follow her round the northern town where the film was set. She appeared to be the quintessence of youthful freedom, liberation and sexiness. An icon of the Sixties.

Julie Christie has always looked gorgeous on screen in movies such as *The GoBetween* (another period film), *McCabe and Mrs Miller*, in which she played a prostitute opposite Warren Beatty, the intriguing *Don't Look Now* when she played a notoriously steamy sex scene with Donald Sutherland, *Shampoo* (again opposite Warren Beatty) and *Heaven Can Wait*. She has had well-publicised cosmetic surgery which has helped her stay beautiful. On that subject, I think there is nothing wrong with such medical help, although I've had none myself, as long as it is not dangerous to a woman's health, or is done so often that the results leave the lady in question looking bizarre. Judging by her recent appearances in Kenneth Branagh's *Hamlet* and Afterglow, Julie Christie's beauty remains intact, which goes to prove that, with a little help, beautiful women can remain beautiful at whatever stage of life they are at. Julie is no longer that swinging young woman of the sixties, but she doesn't need to be. She has moved on and her beauty has changed, but it is still there.

Jane Fonda

I have described my encounter with Henry Fonda in the MGM canteen sometime in the sixties. About that time, his daughter Jane was achieving film stardom under her own steam and also acquiring herself a reputation as a political activist. I have never been fond of actors who dabble in politics and who use their fame to advertise the particular causes they are drawn to. Actors and politicians are alike in some ways:

both are always acting, playing a role, often saying words they do not mean, pretending feelings they do not really feel.

Jane certainly inherited her father's good looks: tall, lean and elegant. It was a shame that Roger Vadim, the French director and her one-time husband, tried to make her into a sexpot because that wasn't Jane Fonda at all. Vadim had done the trick for Bardot, but everyone is unique. You can't replicate another person. Fonda's brand of glamour is very different from Bardot's, and movies such as *Barbarella* did her no favours. Although many people refer to her as sexy, she doesn't so much suggest the bedroom as the outdoors. Perhaps it is not so surprising that she became a fitness guru and made millions out of writing about her methods of staying young and athletic. Jane Fonda's brand of glamour is a particularly American kind: healthy and robust. When you look at her nowadays, it seems astonishing that she had that brief flirtation with Vadim and was a sex kitten. It is well-documented that she had her difficulties with her father and harboured resentment towards him for years because he had walked out on her mother, her brother and herself. I think she has been looking for emotional stability ever since and sought it in relationships with charismatic men like Vadim. Now she is married to media mogul Ted Turner and seems to have found that stability she has craved for. Her fitness regime has paid off in terms of how she still looks.

Goldie Hawn

Goldie Hawn is delicious and is terribly glamorous despite the 'dimwit' roles she has often played. As is often the case, it takes an intelligent actress to play the dumb blonde and Goldie seems very bright to me. She sprang to fame playing dumb in the sixties television show *Rowan and Martin's Laugh-in* and has never looked back, although the range of her roles has expanded. She has an infectious giggle and she seems to enjoy life, which is always attractive in a person, man or woman. The usual adjectives that are used about her are 'kooky', 'wacky' and 'dizzy', but they all come down to the same thing: charm. She is certainly not classically beautiful, but in her own odd way she is glamorous.

Her first success in films was in *Cactus Flower*, then she acted opposite Peter Sellers in *There's a Girl in my Soup* and was very effective in *Butterflies Are Free*. She became a producer, which is further proof that she is no dumb blonde, and acted as executive producer on her *Private Benjamin* and several of her later films. Such contact with the sharp end of filmmaking doesn't seem to have doused her natural warmth, however, and it is this and her ebullient personality that give her that uniquely attractive quality she has.

Barbra Streisand

Streisand is an 'ugly duckling' if ever there was one, but who could deny that she has a glamour all her own? In her case, the glamour comes from her talent, her power, her strength of will, her wit, her sheer determination and her Jewish roots. She is New York to her fingertips and New York is perhaps the most glamorous city in the world. I have been a huge fan of La Streisand ever since I saw her in the stage version of *Funny Girl*, which made her a star. Before I saw the show, I had never even heard of Streisand, so I was quite unprepared for the impact she made. There on the stage was this magical woman, gawky, even a bit ugly, almost raucous in her style, but her performance completely captivated me and the rest of the audience. She was a phenomenon then and she has remained a phenomenon ever since.

As a singer and all-round performer, she broke all the rules I had been taught when I had started as a singer and dancer. She was certainly not conventionally good-looking, she was very loud and at times she looked a mess. But she became a megastar. Perhaps glamour is not the word to use in connection with Streisand. She has never been beautiful and she knows it. What she has is an aura about her. An aural power. This special kind of aura makes Streisand fans among the most devoted and fanatical of them all. And, of course, she pours herself into her performances on stage and screen. She has scarcely ever been restrained, she has always given her all, she is a real showbusiness trouper. Her story is the story of the ugly duckling who turned into a swan right in front of our eyes by sheer force of will and personality. She has controlled her own destiny and in the male-dominated world of films, she has made her presence felt. She has produced and directed her own films for many years now. At times she has been criticized for being too pushy and demanding, but are these complaints mostly from men who do not like ambitious, powerful women? Perhaps so. At any rate, Barbra has retained the affections of millions of fans who see her as a kind of role model and a hugely talented star. She is truly unique and one of the biggest names in the annals of twentieth-century showbusiness.

Bond Girls

I cannot write about glamour in the cinema without a section on the Bond movies, which have become famous partly for the parade of Bond girls who have graced them down through the years. I was fortunate to be in one of the very best of the series and to have made something of an impression in the brief but telling role of Jill Masterson.

In my judgement, Ursula Andress was the most beautiful woman from all the Bond movies. Who can forget her in *Dr No* and that image of her arising from the waves in that white bikini with a belt and dagger? She played Honey Rider, of course, and was one of the glamour girls in the Bond movies who manages to live till the end of the film. Ursula is sexy, but it is a classy sexiness. There is nothing at all common about her looks. She has wonderful bone structure, a sensuous mouth and lovely eyes.

She has something else, too, something that makes a beautiful woman even more beautiful: a quality of vulnerability. Sometimes glamour queens in the movies come over as rather hard, but not Ursula. She is so beautiful that it is not surprising that she starred in *She*, the film of the Rider Haggard story about the woman who seeks eternal beauty. Ursula is around sixty, but recent photographs that I have seen of her confirm that she is still a very beautiful woman.

Of course, the Bond movies have been criticized in some quarters as being sexist in the way they represent women as beautiful objects. But when you look at someone like Ursula Andress in *Dr No* and see the power she projects through her beauty and presence, then how can it be said that she is being exploited or women are being degraded in some way? Women always have had the real power in this world. I like a woman to be a woman and not an imitation man. I love men, but they are all mostly little boys at heart, little boys in long trousers. Don't get me wrong: I like men to take the lead and act powerfully, but I do think they need the support of strong women behind them. I also think that men are much more vulnerable and sensitive than most women realize. At last, they are being allowed to show feelings, which is a good thing. On the other hand, I think that in modern society with all the changing of roles that is going on, men are confused about their own positions and roles. Sometimes I feel sorry for young men because the old certainties seem to have vanished for them.

Honor Blackman, my co-star in *Goldfinger*, was excellent as Pussy Galore and then there was Diana Rigg as Tracy in *On Her Majesty's Secret Service*. Diana is a very elegant lady and a talented actress who has played heavyweight roles in the theatre, as well as the lighter stuff like in *The Avengers* series. She, as Emma Peel, was a perfect foil for the very British Patrick MacNee and because of her athletic build, she was convincing in the action sequences both in *OHMSS* and the television series. I don't think that Diana Rigg was a raving beauty of the class of Ursula Andress, but she is a thoroughbred of real quality.

Britt Ekland as Mary Goodnight in *The Man with the Golden Gun* made a very glamorous Bond girl as did Caroline Munro as Naomi, the villain's helicopter pilot, in *The Spy Who Loved Me*. Caroline started her career as a top photographic model and her beauty has adorned many a calendar, deservedly so because she is very

Helena Bonham Carter

striking. Her career took off after the Bond movie she made and she has acquired millions of fans from her appearances in *The Abominable Dr Phibes*, *Dracula A.D. 1972*, *The Golden Voyage of Sinbad* and *At the Earth's Core*.

Of the more recent Bond ladies, the one who has caught my eye has been Famke Janssen who plays Xenia Onatopp in *Goldeneye*. She has a former model's grace and makes a wonderful femme fatale. She combines a powerful image with a special kind of allure.

More Glamorous Ladies I Admire

Faye Dunaway is a very elegant lady and an actress whom I admire for her talent and innate glamour. I met her once at a party that had been organized for Roger Moore. I was very excited to meet such a big star. At that time she was married to an Englishman, so she was often in England. I loved her in *Bonnie and Clyde* and *The Thomas Crown Affair*.

Of the contemporary Hollywood actresses, I think Sharon Stone is one of the most beautiful. She has a classic beauty and although she acquired a reputation after that scene in Basic Instinct when she appeared not to be wearing underwear, she has much more talent and natural glamour than such notoriety would suggest. I saw her recently on television being interviewed by Ruby Wax; Sharon was wearing a dressing-gown and no makeup, which is a great test of any woman's beauty, but she passed with flying colours because she is a natural beauty. Some cruel critics have written about her as though she is just a sexy lady with no brains, but it is quite obvious that she is highly intelligent and a talented actress. But there is no doubt that she has been burdened with the same kind of baggage that Rita Hayworth from a previous generation had to carry. Her private life has not always been happy and talking to Ruby Wax about a relationship that had failed, she explained that the man 'had thought he had gone to bed with the woman from *Basic Instinct* and had woken up with Sharon Stone. This remark strongly echoes Hayworth's comment about her men

154

who had gone to bed with Gilda and found themselves the next morning with a real woman called Rita Hayworth. But I understand that Sharon Stone is now very happily married and I am sure that she has the resilience and intelligence to withstand the pressures that Hollywood stardom inevitably brings.

Of the current crop of British stars, Helena Bonham Carter strikes me as a beauty, especially in period films such as *Howard's End* and

Julia Roberts

Wings of a Dove. Indeed, *Wings of a Dove* is one of my favourite films that have been made in recent times. The script and story I thought were absolutely brilliant. The three leads in this tale of a three-way love entanglement were simply wonderful. The only thing that spoiled the movie for me was the scene at the end when Bonham Carter and her lover make unsatisfactory love on the bed in her room. This was a very poignant moment in the story when they both realize that the man is still in love with the dead woman and their love has been poisoned because of their plotting. Why did they choose to represent the character's obsession with the dead woman through this loveless coupling with Helena Bonham Carter, which is very explicitly acted out on screen? Apart from that issue, who is it that says that actresses have to do this kind of explicit scene? I found almost every shot of this film like a Monet painting, but it was nearly spoilt for me by this unnecessarily sexually graphic episode that broke into the mood of the film and cheapened it somehow. I can see the box office reasons for its inclusion, but I deplore the fact that it was done in this way in such an artistic film and that an actress like Helena Bonham Carter had to play the scene in this way.

My absolute favourite of contemporary Hollywood actresses is Julia Roberts. When I saw her in *Pretty Woman* I recognized immediately something that Rita Hayworth had all those years ago. Julia hasn't conventionally beautiful features, but she has the kind of glamour we haven't seen since the sixties. It is a joy to see this sultry but vulnerable kind of glamour up there on the screen. When you've got that kind of quality, it comes right out at an audience from the screen. Julia Roberts can act as well, as she proved in *Pretty Woman* and subsequent movies. I gather she dropped out for a while from movie-making because of the stress she was under, but now she

Juliette Binoche

seems to have recovered and is back on track to become a very important star. Julia Roberts is definitely my favourite girl of the eighties and nineties.

Next to Julia Roberts, I would say Kim Basinger was my favourite contemporary American actress. I first saw her in the movie *Nine-and-a-half Weeks* with Mickey Rourke. I was completely mesmerized by her sheer sexiness. Of course, she is not simply sexy. Her face is fascinating and she is a good actress too. I have never met her, but I would like to. She is alluring with a strong feminine aura. Curiously, she has aspects of both Monroe and Lauren Bacall, who were opposite types of glamorous women. Yes, I think Kim Basinger is the sexiest actress to appear on the screen for a very long time! And as she gets older, she is becoming even more appealing and beautiful.

As for Juliette Binoche, that fine French actress has me spellbound. I have, in fact, seen her in only two films: *Damage* and *The English Patient*, but that was enough for me to become a fan. The contrast between the two characters she played in those movies showed, without a doubt, what a fine actress Binoche is. She thoroughly deserved her 1998 Academy Award for Best Supporting Actress for her role in *The English Patient*. As far as I am concerned, she stole the film. In my judgement, her appeal lies in her sense of mystery. She is an actress who doesn't let you in, but leaves you wanting to know more about her. Behind her eyes, there is someone there who is shy and not quite sure about what is happening. She is also tremendously provocative in an offbeat kind of way, which is typically French! Indeed, she epitomizes the particular brand of femaleness that French women are blessed with. She seems beautiful without actually being classically beautiful. I hope we see her in many more films. She is an original woman who seems to have burst upon the movie scene with a freshness and quality all of her own. I like that!

I cannot possibly finish this part of the book concerning glamorous, beautiful women without mentioning the beauty of the century: Diana, Princess of Wales. To have watched a shy young teenager turn into a sophisticated, independent and courageous young woman during her life as a royal was a very interesting

156

phenomenon. She gradually became more like a film star than an actual film star. She was the most photographed woman in the world and she shone brightly whenever the camera caught her. She had that extraordinary gift: star quality. Some of it came from the way she looked and dressed, but even more came from what she was inside. It was there in her eyes, the laughter, the flirt, the sadness, she had everything in her expression. She was not the authentic classical beauty; her nose was too long, as she often remarked herself, but it didn't matter. When she looked at you, you only felt her smile, her eyes, her personality. She has become a great historical figure because of her life and death. Nobody can change that.

I, like millions of people all round the world, was moved almost beyond comprehension by her death. I had been looking forward to Sunday, 31 August 1997. I woke up just before eight o'clock in the morning, knowing I would be seeing both my sons and their families. I was full of happy anticipation. It is not too often we are all together, as my elder son lives on the south coast of England. As I went into the kitchen to start making breakfast, I turned on the radio as usual and a solemn voice announced the devastating news. I couldn't believe what he had said! I was numbed by the news. I thought, 'It can't really be true.' However, I had lunch to prepare for my family and I suppose I just tried to pretend I hadn't heard the dreadful news as I began to get everything ready for their arrival.

Despite a certain sadness in the air, we all had a pleasant day together. We did talk about her and my family were as stunned and as speechless as myself, especially my two daughters-in-law. As they were of a similar age to the Princess, they were unusually quiet.

After they had all left, the first thing I did was to write a letter to the Princes William and Harry. I couldn't stop thinking about them and their heartbreaking loss. To lose a mother at any age is terrible, but Harry was still so young! For me, the full impact came on the Monday as I went to my local shops. I found I was fighting back the tears. Everyone, everywhere, was so quiet and the atmosphere was full of sadness. In the afternoon, I watched the television coverage about Diana and by the evening I knew I too would go to Kensington Palace to place some flowers there as a homage to her death.

On the Tuesday, I arranged to meet a young journalist friend outside Harrods. There were many people queuing three or four deep lined along the pavement all around the store. We both waited for our turn to write in the book of condolences and I left two red roses, one for Diana and one for Dodi. Then we went to Kensington Palace. If you weren't there yourself, it is difficult to describe the atmosphere. But I will try. The warm summer sun somehow made the day even more poignant.

Hundreds of people were walking silently with bunches of flowers in their arms. There were many small children with teddy bears and photographs that they were to lay at the gates of the Palace. There were people of all classes, all ages, all nationalities. Some who had already been to the gates with their offerings were sitting on the grass with stunned faces. Some were giving their children a picnic lunch. Some were smiling wanly, some cried quietly. The overwhelming feeling among all those people was of sharing, like a family, something we couldn't talk about, but felt deeply. I think the weight of the silence was the most moving aspect of the day.

Channel Four News interviewed me as I walked past. One of the remarks I made was that I thought history was being born out of this strange phenomenon. As the week passed and the mass grief continued to build, I was proved to be right.

So much has been written about Diana that I feel there is not much more I can add, except to write my personal view. Unfortunately, I never met her, but my thoughts are that she was a kind, vulnerable person who gained most of her happiness from her two sons and public admiration. Apparently she seemed to light up any room she entered. We lost something very special through her death. She was a complex, desperate young princess who tried, in my view, to please everyone to gain the love she'd never had in her life - the love we all deserve. It was a tragic senseless death, except for the fact that she will never be forgotten and will remain young and beautiful in our memories throughout eternity.

This poem sums up my feelings after watching the funeral.

Into the Abbey she was carried on a wave of love
The coffin rocking gently from side to side on the shoulders of the young Welsh Guards
Whose faces were full of grief, but proud, knowing well they carried the country's symbol of hope.
The pure voices of the choir lifting our souls to join Diana's spirit.
On the coffin a simple bouquet of flowers with the words 'Mummy from her youngest son Harry'.
The beauty of the Abbey's vast windows letting in a rainbow of sunshine,
The ocean of silent people outside following the service as one,
Never more united were we than today, morning the death of Diana, Princess of Wales.

7

A Private Person

In 1972, everything in my personal life was stable. Our sons were doing well at school and Colin's building contracting business was prospering, which, I might add, was not always the case. Like most people, we had our financial ups-and-downs over the years, but, even so, I believe I have lived a very privileged life. Somebody up there loves me! Lady Luck has waved her magic wand over my life more times than I can remember or deserve, perhaps. I am eternally grateful.

Colin and I had spent our honeymoon in the south of France and ever since then, we had been there for our summer holidays en famille. For quite a few years we had rented different apartments along the Cote D'Azur, but in May of 1972, we finally bought our very own large apartment in St Jean Cap Ferrat. For most of his life Somerset Maugham, the famous British novelist who was the author of *Of Human Bondage*, *Cakes and Ale* and *The Razor's Edge* among many other fine novels, had had a large house there. It was, and still is, the most exclusive location in the south of France in which to own a property. Gregory Peck, Andrew Lloyd Webber, Kirk Douglas and numerous other famous people owned holiday villas there. We had rented over the years different apartments in the very same block in which we finally bought our own apartment. We had fallen in love with the area. Suddenly, a large apartment on the third (and top) floor of the block came onto the market. We snapped it up immediately, because we knew they were always in such demand. The process did not take long: we found out about the apartment's availability when we were there on our Easter holiday and by June it was ours.

Our new apartment had wonderful views over the old port, a small bay and the

159

distant mountains near Monte Carlo. It was fabulous. I was so happy! Grant often teases me by saying, 'Do you remember the day you and Dad signed the contract for the apartment, Mum?' I apparently was so thrilled, I jumped up and down with joy.

I have so many wonderful memories that I associate with Cap Ferrat. The boys spent much of their young lives in that beautiful place. Both Grant and Colin had an affinity with the sea and boats. Our first boat was a fifteen-foot motor boat. Colin and an old friend had the amazing luck to have won it in a raffle at the SOS Ball Stars Organization for Spastics), held on the first Monday of December at the Grosvenor House Hotel in London. We used to attend this charity ball every year. And that particular year, Colin and his friend won this boat!

So, for a couple of summers, we dashed about on the sea in our little boat. Then our friend took it to be the tender to his large cruiser. A little later, Colin decided he would like a sailing boat, so he bought a twenty-three foot yacht, which we called Ginny. I remember well towing Ginny behind our big American car, bought especially for the trip, all the way from Dover to the south of France. On that journey, we had two very excited little boys sitting on the back seat of the car watching the boat as it swayed about in the wind on the French motorway. Colin had asked them both to keep an eye on her.

We had just passed the town of Lyons when Grant shouted, 'Dad!'. At the very same time, Colin had noticed the steering of the car becoming heavy. One of the tyres on the trailer carrying Ginny had a slow puncture, which was becoming faster by the second. Colin started to look for a safe place to pull over and stop. By the time he had found a suitable place, the tyre was flat and ribbons of rubber had been shed along the road. He and Grant got out of the car to see if there was anything they could do themselves, but, no, it wasn't possible. By this time Jason and I were standing alongside them in the boiling hot sun and feeling dejected. There was only one solution. Colin thumbed a lift to the nearest garage. An hour and a half later, he and two mechanics arrived back at the car. Luckily Colin spoke French and an hour later we were continuing our journey onwards.

When it began to get dark, we decided to stop for the night at a motorway hotel. When we drove into the car park, all we could see were huge lorries, so Colin manoeuvred the car and parked between them. The day's driving and adventures had suddenly caught up with us all and the boys were getting very tired and hungry. I suggested we find the hotel part of the complex and had something to eat, then go to bed. Instead of agreeing with me, Colin had a wicked gleam in his eye and said, 'Let's all eat and sleep on Ginny tonight.' I replied, 'You mean sleep in the boat on top of the trailer?'. I must have sounded a bit grumpy. Grant suddenly came to life and said,

160

'Please Mummy, please, Mummy, let's do it!'. I was outnumbered by three boys! So that's what we did. Colin climbed up first and put the tiny rope ladder over the side of the boat and trailer for the boys and me to climb up on. There we were in the pitch black night, clambering up a very fragile rope ladder to spend the night on our new boat that had, as yet, not seen the sea. We had a sandwich, then slipped into our cotton sleeping bags and fell fast asleep. In a lorry park. In Ginny. On a trailer. Under the stars.

Early in the morning, we were awoken by two French gendarmes shouting up at us. Apparently what we had done was totally illegal. Colin climbed down from Ginny and used his customary charm on the policemen. Because we were foreigners, we got away with our unintentional misconduct.

We finally arrived safely in St Jean Cap Ferrat the following day and took Ginny to her mooring place in the Port of St Jean. That particular holiday was the beginning of us all learning to be serious sailors. Colin absolutely adored being on the sea and wanted to teach our sons to respect it and there is no better way to learn about the sea than on a sailing boat. So over the years we all became reasonably good sailors, although I have to admit I am what you would call a 'day sailor'. I would never go on long trips as I became seasick easily. But Colin and the boys were in their element. Nearly every holiday we would meet up with Roger Moore, his Italian wife, Luisa, and their three children and spend wonderful days on our boats, theirs and ours. Roger had a villa further up the coast from us. It was near a beautiful little village called St Paul. It was away from the sea on a hill with a wonderful view of the French coastline. Later, when our children were adults, Colin and I would stay with Roger and Luisa for a few days at a time. They were such warm and friendly hosts, especially Luisa.

Luisa and I had become good friends ever since she had met Roger. We continued our friendship throughout her three pregnancies and after the children were born, and we are still friends to this very day. She was, and still is, a very beautiful woman. She is a typical Italian mother, passionate and fiery, but very maternal at the same time. She was the backbone of their family and social life. I love her dearly and see her as often as possible. We will always be friends. She is an elegant and courageous woman. She was the strength behind the successful man: that is how I would describe her life with Roger.

My sons' teenage years passed without too much turmoil. I would say we were lucky in that respect. Or is it down to luck? I know that Colin had given them a lot of loving support and discipline. Perhaps that was more than a contributing factor and I, of course, was the typical doting mother of sons, but I was strict too. Colin and I never argued about the way we wanted to bring up our sons, which was a blessing for us all. Strangely enough, you never really know when you get married what kind of parents you will become. Life is such a gamble, but that's the fun of it.

Talking about gambling, occasionally when we were in France, we would go to a casino for a flutter, but it never became an addiction, thank God! Actually, one night Colin was very lucky and thereby hangs a tale. Some time in the sixties, he had bought me a beautiful gold watch. I was wearing it on the publicity tour for *Goldfinger*. I was staying in a reputable hotel in New York. One morning, after having had breakfast in bed, I stupidly put my watch on the breakfast tray. An hour or so after the tray had been taken away by the waiter, I was dressing to go our for a television interview and was looking around for my watch. 'Oh God!' I said to myself, 'I remember! I've left it on the breakfast tray.' I tried not to get too worried. Knowing that it was a good hotel, I was sure that they would find it. I called the manager and although he tried to be helpful, the watch was never found! That evening when I phoned Colin, I told him what a careless woman I had been. Instead of being angry with me, he said something really lovely and in his own inimitable way told me not to fret! Well, to backtrack for a moment. The evening we were at the casino in France, Colin won more than enough to buy me another watch, identical to the first one. After that sweet occasion, he never gambled again.

During the years when we spent our holidays in Cap Ferrat, we were to see several changes in the village. When we first went there, the port was very small and the whole area was totally unspoilt and that's why we fell in love with it. However, the Mairie (town hall) decided to enlarge the port. During the time it was being constructed, it caused mayhem. It took two whole years to complete and the little beach we had previously enjoyed was now full of cranes, cement and all the paraphernalia that goes with a big building project. However, the first summer, we lived like gypsies with some very good French friends. Their children and ours played together. The two families would sunbathe on the huge lumps of concrete surrounding little pools of water, where the children fished and swam. There wasn't any shade to found anywhere, so the children spent most of the hot summer days swimming in the sea, wearing little white sun hats as protection from the possibly harmful effects of the sun. The adults, including Colin and me, had turned nutbrown by the end of the six week holiday. It was hardly the comfortable, luxurious picture that people conjure up in their minds when they think of a summer spent on a Cote D'Azur beach. But, to tell the truth, it was exciting. We were all terrifically fit by the end of the holiday, mostly from swimming so much to keep ourselves cool.

When the port was completed, to our great relief we realized that they hadn't spoilt the beauty of the place. It still is to this day one of the loveliest places to be in, certainly compared to how the rest of the Cote D'Azur coastline has been ruined by high rise blocks of apartments and overcrowding in general. I grew to love the south of France almost in the same way as Colin did. We never went anywhere else for our holidays because we were content in our own apartment.

Some time in the late seventies, Colin bought a big ChrisCraft motor boat from a friend. We adored Ginny, but she wasn't big

I decided to use this photograph with Roger, as opposed to a professional one i.e. us together in *The Saint*. Unfortunately, I never did a Bond film with Roger, but with the Scottish gentleman (Roger told me to write this!).

enough when we wanted to take friends out to sea for the day. We called our new boat Kep and Kep could carry at least eight people comfortably. Some of our friends preferred motoring to sailing on the boat. Sometimes we would divide ourselves up and go out on both the boats.

We had so many marvellous times on the sea. Often we would take trips to Monte Carlo or travel in the opposite direction towards St Tropez. Life was rich with natural pleasures the sun, the sea, the wind, the boats. Who could ask for anything more? When we motored or sailed along the coastline, we would moor in different bays, put our anchor down and then picnic and swim. At last, I managed to become a good swimmer!

One time when we were having a picnic on Ginny in the little bay of Ville Franche, which is just around the corner from Cap Ferrat, I was feeling quite anxious. It was August 1978. Grant had stayed in the apartment because he was waiting for a very important phone call: his 'A' level results! I don't know who gets more nervous about exams, the parents or the youngsters. Anyway, in the middle of the afternoon as we were lazing in the sun, we heard the engine of our little rubber tender to Ginny coming towards us. Grant was waving his arms and shouting, 'I've passed! I've passed!' Jason, Colin and I all hugged each other, then watched Grant tie the dinghy to Ginny. He had a great big grin across his face as he said, 'My grades are high enough to get me into university!'. I hugged him very hard after he'd climbed aboard Ginny, then I turned away and went down into the cabin where I burst into tears of joy. I know my reaction was over the top, but perhaps because I hadn't had a formal education myself, I felt so passionate about our sons' education. I had had a wonderful, real life education, but it had been by no means an academic one.

At home in England, family life continued to rush by. Jason was working towards taking his 'O' levels and working very hard, I might add! I had stopped attending Art School and had decided to sculpt at home. I felt that there was only so much I could learn at school. If you are lucky enough to have any talent at all, after a certain stage you must go it alone. Most days I managed to fit in at least a couple of hours' work in between the usual activities of the daily round. I had just finished a lifesize head of Colin. He was thrilled with the result and our friends said I had captured him 'to a tee', as the saying goes. By this time, I was really hooked on sculpture. I found it exciting and I liked the feel of clay in my hands and producing something creative out of a simple block of earth. Everyone who visited us was used to seeing a funny shape perched on a pedestal, with a damp cloth covering my next masterpiece. Oh, it was such fun, well, most of the time. I also made a semi-miniature head of Jason, which I love. My parents have the only full figure I ever made.

In February of 1981, my parents sold their hotel in Fowey in that lovely county of Cornwall and went to live in Mallorca in a small village called Andraix. They, like us, had fallen in love with the sunny climate of the Mediterranean (it was Colin's dream to retire to the south of France one day), but it was Spain, not France, they preferred. Finally, they decided to live there. My parents and my brother are very good sailors. In fact, my parents with two old friends took their beloved motor cruiser/sailboat Blue Otter all the way to Mallorca from Cornwall themselves. They made the trip in about six weeks, stopping along the canals in France. I think they were very brave. I couldn't have done it, but that's just typical of their freewheeling spirit. They lived on the boat all the time while they were on holiday, but when they moved there to live permanently, they bought a pretty apartment overlooking the port, where I used to visit them whenever I could. A little later, they saw a house nestling on the side of a small mountain. They had to have it! The view of the sea

Jason, my younger son, aged 21.

164

and mountains was wonderful.

It was there in 1986 that all the family gathered to celebrate my parents' fiftieth wedding anniversary. What a day! Johnnie, my brother, his wife and two sons, went to Mallorca, as well as Colin and myself, Grant and Jason with their girl friends, and many new and old friends of my parents who wanted to be there on this very special day. My mother had arranged everything in her usual organized way, including the making of her own dress. She also made sure that the family had a comfortable place to stay. In fact, we spent a week there, making a holiday out of the occasion.

On the actual day of the celebration, the sun shone brightly for most of the time, but it was not too hot considering we were in Mallorca. There had just been a spell of rainy weather prior to our arrival and we even had a little rain on the day, but that was welcomed by us all. We had been apprehensive that it was going to be far too hot. My mother and father left the house to go to the church in a Malloraian farm cart drawn by a donkey. It was covered in ribbons, balloons and wild flowers and it had a great big 'Just married!' banner on the back. How they both laughed as they edged their way down the dusty road to the village of Andraix with us following behind. We went to the local Catholic church, where the priest welcomed us, even though we were not Catholics. The ceremony meant a great deal to my mother, having been married in a registrar's office fifty years before. The priest performed the ceremony in Spanish and although most of us couldn't understand the language, we understood why we were there. It was a tremendously moving atmosphere in the cool old church. When the blessings were over, we left the church to get into our cars and drive to the Port of Andraix Yacht Club, where they were to have the reception. My parents insisted on staying in the cart with donkey pulling them slowly around the road along the sea shore to the club. It was very romantic and funny! Two hours later, when we'd all finished eating, it was speech time.

By then my father was very tipsy. He stood up to make his speech. He is a natural comic and liked to be the heart and soul of any party. Besides praising my mother for her support and love throughout the years and declaring his deep love for her all over again, he also let a few secrets out of the bag, including me, of course, and how I was conceived in a park! My mother and I were laughing and blushing all through his speech and everyone thought he was hilarious.

Then it was my mother's turn to say a few words. She is not a comedian like my father, but she still has a great sense of humour. In fact, what I remember most about her contribution was the advice she gave about keeping a marriage alive. 'Laughter,' she said, 'is the most important ingredient in marriage.' Then my father interrupted somewhat loudly by saying '...And sex!'. Everyone burst out laughing again, so that's how the afternoon continued. Lots of wine, sunshine and laughter! As I write down my memories of that happy day, my parents have just celebrated their sixtysecond wedding anniversary.

After the festivities in Mallorca were over, Colin and I flew to Cap Ferrat for our annual holiday. 1981 was an important year for weddings and anniversaries. It was our twenty-fourth wedding anniversary on the fifth of August, but before that date there was, of course, the wedding of the decade. On the twenty-ninth of July, Prince Charles would be marrying Lady Diana Spencer. We deliberately neglected to own a television set in our French apartment because we felt we watched too much television when we were in England and there were far better activities to pursue in the south of France. However, that July we were eager to see the Royal Wedding. Fortunately, friends of ours, the late Richard Thomkins, who was the founder of the Green Shield Stamp empire and later Argos stores, and his wife Elisabeth and daughter Melanie invited us to their villa on the Cap to watch their television and share the celebrations with them. I suppose it was partly because we were all English and the fact that we weren't in England at the time of the wedding that we badly didn't want to miss it. So there we all were glued to the set with the French commentator talking so fast that it was difficult to catch all that was said. I got especially irritated when we couldn't hear them take their vows. Even so, it was a happy day with friends sharing the Englishness and the pomp and pageantry of it all. Looking back on it now, what high expectations we had of that romantic union! Alas, it wasn't to be.

Later, when the press exploited the secret activities of both Princess Diana and the Duchess of York, I thought to myself, this is the beginning of the end for the Royal family as I had known it. And as the years pass by, I fear I may be right.

Most of our wedding anniversaries were spent in France simply because we had been married in August. We always tried to visit our favourite restaurant called Le Peintre which was in a quaint old village in the hills. The reason we liked it so much was because we stayed in a little pension in that village on our honeymoon. The memories were romantic, memories which we rekindled every year.

The early 1980s seemed to fly by with the normal ups-and-downs of living. Jason had achieved three good grades in his 'A' level exams when he was eighteen, but didn't want to go to university. What he wanted was to go straight into the world of business. Colin suggested that it might be a good idea if he worked for his firm for a while, just to get acclimatized to the reality of working life. Jason agreed, so for a few months he did everything from making tea to driving vans. Meanwhile, he was having interviews with various advertising companies. Before very long, he joined a firm in a very junior position, but ever since he has been going from strength to strength in the world of advertising. Grant also worked for his father for a period. I believe both our sons look back on that those times as good experience and the first step they took along the road to wherever they intended to go. By 1986, Colin had had enough of life as a building contractor and decided to sell the business and retire. The same year we sold our family house in Hertfordshire and, after much deliberation, made plans to move to Cap Ferrat.

Our sons seemed happy enough. They both had partners to care for them so, as a mother, I thought my job was done, well, as far as a mother's responsibilities are ever done! Colin was tired of London and wanted to fulfil his lifelong dream of living in the south of France.

In January of 1987, on my fiftieth birthday, the boys and girls and Colin and I celebrated the event by going to see Dave Allen's one man show at the theatre. Dave Allen was our favourite comedian at the time. Following the show, we all went on to Tramps. It was a happy and nostalgic evening. I was getting the jitters about leaving our sons and England, but the decision had been made and there was no turning back. We told our sons we intended to live in France for a year, then we would decide if we wanted to stay there permanently, which was the truth. That took the sting out it of for all of us.

So on the last day of April, with our cream Cadillac full to the brim with our belongings, we drove to Dover and boarded the ferry to cross the Channel. The week before there had been a devastating accident when one of the ferry ships had sunk just outside Zeebrugge with major loss of life. I felt nervous as I stood on the deck in the drizzling rain. It wasn't because of a fear of the boat sinking, but because I was wondering what challenges lay ahead for us both, as we sailed across the English Channel to a new life in France.

Only two weeks after we'd arrived in our apartment in St Jean Cap Ferrat, Luisa Moore telephoned and invited us to dinner. There were twelve guests altogether, including Leslie Bricusse and his wife Eve. I hadn't seen them for a few years, so we talked about the last time we'd met. It had been in their house in Los Angeles when I was in Hollywood to make the television film *The Scorpio Letters* and Colin had come over for a week to be with me. Leslie had telephoned us and we were delighted to accept his invitation to spend a lazy Sunday with some other English friends. Richard Attenborough (not at that time yet knighted) was filming in Hollywood too. Richard, as everyone knows, is a lovely man and I talked to him for a long time. We discussed the strains of the separations our work inevitably brought to family life. His wife, Sheila Sims, wasn't able to be with him on that occasion and he was feeling very down and lonely. I reminded him of that day at Queen Charlotte Hospital when he and Colin were pacing up and down the corridor of the maternity unit, while Sheila and I were giving birth to our children. Sheila produced their second daughter and I produced our first son. 'Oh, the memories, the memories we all have!' Richard said as we joined the others to take a swim.

On the same trip, Rex Harrison and his wife Rachel Roberts, whom I had worked all those years ago at the Hammersmith Lyric in the revue, invited us to a show biz party one evening at Vincente Minnelli's house, which they were renting at the time. Rex was also filming in Hollywood. Leslie Bricusse was at the party, as well as Anthony Newley, Joan and Jackie Collins. There were also a host of American stars including Warren Beatty, the biggest heartthrob and womanizer of that era. Funnily enough, after speaking to him for a short while, I soon realized there were other far more interesting men at the party to be with. It was a real Hollywood shindig and all that that stands for. There were wives, husbands, lovers and mistresses all eyeing each other. What a laugh! It was the only party of that kind I ever went to. For me the highlight of the evening was seeing Rachel Roberts again after so many years. We laughed and talked about our lives, marriages and careers. She said to me in her lilting Welsh accent, 'For the daughters of a mattress-maker and a country vicar, look where we are now! Who would have believed it?' I adored Rachel's Celtic earthiness. Little did I know then that she would become so unhappy and take her own life a few years later. Poor, dear Rachel.

Back to France and our evening with Roger and Luisa. As the guests were all talking, Leslie asked Colin if he was a motor racing fan. Well, besides me, the boys and France, Colin's next love were the Grand Prix! To Colin's great joy, Leslie invited us to the May Monte Carlo Grand Prix. Graham Hill and his wife, Betty, had been close friends during the heady times of Graham winning the World Championship twice and the Monaco Grand Prix a total of five times. Then our lives had drifted apart, not for any particular reason but because all of us were doing different things with our lives. But I have tried to keep in touch with Betty on and off ever since Graham's fateful aeroplane crash. I will never forget that cold foggy November night in 1975. Colin and I were sitting having our supper while watching television. Suddenly, a news flash appeared on the screen saying that Graham Hill had been killed in an air crash. 'Oh, my God!' I said as I turned towards Colin. Then a short while passed and it was confirmed on the news. Graham, who was piloting his own plane, had been trying to land in an airfield close to our house in dense fog and had crashed into trees at the Arkly Golf Club. He and all his passengers had died, all of them. We couldn't take it in, we were so shocked. I rang Betty straight away. Later she told us that Damon, their son, had been watching television too that dreadful night. Imagine a small boy finding out about his father's death in such a horrendous way. Betty then had years of worry and court cases to cope with as well as her own, and the children's, grief. Alone, she had to continue to care for Bridget, Damon and Samantha. Thank God, she is a woman of great strength. My admiration for her is endless. When Damon won the world motor racing championship in 1996, I have to admit I cried with joy, but it was tinged with the sadness of Graham not being able to share that wonderful moment with his son.

Colin and I settled down in our apartment after our first few weeks of 'the new life' in France. Colin sailed on of our boats on the sea almost every day and I would join him when I felt like it. Life was good and it seemed as though we were living in a kind of dream. The boys came over to spend time with us whenever they could and I returned to England at least once a year to see them and friends. I naturally missed our sons, but they had their own lives to live and Colin and I were very happy in Cap Ferrat. Then one day as we were both sitting on our balcony looking at the mountains near Monte Carlo, Colin asked me if I missed not having a garden. I replied, 'Yes, but the sea is my garden.' All our lives we had had a garden and, in truth, I did miss not having one because I love growing things. That was the beginning of the idea of us perhaps buying a house on the mountain we could see from our apartment.

As the hot summer of 1989 faded, we started to house hunt. In 1990, after living in France for nearly three years, we found our dream house. It was a 300-year-old farmhouse perched on the side of a mountain. It overlooked the sea and the coastline all the way to St Tropez. The view just took your breath away. It was situated fifteen minutes from St Jean Cap Ferrat with incredible views of the mountains as well. The position and the house itself were spectacular. However, there was just one problem: the young French family who owned it had started a large extension to the house and couldn't afford to complete it, so we knew when we bought it, there would be problems! But we loved it so much we weren't going to be deterred by a few building problems. After all, Colin had been in the building business for years! We got to know the young couple and their four small children well, as we visited the house on numerous occasions to work out exactly how we wanted to finish the extension. They always made us more than welcome. However, their German Shepherd dog, Darling, used to scare us somewhat, but as she began to see us more often, she became affectionate towards us and we began to like her.

The evening before we were to take possession of the house, the family asked us up to say goodbye and tell us a few things about the surroundings. We sat under a beautiful olive tree and talked with the children who were being well-behaved, as

French children usually are. Darling, the dog, nudged our legs and I was caressing her when the husband said, 'We can't find a new home for Darling. We are so worried as there is no room for her to live with us when we move from here so we wondered if you could possibly have her.' Colin immediately said yes, which surprised me. I was more of a doggy person than he was. Although we had always had a dog in the house, I never thought he would accept living with a German Shepherd because of the reputation they have. Anyway, the family were thrilled that she was going to be cared for by us.

All their belongings and furniture had been cleared out of the house earlier in the day and the time came for them to leave. We said our goodbyes, the children hugged Darling woefully, then they left in two cars which were full to the brim with last minute belongings and four tired little children. We stood watching them wind their way down the narrow steep hill, all of us waving to each other until we could see them no more.

We stayed on at the house for a while. We had mugs and a kettle in the kitchen for the inevitable river of tea we would all need the next day when we moved in. Just before night came, after watching the sunset for the first time in our new home and feeling full of anticipation, we left to go back to St Jean, leaving Darling alone to guard the house.

At 8 am, everything was ready for the move. The apartment seemed to look sad, or was that just a projection of my own sadness? After all, we were leaving somewhere we had loved. As I sat amongst the boxes and furniture waiting for the removal men to arrive, I felt very mixed emotions.

Colin decided he would go straight to the house to be ready to receive everything and I would stay at the apartment to oversee the removals. As he went out of the door, he was holding a French baguette and a bar of chocolate in his hands this was insurance so that Darling would give him a friendly welcome! He told me much later that day that the ploy had worked: she had gobbled up the baguette and the chocolate in an instant and then given him big slobbery licks. I'd made a plan of the house and individual rooms to make it easy for Colin to direct the men exactly to where everything should go. I let the removal men into the apartment and they started to fill a large van with our furniture. We had forewarned the removal company that the road to our new house was only wide enough for one vehicle and that it was also extraordinarily steep. In fact, the manager himself had been up to the house the week before to examine the road. So, when I saw the size of the van that our furniture was being piled into, I had a sense of foreboding. However, the first load was finished and the men left saying they would be back in an hour for another load. I waited and waited. Two hours had passed and there was still no sight of the men. It was July and the day was becoming very hot and I was getting very worried. Eventually Colin arrived at the apartment at noon; he was looking more than a little angry. We hadn't been able to reach one another by telephone, even though we had arranged with French Telecom for our line to be connected that very day. Telecom simply hadn't done it! Colin then began to explain why the men hadn't returned as expected. My forebodings had been justified.

Apparently, when they had tried to drive the removal van up the steepest part of the hill leading to our new house, the van had started to tip backwards and the front wheels had left the road (they did a wheely!) and the removal men had panicked. After finally regaining control of the vehicle and carefully reversing down the hill, they had refused to continue with the job. Fortunately, after much heated discussion and frenzied communication with their boss, everyone had agreed that the only way they could possibly deliver all our furniture was to unload piecemeal from the large van and ferry it in small quantities in a very small van up and down the hill.

This they did. They spent the whole afternoon going up and down that hill. Colin took me to the house after the last loading of the big van was finished. It had been frustrating, annoying and yet somehow funny too. You have to have a good sense of humour if you want to survive living in France. Finally, around five in the afternoon, I saw the little white van slowly creeping up the hill with its last load. It had our dining room table strapped to its roof and three very weary removal men inside.

While we had all been working, Colin had tried to turn on the electricity in the house. To our total disgust, that, too, had not been connected, although it had been previously arranged that this would happen. Ooh-la-la, the French! The men were exhausted, in fact, we all were. They came into the house to cool down and all I could offer them were warm beers. However, we all saw the funny side of things and had a good laugh about it. As they left, we thanked them for finally getting us safely moved in, even though it had taken all day rather than the two hours they had quoted for the move. On that first night in our new home, there were two very sleepy people eating a sandwich by candlelight, then falling exhausted into bed. It had been a gruelling experience, but we had made it.

7

Living on a Mountainside

We called our house 'Rose Grange', the French equivalent to the name of our family house in Hertfordshire 'Rose Barn'. I was particularly sentimental about the name, as 'Rose' rhymed with Colin's surname.

The weeks following the move were exciting and hectic. Every time we looked out of a window, or stood on the terraces or in the garden, the view we saw almost brought us to tears. It was just so beautiful. We lived in the very old part of the house, while we planned the final design of the interior of the new extension. Every week a French architect came for a meeting with us to draw up plans for the builder.

I should explain that the previous owners had obtained building permission from the Mairie (the Town Hall) for the extension, so therefore we thought there wouldn't be any problems, but little did we know! I suppose you might say that the eventual problems we did have stemmed from a neighbour - not the Mairie although they certainly played their full part in building up our frustrations. There were three neighbours round us, who were not exactly next door, but we could see each others' houses. One family lived directly behind our house but further up the mountain. The husband was Dutch, his wife American and they had two small children. They were an absolute joy as neighbours. A day or two after we'd moved in, they invited us up to their home to welcome us to the area. During the time we lived in Rose Grange, we became good friends with them. The other two neighbours were quite pleasant to us at first; one was an Italian family, the other French. I am sorry to say that the French family turned out to be the neighbours from hell. Thank God they lived further down the mountain, but unfortunately their private road which they used every day ran along the perimeter of our property. To get down to Eze, our local village, both the French and the Italian families had the use of the tiny road in front of our house. Therefore, they never missed a trick!

Our French architect, Monsieur Chevalier, was a generous and warmhearted man and a godsend when things became difficult during the construction, that is, helping us get through the spidery web of French bureaucracy.

At last the plans were completed. They included a large swimming pool and the work was scheduled to start in the first week of October. We had three months of bliss before the onslaught began. I wanted to make myself useful during that time, so I started to make a garden round the house among the rocks and earth terraces. We wanted to leave the rest of the land with its twelve olive trees wild. It was very hard work as the earth was almost non-existent. Colin bought large quantities of bagged soil for me to plant the flowers and shrubs in. It took time to get used to the everyday insects being three times as big as ours in England. There were scorpions in the garden as well (only little ones). When I moved rocks, I saw them, but luckily we were never stung by any. There was also the odd viper slithering about. Colin found a discarded viper skin one day, but we never encountered any snakes face to face. Without doubt, the adventure of living on a mountainside more than compensated for the slight inconvenience of a few troublesome insects. Although it was like living in the country, the sea was always within our view, so we had the best of both worlds. The house was located just beneath the Grand Corniche and ten minutes from Monte Carlo. Eze, the ancient local village, had many historical associations. Tourists came from everywhere to see the spectacular view along the entire length of the Cote D'Azur and we actually lived there! I could hardly believe it.

One day, as we were driving along the Moyen Corniche, I said to Colin, 'This road has some childhood memories for me. When I was twelve years old, my parents and my best friend Maureen were driving along this road during a camping holiday. It was our first visit to the south of France and we were loving it. But because the road twists and turns so much, I became dreadfully car sick and wanted my father to stop the car.' Colin looked at me with a smirk on his face and asked what had happened. I told him that my mother just passed me a chunk of French bread and told me to eat it and I would feel much better. Colin and I smiled at each other as I thought about that day so long ago. I never dreamt then that one day I would live there.

About a month after we moved in, Colin bought me a four-wheel drive Fiat Panda.

I called her Poppy, because she was bright red. He thought that, with that kind of car to drive, I would get over my awful fear of the steep hill leading up to our house. I had tried to drive our Peugeot up the hill several times without success. On one of those occasions I panicked and froze halfway up, as I saw the bonnet of another car bearing down on me. There I was stuck, with the handbrake slipping - I was terrified! However, I was also angry with myself because I had always enjoyed driving. I just had to overcome my terrible fear. Finally I did driving Poppy! I remember the exhilaration I felt the first time I drove up that steep hill alone. That time I was lucky because I didn't meet a car coming down the hill. Slowly, with a lot of practice, my confidence grew and I came to enjoy the challenge of the hill. Just a little sidenote on this topic: we had many friends of both sexes who wouldn't attempt to drive up our hill. When they came to visit, Colin collected them from the village.

During that first summer our sons came to visit us with their girl friends and fell in love with house and the view. We showed them the plans for the extension and they were as excited as us about how the house would look when it was finished.

October arrived and so did the builders and the rain! The builders couldn't start their work for two weeks because of the treacherous conditions on the hill. Then as always in the south of France, the storms cleared away and the building work began in earnest. None of the men spoke English, including the architect, so, out of necessity my French became almost fluent during the fifteen months they were with us. The work was meant to be completed in nine months - but everyone knows what builders are like! We were in an ideal situation, living on site which meant we were there every day and able to watch the progress the men made - or rather the lack of it! Actually, they were a wonderful group of people most of the time. They were all different nationalities: Italian, French and Arab. We lived every moment of joy and disaster with them.

The first problem arose after the men had been working for two weeks on the front part of the house. The original owners had built a shell with small windows facing the fabulous view, so naturally we changed these for big French doors and curved topped windows. Halfway through knocking out the small windows, we suddenly had a visit from the local police. After much confusion and jabbering, we found out that our French neighbour had contacted the Mairie to tell them that the 'Anglais' were breaking the rules about building permission by changing the windows. Colin rang Monsieur Chevalier, the architect; he contacted the foreman builder and that afternoon they all went for a rendezvous down at the local police station.

Apparently our French neighbour (being the type of fellow he was) had told the police we were extending the front wall of the house, which was not only untrue but infuriating as we knew only too well we weren't allowed to make the basic extension any bigger than the way it stood when we bought the property, but of course we could change anything we wanted inside the building - which we promptly did.

To add to the nonsensical disruption, the view from our house didn't overlook any other houses in the vicinity, no one was affected by us having larger windows! However, the outcome of the meeting at the Mairie was that all work had to be stopped for three months! Three months! We couldn't believe it. Our Italian builder calmed us down by proposing that his men could start excavating the ground for the building of the swimming pool, so time wouldn't be wasted. As we were foreigners, we had little choice but to agree. However, after a couple of weeks when most of the earth had been dug out of the area for the pool, we had another visit from the police asking us if we had permission to build a swimming pool. They told us that no plans had been registered at the Mairie.

Well, by now, Colin was beginning to lose his patience. He looked into the detail of the contract for the sale of the house and found that the previous owners had received permission from the Mairie to build a pool, but they had never had it built. The problem we now faced was the fact that the Mayor who had given them the permission was no longer in office. So once again the new Mayor made us wait a month before we could continue with the building of the pool. The irony of our situation was that all the people on that particular part of the mountain had built their swimming pools without the consent of the Mairie, so to say we felt somewhat victimized would be to put it mildly! We were all very aware of the advantages of having pools (including the Mayor) as the whole area had a high risk fire factor. Indeed, in the mid-eighties a catastrophic fire had swept through the area including the property we now owned and by some miracle it hadn't burnt our old house, but had decimated many of the pine trees and wild grass around the house. But if people had their own pools, at least the fire brigade could use the pool water if another catastrophic fire were to start again.

Our French neighbour would pass every day during the hold-up with a smug smile on his face. He was an out-of-work architect, which goes halfway to explaining his attitude towards us and, after all, we were also 'les Anglais', the foreigners. What self-respecting Frenchman wants an Englishman as a neighbour! I must say, though, that I found his hostility towards us hurtful. To make matters even more confusing, sometimes when he went to collect his mail from the box directly situated outside the entrance to our house, he would smile up at me and wish us a merry 'bonjour'!

The weather remained beautiful through November and December. We put aside the building aggravations, the nasty neighbour and the ridiculous French bureaucracy and began to prepare for Christmas. Grant and Jill were coming to share it with us - our first Christmas in the mountains. We felt very happy. We had plenty of space in the old house for them and as I busied myself with the decorations and cooking, I felt content.

The day they arrived, the warm winter sun shone. We waited for them on the terrace, watching them wind their way up the hill in their car. Having previously managed the drive up the hill in the summer, Grant told us he was looking forward to the final leap (!) just before the house.

The week they were with us passed far too quickly. The weather was so good we were able to go sailing in Ginny. We also visited some very good French friends in St Jean Cap Ferrat and generally had a wonderful time together. Colin noticed the growing relationship between Grant and Jill and thought how well-suited they were to each other. Jill is a very affectionate and tactile person and I was growing very fond of her. Like me, she absolutely hates goodbyes. When they left and the hugs and kisses were over, I saw her hazel eyes were full of tears.

January arrived and the builders began working furiously. At last the three months of work suspension were over - what a relief! The Mairie are a law unto themselves. They have laws, of course, but they are made to be broken, especially by the Mayor if he feels it is of benefit to him or the community. Ummmm! Living in France as foreigners, we found it best to play the game by the rules but even then you can meet complications quite unexpectedly. Some of our English friends said to us during the building of our extension, 'Have you read the book called *A Year in Provence* by Peter Mayle? It's very funny.' I replied without much humour, 'No, we are living it.'

We woke up one morning in February and noticed how quiet everywhere seemed no noise of workmen, just a very still silence. Colin got up and looked out of the bedroom window. He smiled with surprise, then turned to me and said, 'Darling, come here and have a look.' Crossing over to the window, I asked, 'What's the matter?' As we both stood looking out of the window, we saw spread before us a white fairyland. It had been snowing all night and the view around us was quite magical. The pine trees were dripping with snow; the landscape had been transformed into a white fluffy blanket. We went downstairs into the kitchen and opened the door to let Darling out. She ran a few steps, then stopped, looked back at us, then at the ground and started to sniff the snow. I think she was mystified as she had never seen snow before. I wrapped myself up warmly and went out into the garden with her. The snow was about five inches deep and both of us were making footprints wherever we trod. She began to get frisky, realizing that the funny cold fluff on the ground wouldn't hurt her and she started to roll over and over in the snow. I rushed back into the house to fetch my camera. Snow is rare in the winter in the south of France, especially in a location so close to the sea but there it was in all its beauty. Obviously no work was done on the house that day because the hill was impassable for any vehicle. We were snowed in for three days and we loved every minute of it.

When the men cleared the ground where the swimming pool was to be built, they had to cut down a beautiful olive tree. Not only was this illegal as olive trees had preservation orders on them, but Colin and I were sad to demolish such an old tree. We had all put our heads together trying to think of a way round the problem, but unfortunately there was no other solution. The builders decided to do it surreptitiously. One morning when we had been out to a specialist tile store to choose the new flooring for the house, they proceeded to cut the tree down in our absence.

We arrived back early in the afternoon and the dirty deed had been completed, all except for a six foot square stump, which they would have to get out of the ground by means of a mechanical digger.

Later that week a chap came creeping up the hill in a mechanical digger, puttputting all the way to our house. It could only be a small machine to allow its entry onto our property. Well! In mid-afternoon, when Colin and I were busy doing odd jobs in the house, we heard the men all shouting, so naturally we rushed to see what was happening. The driver of the digger looked as white as a sheet and the foreman began to explain what had just occurred. Apparently, as the driver was trundling the digger along the perimeter of our land, with the mighty clump of olive stump precariously balanced on the small fork at the front, the digger had turned on its side, the olive stump had fallen off the digger and crashed through our iron railings down onto our French neighbour's private road. The great ball had continued to roll over and over the neighbour's land. Down, down it went demolishing five young fruit trees on its journey until it finally came to a halt way down the slope of his land.

Our first reaction was to thank God that no one had been walking or driving along the narrow road where the stump started its journey, because had they been, they would have been killed instantly by the remains of the tree. If something like that was going to happen, Sod's Law would have it happen to that particular neighbour of ours.

Although it was a serious matter, we all leaned over the broken railings and began to laugh, even though the men had been hassled by our neighbour when they were coming up and down the hill in their lorries. After a while, the men continued with their work and Colin and I went back into the house. All that evening we waited with bated breath for the telephone to ring waiting for a call from the neighbour. It never came! That astonished us at the time. We found out later that the olive tree stump was valuable. Our neighbour would have been able to sell it to an artisan wood carver to make wooden artefacts.

Spring had given way to summer. The weather was gorgeous, not too hot. Jason had called us to say he and Dulcie (his girl friend) were coming down for a twoweek holiday with us. I was very excited at the prospect. I adored living in France, but, in truth, I did miss our sons more than I care to admit. Jason and Dulcie had been together for a few years and seemed happy. I liked Dulcie very much. We had a lot in common, although she wasn't an actress. We were, and still are, tall slim blondes and creative people by nature.

Years ago when the boys were young, I made a promise to myself. I vowed that when they were adult men, I would love whoever they chose as their partners I believe it is the only way to keep a family together. I had seen examples of conflict between parents and their children, because of the parents taking a negative attitude towards their offsprings - wives or husbands. As a mother of sons, I was determined not to go down that road. It takes patience, understanding and tolerance on all sides but most obviously it takes love.

On the day they arrived, we went to meet them at Nice Airport. I never tired of the scenery along the Avenue des Anglais. As we drove along passing the huge pine trees and flower beds in the centre of the road, with the sea lapping gently on one side and the hotels on the other, it seemed this was the epitome of the Cote D'Azur. I suppose it was because I had travelled that particular route so many times before over the years and I still have so many wonderful memories connected with it.

We talked ceaselessly on the way back to the house, catching up on each other's news. They were eager to see the progress that had been made on the house since their last visit. We were still living in the old part, but the extension was taking shape nicely. During the holiday, we went sailing whenever we had to get away from the daily building activities. We met Roger and Luisa in the port St Jean Cap Ferrat and went out in their boat to swim and picnic. After Jason and Dulcie had left, Roger and Luisa came to see our new house and loved it, as did a few other friends who came to the south of France during the summer.

By now the shopkeepers in our local village of Eze treated me as a celebrity in a low key kind of way. They had seen *Goldfinger* and some of my other films on television and they recognized me now. The French fans are very civilised about the way they treat famous people. They don't pester them, they just enjoy seeing them around and joining in village life and behaving normally.

By the time our second Christmas in Rose Grange arrived, the builders had almost finished their work and we hoped to move into the new part of the house early in the new year.

Taking the risk of boring you, I just cannot help but emphasize how gloriously happy Colin and I were living together in France. We called it 'our time'. In fact, my happiness translated itself into the joy of writing poetry. I wrote almost continuously while we lived there. I also started writing this book then, hoping that one day it would be shared with you. At last I seemed to have time on my hands, enough time to enjoy the new challenge. As I mentioned earlier in the book, we didn't have a television set, so I had plenty of time to read. I read non-stop, all different kinds of books and in a way it gave me the courage to start writing myself. I did the two activities at the same time and one led to the other.

The extension was finally finished early in 1992. I have only written about a few of the ups-and-downs that happened during the first eighteen months of our lives at Rose Grange. Mostly it was a wonderful adventure that we shared and enjoyed together. We had created our dream home, which only happens once in a lifetime (if you are lucky). I consider us to be very lucky.

Grant and Jill got married in June, 1992 and we went back to England for the wedding and the family reunion with relatives. We both felt very happy about the marriage. While we were in London, I did an interview for London Weekend Television, talking about the Bond films and *Goldfinger* in particular. Over the years I had often been contacted to appear on television game or talk shows. Sometimes I had said yes and sometimes no! My life seemed so complete with Colin that I still didn't consider work as one of my priorities, even though I have always regarded my fans as special. However, having written that, I did have the urge to be in front of the camera again, but this time I wanted to produce and direct. The idea came to me as I had just finished writing my ninetieth poem. I decided to produce a video of my poetry. I became very enthusiastic about the idea, so while I was in London I contacted a few people and arranged for a talented young crew to come over to the south of France, stay with us and do a week's filming. Robert Mansfield was on camera and Brenig Hester was the sound technician. Funnily enough, Brenig I had known since he was a child, as he was the son of a very dear friend of mine. They came to France in the early autumn and we made the video. It was a terrific experience, half a holiday for them and half work! We all took our share of acting as the director and Colin was the general 'gopher'. I knew where I wanted each poem to be filmed exactly at each location where I'd previously found the inspiration to write them.

The 'crew' were as overwhelmed as we were by the beauty of the scenery and views. Although it was hard work making video, we all thoroughly enjoyed ourselves. Some days the sun shone, on others it rained heavily. By some miracle we managed to finish a forty-five minute tape in a week. I simply loved being in front of a camera again delivering a performance of something I really believed in. It was a great feeling! We actually shot four hours of tape. I still have the uncut version and some of it is very funny. It has been put away as a memento for my grandchildren to have.

After the crew left, Colin and I went back to work on the house and garden. There were many small things to be done, even though the main work was completed. I was still trying to make something out of our stony garden and the wild part had to be strimmed in the autumn. I also planted ten fir trees to remind me somewhat of England, the kind of fir tree that grows like the devil. We had plenty of space for them so they could grow to their hearts' content.

In November we went to England because Colin needed some very special dental treatment and only trusted his own dentist in England. We stayed with our dear friends Dolly and Gerald Frankel and at the same time visited our sons at their homes. On one of our visits, Jason and Dulcie presented us with some very important news. While we were having dinner, Jason suddenly announced that he and Dulcie were going to get married. There was a slight pause and then he added, 'Next March in Mexico!'. I was pleased for them but somewhat surprised at the location they had chosen. However, we understood the underlying reasons (past family problems) so Jason opened a bottle of Champagne and we toasted the couple, wishing them all the love and luck in the world.

On the plane back to France, my thoughts wandered - it seemed like only yesterday my two sons were schoolboys! And soon they would both be married men.

Our third Christmas in Rose Grange arrived and both couples came to be with us. During that holiday Grant told us that Jill was expecting a baby in the new year. We were all overjoyed at the news and had the most wonderful time together. It was a very special Christmas. Little did I know at the time that we would never have another one like that again.

February of 1993 was cold and wet, but there was no snow that year. Darling, our dog, had become a very close friend to us and we loved her. She was a wonderful guard dog for the house. With her around and that steep hill, there was little chance of our being burgled, which was an everyday occurrence along some parts of the Cote D_Azzur.

When March came, we rang Jason just before they were due to leave for Mexico. We wished them a wonderful wedding. They had three young couples who were close friends who went with them to celebrate the weddding. Obviously it wasn't to be a traditional family ceremony, but they were happy and that's all that mattered.

Summer was very hot. When we weren't sailing or cruising on the sea, we were swimming in our pool. It seems funny now, but it was Colin who insisted we have a pool built. I didn't mind one way or another, but it was me who swam in it most of the time! I think he just needed to be near water. My favourite time to swim (because it seemed so luxurious) was at night, naked. I would go down from the house just before we went to bed and have a moonlight swim. We had lights in the pool, but everywhere else was black, except for the starry sky and fireflies dancing like miniature fairies all around the pool and garden. It was magical.

I went back to England in October to stay with Grant and Jill. They had asked me to be with them for the birth of their baby. It was a very emotional time. During the days before the baby arrived, Jill was full of energy. She buzzed about cooking and cleaning. She was on a high, just longing for the baby to arrive. Everything was ready for the great event. The night before the baby was born, she had got out of bed about one in the morning with labour pains. She had taken herself down into the sitting-room. I heard her, so I got up too. She was excited and frightened and needed comforting. I made her some herb tea and we talked for a while, wondering how long she would be in labour. Grant came down and held her closely to him, rocking her gently. As I write this, I can still see those two young people in a world of their own and so close to each other - so loving.

Finally, Jill asked him to take her to hospital. She was in labour that night and all the next day, then at eight o'clock on the evening of the twentieth of October, their daughter Morgan was born. Grant came back to the house at midnight. Although he hadn't slept for twenty-four hours, he had to tell me everything about the birth. His adrenaline was flowing and he needed to share the joy of the experience. I listened spellbound - my boy was now a father. When I went to the hospital the following morning to see them, I held the new life in my arms and was intimidated by the miracle of birth. Our first grandchild I wanted to cry.

I stayed with them for a few more days, then went back to France and Colin. When he met me at the airport, his first words were, 'How are you, Grandma?', then, as he hugged me, he whispered in my ear, 'I love you.'

9
Tragedy

Silent Pain

Silent Night

Silent Heart

Without Him

Lonely Hours

Lonely Soul

Without Him

No more his touch

No more his kisses

No more his body

Beside mine

The vivid feelings

Of so many years

Lay like burning embers

In my mind

Silent Pain

Silent pain

Silent Pain

Without Him

November 1993

Colin had just entered the house. It was one of those evenings when the sunset was misty. It had been a dull day with fine rain occasionally. Having the rain was a blessing because we always needed it to refresh the earth in such a hot, sunny climate. He looked tired and pale. He had spent four hours scrimming the wild part of our land. I was worried about him because he had lost weight over the past year. I thought perhaps it was because he had been working very hard on the house and gardens.

We sat and talked about the joy of living in our mountain home. It gave us such pleasure and an enormous sense of peace. We had dinner and then went to bed early, feeling the satisfaction we always felt after working outside in that beautiful place. Just as I put out the lights and sleep was approaching, he said suddenly, 'I don't feel well.'

The next morning he clearly was very ill. I called the French doctor and he diagnosed pleurisy. He gave Colin a three week course of antibiotics. Initially, he seemed to get a little better, but after three weeks had passed, he was still in pain. The doctor looked concerned and suggested Colin should go to hospital in Monte Carlo for tests to be carried out. After Colin had agreed, which was no mean task because he disliked everything to do with illness, having enjoyed good health all his life. He was told he would only be in hospital for a few days. I took him to the Princess Grace Hospital which lies high on a hill in Monaco with a most spectacular view of the sea and the Palace.

We were shown into a spacious private room. I felt nervous. We looked at each other, unpacked his small holdall and he said, 'I better get into bed.'

The week that followed was to turn into a living nightmare for us both. I had been praying that the dark seed of fear in the back of my mind would be erased, but it wasn't to be.

After he had undergone many tests, he then had major surgery and we were told he had cancer.

The days and nights that followed took on a dream-like quality. I didn't feel real any more. My mind was screaming, 'It can't be true! It can't be true!'. The nurses helped me arrange his bed so he could see the sea through the large windows, which led onto his balcony. How many hours over the coming weeks would I stand on that balcony looking at the sea and the beauty of Monaco and think to myself that this could not be happening to us.

We never talked about dying. We never gave up until everything became hopeless, but both of us knew in the back of our minds what was going to happen. I forced it away; I couldn't take it in. I just could not come to terms with the fact that I was going to lose him. He had not only been a husband and a lover, but he had been a father figure to me as well. He had been so many things, giving me two wonderful sons whom we both doted on. We had been together for 38 years. How could I live if I lost him? He had taught me so much and our love for each other was deeper now than when we had first met. How could I comprehend what was happening to us both? The truth was I couldn't. So I went through weeks and months at the hospital and at our home, as though I wasn't there. I was in a dreadful trance. I would spend most of the day with him at the hospital, then go back up the winding, steep hill to our mountain home, alone and feeling numb.

I did all the everyday things to stop myself from going mad. Our German Shepherd dog, Darling, was a comfort to me. Dogs are a wonderful panacea for human beings. She seemed to know how much I needed her. It was just she and I together, trying to cope without him.

Not long after he had his operation, the Professor at the hospital put him on a course of chemotherapy. Watching the side effects of that barbaric treatment was horrific and it turned out to be of no avail, in fact, it hastened his death.

Jason, our younger son, was a wonderful support to me. He would telephone from London several times a week to find out how his father was and ask whether there had been any progress one way or another. He was the only family member I could bear to speak about the situation without breaking down. Somehow he gave me the strength to carry on.

Colin came out of hospital in May, having been there since January and for a while he seemed a little better. He was content to be in our peaceful home again. I was happy to see him and have him near me at night. I thought maybe a miracle would happen. I began to eat properly again. Before, everything I put in my mouth seemed to be choking me. I had lost a lot of weight and sleep never came. That last time in our home together did have some joy in it. Being together for 24 hours a day was everything to us. That's where he wanted to be and I wanted whatever he wanted.

Unfortunately, after a couple of weeks he began to deteriorate badly. I had done all that I could to nurse him, but the time had now arrived when he needed the professional care only a hospital could give him. He was extremely weak, could only speak with great difficulty and had lost the use of his right arm and leg. The cancer had also spread to his brain. Reluctantly I called an ambulance and he went back to the Princess Grace Hospital.

The doctors gave him blood transfusions and more tests and scans, only to discover the cancer was spreading through his body rapidly. I continued to be at his side during the day, watching the impending horror, the drips, the tubes, the life ebbing away, through eyes that couldn't see and didn't want to see. I loved that man and he was disintegrating before my eyes.

Then one evening when I returned home, I rang our sons in England and said I could no longer carry on alone. I was scared out of my mind. The next day, they both came to France. That particular night, instinct had told me to phone them. Colin had very little time left and I knew Grant and Jason must be with him before it was too late. I needed them desperately too. I had coped quite well without family around me, but now I was in a state of collapse.

We three visited him every day. Jason would read to him and Grant would sit and hold his hand, each taking turns to catch their breath out on the balcony. He could no longer speak. I sang 'How Deep Is the Ocean' quietly to him, which was our favourite song from way back when we first met and he used to watch me on stage. So many memories were flashing through the fog of my mind. I hope he heard me. His eyes would open from time to time.

On a Friday Grant and I went to visit Colin in the evening and were greatly shocked to see how much he had deteriorated in just a few hours. I could barely recognize him. We held both his hands, sitting on each side of the bed. We didn't speak, our hearts were leaden with sorrow. I don't think he knew we were there.

Time stood still. I felt as if I didn't exist.

Later, as we closed the door of his room, my son and I walked slowly along the hospital corridor. I felt anger rising up in my throat. Without saying a word, Grant put his arm around me and we left the hospital. I tried to talk to Grant in the car on the way back to our house, but the words wouldn't come. Only the horror of the way Colin looked filled my mind.

The next day as we were getting ready to visit him, the hospital telephoned us at 10.45 in the morning to say he had slipped away. It was the fourth of June, 1994.

My sons went to see him, but I couldn't. The spirit of the Colin I knew had flown to me in our house. What was left of him in the hospital was an empty shell.

The boys took care of the funeral arrangements over the following four days. We decided to have his body cremated. They went to a funeral parlour and chose a beautiful bronze sculpture of two hands entwined together to put his ashes in. We also had two tiny pots with a few ashes inside. I opened mine and scattered them at the base of a small tree in our garden. Colin had given it to me on Valentine's Day of the previous year.

Friends and family arrived for his funeral on the following Wednesday. It was a simple service in an English church in the village. My brother Johnny carried Colin's ashes all the way to the church. He had loved Colin too. The bronze statue with his ashes in it was placed on a high pedestal in front of the alter. We didn't have any music, so the Vicar, whom we knew, suggested that our sons read one of my poems.

I did not cry during the service, but nearly everybody else did. I kept thinking and saying to his close family we are celebrating his life, not his death. His two baby granddaughters were with us in the church. He would have smiled, had he been able to see them. I didn't cry. If I had, I knew I would never have stopped. That's how it was for weeks after his death. Periodically, as I was doing quite ordinary activities around the house and garden, I would become aware of hot tears running down my face. They came without warning. Silent pain gripped my heart like a steel vice.

I stayed on in France for another year. The dream home we had made together was full of his presence. Everywhere around, I felt him there and it helped me. That year my elder son, Grant, and his wife Jill and their baby daughter, Morgan, lived with me to help me survive. For a time I wanted to die too. Slowly, with their care and love, I realized I had to go on living. Jason and his wife Dulcie also had a baby, Jessica, so I concentrated my mind on the family and somehow, by a miracle of love, I began the long journey back to life.

10
Starting Again

1995-1998

When the rage of pain slowly subsides,
We're left in a void hard to describe.
To start again with hope and love
And ask god's help for courage and strength.
If we believe and have faith all will be well
For everything changes like the tide and the swell;
Nothing is absolute as we make our way,
Only his love which we see every day,
The miracle of nature heals our distress,
To recognise that, we must know we are blessed;
When we see people who suffer content in their lives,
It must surely teach us to be humble and wise
To open our hearts to all that is good
For it's everywhere around us but not understood,
To believe in nothing but worldly success
Leaves us barren, soulless and sadly depressed.
My meaning is deep, but simply expressed,
I have tried all my life to do of my best.
Forgive me, dear lord, for my failures and sins
As now my belief in true wonder begins.

My mind spins when I think how everything has changed. I arrived back in England on the first of July, 1995, a year and a month after Colin's death. Jason and Dulcie had organized a rented house for me in north London, not far from where they lived. I had never lived alone before - the thought scared me beyond belief.

My dear friend Dolly, who had kept in touch with me all through the years I lived in France, kindly allowed me to stay at her house when I first arrived back, knowing how sad and petrified I was of being alone. Dolly is one of those rare human beings; she gives love without wanting anything in return. She gives her time, as though it wasn't precious, to anyone in need. She gives confidence where none exists, she sees hope when all seems hopeless. She is an incredible woman. I could never have got through the first couple of weeks back in England without her. I will be in her debt forever. Jason had collected me from the airport when I returned, welcoming me home. He is like his father in many ways, both my sons are; it's almost uncanny. When I'm with them, I feel Colin is there too.

He drove me straight to Dolly's home and after she'd given him something to eat (no one visits Dolly's house without eating a plate full of delicious food), he then went home to his family. The next day they all came to Dolly's for lunch. I was longing to see Jake, my new grandson, who was just five weeks old. I made a big fuss of Jessica, so she wouldn't feel jealous, then held the tiny, wrinkled son of my son in my arms. We all had tears in our eyes thinking of Colin and how much he would have loved his grandchildren. I now had three, two girls and a boy, but nothing could appease the pain in my heart. I was still numb, although I seemed to be coping, with the help of Dolly's love. She stopped me from falling back into a deep black hole. In a way, she continued the healing process that Grant and his family had started throughout the year we lived together in France.

I didn't realize then that I still had a lot of love to give. I'd locked it in a tight ball somewhere deep inside of me. My emotional condition, if compared with the physical, was of a woman trying to lift each of her feet out of thick boggy mud without falling over, desperately trying to keep on walking. One day at a time, I kept saying to myself, one day at a time. Even though I had the family and Dolly's love, I still felt isolated coming back to England without my soulmate. Many times when Dolly and I were alone, I'd find myself crying. Somehow, because I was with her, I allowed myself to cry. She understands grief more than anyone I've ever met. It must be because her basic nature is that of a happy, optimistic person. She urged me to get on with the practical side of my life, hoping at least it would give some respite to my silent pain.

We went to my rented house every day to get to know the feel of the place and to meet the owners. They were a lovely Greek family and we liked each other instantly.

The wife, Anthea, was a warm, outgoing young woman and full of energy. The husband, Sid, was kind and protective. They reassured Dolly that they would look after me when I moved in. The house was unfurnished, which is what I wanted. I needed all my own things around me, more now than ever before. When the removal men arrived with all my furniture, Dolly was with me to help sort things out and for moral support. For the next few days, I went there alone for a couple of hours unpacking the piles of boxes and trying to imagine what it would be like when I lived there.

Then one morning, as I was having breakfast at Dolly's house, the telephone rang. A frantic voice said, 'Shirley, come over quickly!' It was Anthea telling me that I had been burgled. The look of horror on Dolly's face when I told her gave me the courage to keep calm and go to the house immediately. When I arrived, I was greeted by two policemen, Anthea and a friend of hers. Anthea was in tears. I looked around to see what exactly was missing. It didn't take me long to realize that almost all of my antique furniture was now gone. The rage and shock welled up inside me. I couldn't believe that all the things I'd carefully collected over thirty years were now gone. 'Welcome back to England, Shirley!' I thought to myself, as the policemen were asking their usual questions after such an event. I felt so angry! When the police were finally finished with their questioning, telling me there wasn't a hope in hell of ever finding the villains who had committed the crime, I then left and went to Dolly's. As I was driving over, I mulled over the information the police had given me. They thought the burglars had come during the night and somehow they had been disturbed. In fact, they commented that I was lucky the whole house had not been completely stripped. I sat in Dolly's kitchen telling her everything. I was shattered. My adrenaline subsided and my anger drained away. I just felt very, very tired. When I told my sons later that day about the burglary, I even laughed down the telephone, saying, 'Guess what? I wasn't insured either!'. Well, it was one of those situations where you either laugh or cry. I chose to laugh, but rather hysterically, I must admit.

Five days later, I moved into the house with fear and trepidation. I knew the longer I stayed with Dolly, the harder it would be to leave. I had to brave the next step of my journey. I busied myself every day with the sorting out of the house, as there were still boxes to unpack. I also had to replace the furniture that had been stolen, but not with antiques again, I might add. I was just trying to feel the earth beneath my feet again. I still went back to Dolly's for a night or so every week - it was a little like going back to mother for reassurance.

My next practical task was to go househunting to buy a place of my own. The first estate agent I went to see took me to a small house he thought I might like and I did. I bought it straightaway. Everyone said I was mad. They just couldn't believe I'd buy

With Dirk Bogarde at Pinewood, reunited to celebrate Peter Rogers and Betty Box's forty years as film producers.

the first house I had viewed, but that's exactly what I did. I have a history of getting what I want in a rather impromptu manner. There was one feature of the house, I didn't like, however, and that was the kitchen, which was minute. I couldn't live with a kitchen that was so tiny. So I made plans to have an extension built by now I was a wizard at building extensions! Jason put me in touch with a reliable Irish builder called Noel O'Sullivan and I proceeded from there, designing the way I wanted the extension to look.

I stayed at the rented house while the men were working on my own. They started the extension in November, 1995. Somebody up there loves me, I thought, as I got to know my Irish friends. Noel and his band of men, Brefni, David, Dennis and Willy, were not only good at their job, but were extraordinarily loveable people. As my own house was just around the corner from the rented one, I spent most of my days with the men seeing how they were progressing. Among the dust and debris, I made them gallons of tea. We'd laugh a lot and tell each other stories. I became very fond of them all. When I mentioned that my mother was half-Irish, they took me into the fold. The four months we all worked together on the house became part of the healing process because they made me feel alive and needed. I told them about the burglary and immediately they offered to move all my furniture from the rented house to my house when it was finished. Oh, the Irish can be so generous. I shall never forget them.

Except for a short spell of snow in February, my first winter back in England was mild I thanked God for that, the work of my Irish friends would have been terribly delayed if the weather had been bad. Ironically, the day I moved into my new house (in late February, 1996), it snowed, but the place was small and cosy and I wasn't too perturbed. I felt a certain joy in having a home of my own again, even though it was entirely different from the one in France. The big house, the pool, the grounds and the general luxury I'd had then slipped away easily. For, without Colin being there to share it with me, I didn't want it any more. People often ask me if I miss not living in the south of France. I tell them no! My roots are here in England where my sons and closest friends are. Life has a strange way of whirling you around. I now live two minutes from the hospital where I was born. I seem to have come home in a sense - made a complete circle! However, there is one aspect of my life in France that I miss dearly - no, not the sun, the sea! I miss not being able to swim in the warm, mother sea whenever I feel like it. Yes, I miss the sea.

About a month after I'd settled into my new house, my spirits were low, very low I hated living alone, but there was no alternative. One night I said to myself, I must not let myself sink back, I've come so far and been given so much help I have to go on. Then suddenly another thought struck me, telling me not to be a weeping widow for the rest of my life. The seed had been sown!

Spring arrived and I made myself busy in the garden. Then, on the fifth of April, Grant and Jill had their second baby daughter, Isla. My spirit lifted as new life began to emerge all around me and my fear of being alone began to subside. I found out I could do it - by doing it.

Luisa Moore telephones me every time she is in London and I go and stay with her for a couple of days. We shop, talk and just enjoy being women together. She has now been living apart from Roger almost as long as I have been a single woman we have much in common. Maybe by a quirk of fate, she and Roger could get together again. One never knows what lies in store for us, as we fight through the jungle of life. She, to me, is one of those friends we can count on one hand, if you understand my meaning. We are both alone - but for entirely different reasons and are determined to live our lives fully once more.

Another friend I count on that one hand is Maureen Timms. We've known each other since we were babies. We are the closest you can get to being sisters without being sisters. She was matron of honour at my wedding, as I was at hers. She has been a faithful friend throughout the years and especially so since Colin died. She spent many a holiday with us in France. The closeness of female friends cannot be taken for granted, but when you are close, it's really special.

I am trying to start my life all over again. At times, I thought I would never survive, and but for family and a few friends, I don't think I would have. But, as the old saying goes, time heals and it's absolutely true. You never, never forget the pain, but the sharp edges soften and strength seems to come from somewhere. The times I've said to myself, 'Somebody up there is looking after me.' Who is it, I wonder? God? Colin? Some unknown force is guiding us, I'm convinced of that. My mind has widened tremendously since I've now learnt to live alone, which couldn't conceivably have been the case while I had Colin's protective arm around me. It has occurred to me recently that the cruel twists of fate sometimes have a deeper meaning that we are certainly not aware of at the time. Personally, I've realized that endings can also be

Paul Hancock, a talented young photographer, took this recent glamour pose of me.

beginnings.

I remember the Daily Mail kept telephoning me, asking for an interview, just after I'd arrived back in England. As I was still in a haze of grief, I trustingly agreed. So they sent a young woman journalist to the house I was renting. We sat and talked for about an hour over a cup of coffee, then she left. When I read the article a few days later, I was very upset. I hadn't realized that the editor had wanted to print a 'Poor Shirley!' article. The headline to the story was something like 'Shirley Eaton's Golden Days Are Over'. Oh, how wrong they were!

It was not only untrue, but the paper has found it advantageous over the last eighteen months to print several photographs of me painted in gold. Oh, well, newspaper editors are a law unto themselves. Strangely enough, because of the contents of the article they

192

published, I received many moving letters from the public, which were heartwarming.

I rapidly grew to love my little house. I began to grow roots, both emotionally and practically. I remember when I first began to feel the earth beneath my feet again that if I came through that phase, I would like to continue my career in one form or another. It was like a tiny light in the back of my mind urging me on helping me not to give up. Well, now that time has arrived. Instead of saying no to the many invitations I receive, I welcome them. Since I took that attitude, there has been no looking back. My life has taken on a certain glow, but most of all I felt needed once more.

I make personal appearances both here and in the USA, signing autographs by the hundred, meeting film fans from all over the world. The thrill is mutual. I attend important film and book functions and generally let it be known I am here again and very much alive! In September, 1998, Christie's, the famous auction house, had a sale of James Bond memorabilia. I auctioned the pink lace panties I wore around the time of filming *Goldfinger* and they were bought for a high price. I was flattered, but at the same time I found it hysterically funny. My sense of humour these days is riding high and I seem to see the funny side of life more now than ever before. On a more serious note, I'm now a published poet, having released a limited edition of my poetry on video. The feedback I am receiving from everyone is genuinely overwhelming. I'm laughing again now, thinking about the little gold dolls that are in my image as Jill Masterson in *Goldfinger*, which were available in movie memorabilia stores worldwide in 1998. I'm giggling so much I can hardly concentrate on my typing!

OK, I have control of myself again. To my delight, I have also had several articles published and now I have the pleasure of sharing my life and thoughts with you what could be better than that? You might ask what I want to do now? I would answer, 'Just to go on living and continuing to be creative in some way', and I might add, 'To finish the novel I've started to write.' When I look back on my working life as a whole, I realize I've been a very fortunate person. In fourteen years, I made twenty-nine films, worked with some of the world's most famous, handsome and talented actors and travelled to many exciting countries during the course of my film career. In all honesty, I must admit I had a wonderful time.

The highs, the lows and the inbetweens were all a learning experience, as is all of life. The aspect that brought me most pleasure during my career was the comradeship between the people concerned in films, the theatre or on television. We were all working together trying to create something good, something special and while trying to achieve our aims, a close bond formed among us. Everyone is very supportive of each other, they have to be. Nobody, just nobody, becomes famous purely as a result of their own talent. Imagine the Spice Girls, for instance, and ask yourself where they would be now if it weren't for the brilliance of the marketing moguls behind the group and the new sound and visual effects. Whether you like them or not, it is surely a fact that without all these aids they wouldn't have got anywhere! We all need help, guidance and advice behind the scenes, plus the intervention of Lady Luck. But let's hope we don't dehumanize the arts.

Paradoxically, when you are a huge success, the pressure can be insupportable. You don't need to look far to see what success has done to some of our young footballers today. It's a case of too much, too soon, and they just can't handle it. They seem to have everything, but in truth they are spoilt little boys. Showbusiness has some of the same pitfalls. It's a very tough life, not the bed of roses that many people might think it is. Money and fame are fine, if you've got the guts to keep your feet on the ground and don't let those two blessed evils dominate your life. Just a few rare human beings seem able to cope with megasuccess. They have that sort of quality   strength of character!

I had a very interesting evening with EON, the producers of the Bond films. They have taken me under their wing, so to speak, because they say I am part of James Bond history. Michael G. Wilson and Barbara Broccoli are delightful people, endeavouring to live up to the genius of their father, Cubby, both professionally and socially. On the many occasions that we've met and talked, I'd say their father would have been extremely proud of them.

The evening in question was to celebrate the launch of Cubby Broccoli's biography written by the famous showbiz journalist and author, Donald Zec. In the fifties, sixties and seventies, he was the number one film journalist for the *Daily Mirror* (when it was the authentic *Daily Mirror*, not the tabloid we know today). He interviewed me several times during that era. That particular evening, I also met the young writers of the next Bond film (the 19th of the series), Neil Purvis and Michael Wade, and the director, Michael Apted. I was very pleased to meet them all. Later I found out they had all been anxious to meet me too! The two writers are only in their twenties. I thought, what a responsibility these young men have on their shoulders, writing for a James Bond film. However, I found them attractive and intelligent people. While we were chatting enthusiastically, I suggested an idea I'd had for me to appear in the new film (a cameo role). They listened intently, then we all laughed and spoke of the different possibilities there might be for this cameo spot. We even discussed my being painted gold again.It was certainly fun exchanging ideas together. Everything in the arts, or even other areas of life, begins with someone thinking of an idea. That's part of life's excitement!

John Glen was there too. He directed five of the Bond movies and while we were talking to one another, he complimented me on how I played the short but sensational role in *Goldfinger*. I was pleased because it's always gratifying for an actress to receive recognition from another professional. But I try never to forget that all of the entertainment business is an illusion, a fantasy made to look real. The better the actor, the better the script, the better the technicians, the more real it appears. Nevertheless, it is an illusion. One must not lose sight of that fact, especially the performer. The people who bring us these fantasies are often in some way living out their own dreams and demons. Well, that's my theory. What a way to earn a living!

In my life, I've always needed to feel I'm achieving something, whether it be as a mother, wife, actress or even a distant dream. I have to try and make sense out of this crazy world we live in. I need mental stimulation in my everyday life, so that I feel useful, and of course, I need LOVE.

Latest portrait by Paul Hancock.

It seems to me that most actors and performers have an abundance of nervous energy, which needs to be channeled somewhere positive. Acting, dancing, singing, all the arts indeed, are a wonderful way of expressing yourself. I also believe there is a latent psychological need to be loved by one and all. Whether we recognize it or not, most artists get a buzz out of being 'famous'.

On Sunday, 11 October 1998, I was invited to Pinewood Studios for a Gala Luncheon to celebrate the world's longest running television comedy series *Last of the Summer Wine*. The British Comedy Society, which I am a member of, were the organizers of the event. The cast of the series were all there: veteran actors Bill Owen, Peter Sallis, Frank Thornton, Dame Thora Hird and Jean Ferguson, to mention just a few. After the lunch, they held an auction for charity. Scripts, photographs, stars' chairs and costumes, all sorts of memorabilia, were there for the taking. Halfway through the auction, when Bill Owen, Peter Sallis and Frank Thornton were sitting in their chairs on the auction podium, Michael Aspel, the television presenter of *This Is Your Life*, suddenly appeared, much to everyone's surprise, and presented this big, red book to Frank Thornton. An excited murmur went through the room, then Frank looked round at the many guests and commented drily, 'Someone has betrayed me.' He was stunned, but managed to give Michael a nice smile and everyone gave him a big round of applause. I took some photographs of the scene. I've always wanted to be there 'live' when Michael pounced on someone. Before the film crew left to go to the studio for the show, I had a quick word with Michael, whom I'd never met. Besides wanting to say hello, I wanted to tell him we shared the same birth date, to which he replied with

With Jeffrey Archer at Pinewood studios October 1998, celebrating the long running series *Last of the Summer Wine*

a wry grin on his face, 'But I got there before you.' We talked for a short while, had a photograph taken together, then he left Pinewood to go and do the show.

Lord Jeffrey Archer, the author/politician, was the auctioneer for the event. He was sitting at the next table to me, so just before the auction started, I spoke to him. I thought we'd never met before, but he reminded me that we had met a long time ago at the annual SOS Ball at the Grosvenor House Hotel. I liked him for his wit and forthright manner. While we were talking, I couldn't stop myself from showing my admiration for the way he handles awkward interviewers on television. I've seen several of them and he is just great. We had our photo taken together in front of an original poster for the first *Carry On* film, *Carry On Sergeant*, which was one of the items to be auctioned. He is not only a talented writer, he is also a terrific auctioneer because he raised over twenty thousand pounds that afternoon. One amazing lady paid £14,000 to spend a day on the set of the next episode of *Last of the Summer Wine*, which is to be filmed in 1999 and which includes a bit part for her. The lengths people will go to be involved with the entertainment world! There was huge applause for her at the end of her bid. It was wonderful, for the proceeds were going to the MacMillan Cancer Relief Fund and The Stroke Association. It was a most enjoyable day spent at Pinewood, meeting old friends and making new ones.

Late in the evening of November 9, my agent rang me asking if I would like to go to Argentina the following day to be part of an international panel of judges to attend the Argentina Film Festival. My immediate reaction to the idea was to say no. I had only been home three days from a trip to New York. After talking with her for awhile the thought of going began to intrigue me, but could I be ready to leave at such short notice. I'd already made plans for that week. She explained I was being asked to replace Ken Russell, the famous film Director, who had dropped out at the last moment, hence my late invitation.

She told me there would be no fee, but everything would be first-class, the airflight hotel etc, I began to weaken, if the long journey was in luxury maybe I would consider going. She also mentioned there would be some very interesting people on the panel, including the actress Shirley Anne Field. Finally, that same evening, I spoke to the man who was organizing the trip, and would accompany Shirley Anne and myself on the journey and look after us while we were there. I told him I would go, therefore helping him out of a difficult situation, and recognizing it would be an intellectual exercise for me judging films at a festival. I had never done anything like that before. By now it

With Shirley Anne Field and President Carlos Menem in Argentina, November 1998.

was midnight but he needed a photograph of myself to be sent to Argentina by fax, and asked me if he could come to my house to collect it. I said okay, so there I was waiting for a complete stranger to come over to my home. He arrived at 1.30 am and we had a quick conversation about the trip which reassured me that everything would go smoothly. Then he left saying he'd meet me the next evening at Gatwick Airport with Shirley Anne. As I closed my front door after he left, I thought I must be crazy! I didn't go to bed straight away, I began to arrange a few things that had to be sorted out quickly. What clothes would I take now summer had begun in Argentina? Eventually I went to bed wondering what I had let myself in for. I hoped it would be an adventure.

The next morning I made several phone calls re-arranging my schedule for the following two weeks. The one thing I was concerned about was a TV interview I had agreed to do and I didn't want to cancel it because it was a programme called *Biography* for the USA market featuring Sean Connery. I'd seen the programme while I'd been in the USA, and had actually appeared on it before when it featured Mickey Spillane. My agent said she would take care of the problem for me explaining what had happened to the company, and arrange for me to do it when I came back from Argentina.

I packed my suitcase, went to the hairdresser's and got myself ready to leave as planned by 5.30 pm, feeling pleased with myself. Just as I was about to leave, (as I was closing my front door) the telephone rang. I put my suitcase down went back inside my house and went to answer it. It was the man telling me he'd made a mistake and the flight wasn't until the next day. Oh God, I thought, how could he get it wrong, I felt very let down, especially as it had taken a great deal of effort for me to be ready to go in under twenty-four hours. I couldn't believe it. I let my driver go explaining that everything was out of my hands, and asked him to come and collect me the same time the next day. I left everything in my suitcase, made myself something to eat and finally settled in font of the television for the evening wondering if it were an omen.

The next day went pretty smoothly, and at least I could do the television interview after all. I would be somewhat pressurized as the crew were coming to my house at 4 pm, but I thought if I was all ready to go immediately after the interview I would be in time. Four o'clock arrived and no film crew. I began to get edgy - at 4.30 they rang me and apologized for being late, they were still on the road stuck in traffic. By 5 pm I was really getting nervous. They arrived at 5.05 pm, fraught and apologetic. I told them it was too late to do the interview as I had to leave, and suggested we do the filming when I got back from Argentina. They looked very upset telling me they had to do it today to meet their deadline. So we did it in twenty minutes, and it went very well. We all left my house together.

On the two hour drive to Gatwick I managed to relax knowing I would be at the airport in good time. I must say I did wonder if there were any more sudden suprises awaiting me. It wasn't long before I found out there was. I arrived at the airport to meet Shirley Anne and the man as arranged. I was looking forward to meeting her, I hadn't seen her for years, and secretly I was glad there would be another English actress on the long trip. I went strolling over to the British Airways desk to ask for my reserved ticket, and when the young woman looked on the computer for my first-class ticket, she said she couldn't find it, I said 'It has to be there, it's all been arranged for me.' She saw my anxious expression, and started to look again. After what seemed to me to be an eternity, she said, 'Oh yes, I've found your name on the screen, but you've been booked in an economy seat.' I was astounded! No way was I going to travel all the way to Argentina in economy. Travelling first-class was one of the reasons I had agreed to go at such late notice, it was part of the deal. I began to panic and looked around for the man I was meant to meet, when suddenly I saw Shirley Anne walking towards the desk. We greeted each other warmly, and I told her what had happened. We waited an hour for the man to arrive to sort the problem out. I told her I wouldn't be going to Argentina unless it was. She reassured me that she wouldn't go either unless I traveled first-class with her. She apparently knew the man from a previous experience and had become suspicious. She left me a half an hour before take off, and checked herself in saying she'd know what was happening to me by keeping informed by the BA staff. Eventually the man arrived, there was no time to change my ticket officially, so we exchanged boarding cards as we stepped on the aircraft. By some mysterious means he now had a club-class ticket, which was in my name, and he had the first-class ticket in his name.

As I settled down in my seat near Shirley Anne I tried to forget all the airport hassle. The thirteen hour flight went well, I managed to sleep a little. The BA crew were so helpful and friendly. On those long night flights they change crew halfway through the journey, and both captains invited us up onto the flight deck, I like the flight deck, its so interesting. Shirley Anne and I stayed there for quite a while talking about the aircraft and other subjects, it was fun.

In the morning we arrived in Buenos Aires feeling somewhat tired. We still had another flight to catch from a different airport at lunchtime before we eventually would arrive at our final destination, being the beautiful holiday resort of Mar Del Plata, where the Festival was being held. Meanwhile the man took us to a cafÈ in the heart of Buenos Aires to have a little snack and to meet his brother and a friend who lived there. As we sat under a parasol in the warm sunshine relaxing we began to forget that later that day, in the evening in fact, we were to be making personal appearances on the stage of the cinema in Mar Del Platt.

Quite close to the cafÈ there was a huge cemetery where Eva Person was entombed. After we'd eaten we walked through a park to see the cemetery. What we saw amazed Shirley Anne and myself. The place was enormous, it consisted of long narrow alleyways with ornamental tombs each side, quite awesome. The sun never reached the ground because the tombs were close together and very high. We wandered about for a while completely mesmerized. With some difficulty we eventually found Eva Peron's burial place. We were rather disillusioned when we saw it. It was the same size as many others we had passed. It was built in black marble, very bleak and austere-looking. We paused for a while thinking of her legendary status, then I took a few photographs and we left the rows of marble tombs wanting to get back in the warmth of the sunshine.

We left the city of Buenos Aires and were driven to a small Airport. When we got there and checked in, we found ourselves waiting for the flight in an area that was being rebuilt. There were workmen everywhere, banging and crashing all around us and the other passenger's. The place was full of dust, like a cloud of smoke! We managed to find ourselves a seat, longing to get out of the place and onto the plane. We awaited and waited; no one called us to the aircraft. After an hour of waiting the ground staff made an announcement. They apologized for the delay saying they did not know exactly when the aircraft would leave, as there were very bad storms on the way to Mar Del Plata. We couldn't leave the area in case they called us. We all felt like refugees in a war zone!

Finally, after two hours had passed, we were called to the plane for take-off, at the same time warning us that we might have to return to Buenos Aires if the captain found it necessary. I was only a forty-five minute flight, so obviously the pilot couldn't fly over the top of the storm. All the passengers were nervous wondering exactly what was going to happen. By some miracle we made the journey without being tossed everywhere. As I looked out of the window I noticed the pilot had skillfully missed the worst of the weather, and although the flight took longer, we thankfully arrived safely.

When we arrived at the airport in Mar Del Plata we then had an hours' drive to the hotel. By the time we got there, we had been travelling for twenty-seven hours, to say Shirley Anne and I were tired would be a gross understatement. We only had two hours to unpack and get prepared for the gala opening of the Festival. Somehow we found the energy from somewhere to look our best and be ready in time to be presented at the cinema along with the other seven judges. We all met briefly in the lobby of the hotel, then we were driven to the cinema. The cinema was enormous with a very wide entrance with stairs cascading down to street level. The area was covered in red carpet, almost like the entrance to an imaginary Arabian palace, only this was real. There were hundreds of people behind the crowd control barriers, and as Shirley Anne and I made our way up the stairs to the cinema, a great roar come from all the people watching us. We waved and waved at them feeling revitalized and moved.

The opening ceremony lasted for three hours, then we all returned to the hotel absolutely exhausted. Little did I know as I fell into bed that night that the entire time I was to spend in Mar Del Plata I would feel exhausted. Having never been on a panel of judges before we'd no idea how gruelling the task would be. Every day the schedule was changed, we never saw the films we expected to see at the time we thought we would. We watched between two and four films a day, taking short breaks in between to get some fresh air and eat something. Most evenings were spent either watching a film or going to a social gathering that had been organized, and sometimes we did both. The whole time we were there, we never went to bed before 2 am. Everything is done late in Argentina, but at least the first film we viewed in the mornings wasn't until 11 am. In between the screenings Shirley Anne and I had to look glamorous for television interviews and photo sessions and radio and newspaper interviews, we were on a kind of merry-go-round, but being hard-working actresses we rose to the occasion and never disappointed anyone. I spoke French a lot of the time, because I can't speak Spanish, in fact I did my first ever radio interview in French. It was fun!

We viewed twenty-one films in ten days. Halfway through I thought to myself, I never want to go to the cinema again for at least a year! The films came from Spain, Italy, Germany, Brazil, Iran, Canada, Yugoslavia and the USA and Greece. Most of them were spoken in their original language, only one was in English, and a few had English sub-titles. I became frustrated when I realized that I'd be watching most of the films with ear phones on. Ear phones are bad enough in themselves, but when the voice dubbing the actor's is a young woman giving a commentary-type delivery of the dialogue for both men and women, it's impossible to give a genuine appraisal of the films. Together with the loud original dialogue booming from the screen and an irritating shushing noise radiating from the ear phones, it was enough to make any sane person go mad. By the end of the ten days' screenings I felt I'd been brainwashed!

However, Shirley Anne and myself took our responsibility seriously and did our utmost to judge the films fairly. The Argentinian people who organized the daily routine were lovely, even though they were disorganized. In general I liked them all. They tried to be so helpful to us knowing the pressure we were under. The man that came with us and was meant to smooth our path when necessary was never to be seen, except when there was an important social event to attend, then he was with us!

During the days we were there the judges got to know each other somewhat. We were all different nationalities, except for Shirley Anne and me. There were four women and five men. A beautiful young Italian actress called Maria Grazia Cucinotta (who is appearing in the next Bond movie released in November 1999) and a German woman director were the other two females. We all got on well with each other, even though we were entirely different personalities. I especially grew fond of Maria Grazia. The five men were complete contrasts. One came from Iran another from Brazil, another from France, although his birth place had been Argentina, and two from Argentina. They were all either directors or producers. We were a very mixed bunch of people. We'd had a jury meeting halfway through the screenings just to get to know each other and to try and guess who liked what film and why. But largely it was a waste of time. One particular judge didn't really let anyone else have their say. Two or three of us would talk to each other after some of the films, and that method worked well.

The last day of screening arrived and we saw four films. After a short break we all met at 8.30 pm and went to a quiet room and sat down around an oval table to get to grips with our choices for the awards. We had three people to translate for us, as there wasn't one common language between us, we knew it would be a long session. I sat next to my favourite man on the panel, the Iranian director. He had such a peaceful aura about him, he made me feel calm and relaxed unlike some of the others around the table. For a couple of hours although everyone had been talking we seemed to be getting nowhere. Twelve o'clock arrived and still no black and white decisions had been taken, we were all getting very tired, it had been a long ten days. I knew exactly who I was going to vote for, I had them written clearly on the note pad I had carried around with me all of the time. Naturally I wanted my vote to win, but I knew it would be a majority decision that would count finally, so I was being quiet and trying to be philosophical, even though I was passionate about one particular film.

It was now 2 am and we still hadn't reached a final decision. One of the jury got up to leave because she was so tired, and suggested we continue in the morning - we were all tired! There was no time for long debates in the morning the schedule was too hectic. The majority of the panel wanted to continue, so she was out-voted.

Finally, by 3am we had made all our decisions. The best film award went to a poetic movie made by an Iranian company. I personally hadn't voted for it although I liked it very much. The film I had voted for was called *La Cara Del Angel* (The Angel Face). It was made by a brave Argentinian man, Pablo Torre. The theme of the story concerned one family during the reign of terror in Argentina's Junta period. Pablo

Torre produced wrote and directed it. I voted for all three awards to go to his film, but finally he won the best screenplay, I was so pleased. The next day before the awards were presented, but the results had been announced he came up to Shirley Anne and me and hugged us passionately. He told us he had been working on the story for twenty years, even though he was only in his forties now, he'd managed to get the movie made at last. I thought the film was courageous, honest and terrifically moving. After I had seen it earlier in the week I found myself crying uncontrollably. Somehow his film represented cinematically all the evil military regimes in the world, both past and present. It affected me profoundly.

Although being on the Jury had been a worthwhile experience, even with its ups-and-downs. I wouldn't like to do it too often, there is too much political maneuvering for my taste. However I believe the particular mix of different types of intellectual personalities on our jury was a healthy combination, as the final judgements were to prove.

There were many times during the ten day s of screening that Shirley Anne and I were very grateful for each others company. Mostly, I suppose because we were the only English people there, we supported one another on the really tough days! We would laugh a lot, we have the same kind of mischievous humour, we also helped each other by sticking together to keep the wolves away!! She is funny, warm-hearted and still beautiful.

The last day of the Festival came amid a torrent of activity. First thing in the morning was a meeting of the jury, to verify the choices of Awards we'd made in the small hours of the morning. Then there was a press conference announcing the winners. Afterwards we were whisked off to be lunch guests of the President of Argentina, Dr Carlos Menem at his summer residence, an hours drive from the Hotel. There were about forty of us, the jury members sat at his table. He was charming and very friendly, obviously enjoying the company of people from the film world. Although his English wasn't fluent, it didn't seem to matter because his smile was so warm and he was very natural with everyone. I took photos of him with my own camera. He took a group of us down to see his private beach saying, we could use it any time we liked. As we walked back to the house, we saw a helicopter landing in the grounds, he then turned to Shirley Anne, Maria Grazia and myself asking us if we would like to go up for a ten minute sight seeing trip. We said yes. He then politely ushered us into the helicopter and waved at us as we were lifted into the air. It sat eight people, had his presidential crest everywhere. It was comfortable and felt like a Presidents' helicopter. The day had taken on a character all of its own. We came down to earth fifteen minutes later, and there he was again helping us down the steps of his personal aircraft. Our party had to leave late afternoon to get ready for the last night Gala at the cinema.

We said our farewells to the President and were driven back to the Hotel. We had an hour to rest before we went to the cinema for the awards to be presented. As I lay resting I thought to myself that after the presentation I could finally relax and enjoy the last twenty-four hours in Mar Del Plata. I sighed with relief after the three hour presentation was over. Once again like the opening night of the Festival when Shirley Anne and I walked down the huge stage like stairs outside the cinema as we left, the crowds of people cheered and shouted. We waved goodbye to them, our final farewell to the Argentinian people.

We were driven to the hotel and went straight into the ballroom for a celebratory dinner. I was feeling good, knowing we had worked very hard and done our best throughout our stay and the Festival was coming to a close. After the dinner we went to a disco in the hotel to dance. Only God knows how I found the energy, but I've always enjoyed dancing and after all it was the last night. I went to bed at 2.30, it had been a long long day. Sunday we stayed on at the hotel to recuperate. Shirley Anne and myself even swam in the pool at the hotel and slept for a while under a parasol - bliss! We needed it before our long journey home on the Monday.

If you should ask me, would I do it all again - with a slight pause - I would say, yes because I met a handful of very special people while I was away, and mean to keep in contact with them. I found Mar Del Plata a very beautiful place, even though I was too busy to enjoy it, and because I've found a new friend in Shirley Anne Field. After being together in many different circumstances, we almost feel like sisters! A shared experience is special. Whatever happens in the future, we will never forget our Argentinian adventure.

Getting older is a somewhat touchy subject with many beautiful women and actresses are no exception. Brigitte Bardot made a brave comment when a journalist asked her about her wrinkles. 'I love them', she said, 'it has taken years of hard work to get them.' I liked that response. As for me, I don't worry about them either, well, not too much! It's a perfectly natural process, after all, and beauty goes deeper than a few wrinkles on your face.

There is no sense in chasing our youth. We have lived it, it has gone forever, far too quickly, of course. Nonetheless, there are certain joys in being older. Sometimes, with the fullness of time, glamorous women become even more beautiful. Their life and character shine out from their eyes, the eyes of experience. The actress Francesca Annis is a wonderful example of beauty and sexuality in an older woman. Not only is she still a beauty, she is still a fabulous actress. Her looks and talent have matured simultaneously like a rich red wine. Of the many roles she's played (including a part in one of the early Saint series on television), my favourites are the television adaptation of the life of King Edward VII, in which she played his mistress, Mrs Hepple, and was entrancing, and more recently in the television drama *Reckless,* a love story concerning an older woman involved with a younger man. Robson Green played the man, lucky fellow! The whole production was brilliant, British television drama at its best.

Another older actress I like very much is Helen Mirren. She's not a classical beauty, but she has a sensual charm all her own and she's an excellent actress. She was fabulous as a detective in the television series, *Prime Suspect.* Personally, I hate all the blood and gore that was shown in this series, but the good script, combined with great direction and the wonderful acting of Helen, kept me glued to my television set.

We older women have Joan Collins to thank. In a strange way, she set the pattern when she played Alexis in *Dynasty.* Ever since then, women over forty have felt much better about themselves. Women are young until they let themselves FEEL old!

What I also find fascinating when you gather up the years is the sense of what has gone before our own individual history and what we have achieved on the journey. If by the grace of God we remain healthy, we can become more philosophical, more understanding and, dare I say, even serene. But make no mistake, I'm still on a voyage of discovery, that's what it's all about. I know I've been lucky, I've had much love given to me over the years and now I have four small grandchildren, two wonderful sons, born from a stimulating marriage and it all began because my father had a twinkle in his eye when he met my teenage mother. I owe so much to all of them. They moulded the person I am today, never forgetting the marvellous fans out there.

I've been writing this book for quite a while and during that time I've had a lot of late nights, some headaches and a great deal of joy. Now as it is coming to a close, I feel a large part of me has been set free. I have shared myself with you, but never selling my soul or anyone else's. To share our joys and sorrows with one another is what life is all about. It brings us all together, even if it be through the pages of a book.

This little poem expresses my thoughts about joy:

What is this joy I feel?

Can it be truly real?

Is it a passing moment

To fly away and disappear

Or will it stay forever near?

I know not what but that it's exquisite

Here glowing inside me to visit.

Destiny took me on her wings and carried me through life high above the mountains and deep into the valley. I am grateful.

Apart from making personal appearances, giving interviews to the press and doing television talk shows etcetera, I've now become totally absorbed with writing. I love it, it's so challenging. But writing is a somewhat solitary occupation so I enjoy the contrast of making personal appearances, doing both suits me fine. At last, I have the time to do what I want to do. Time is a gift. What I do with it is what really matters.

I have attempted many creative activities along the way. Now I've put pen to paper. I am currently working on a new CD to be released later this year. I chose the beautiful ballad, 'Fly me to the moon'. I am fulfilling a dream I had when I first went into Show Business. It will be released late in 1999. Dreams never die and just sometimes they come true. Acting? If you asked me if I wanted to act again, I would say, 'I'm contemplating two offers of cameo roles at the moment. If they are interesting or fun, I will accept them, as now all my doors are open.'

The golden days are never over.

Here I am like a dolphin plunging once more into the sea we call life.

James bond never dies and neither does gold paint!

I would like to leave you with this thought.

There is nothing as sweet as promise,
What is to come before it comes.
The dream, the idea, is rich with pleasure,
It has no end that we can measure.

INDEX